The Philosophical Background to Friedrich Schiller's Aesthetics of Living Form

D0841745

European University Studies

Europäische Hochschulschriften
Publications Universitaires Européennes

Series I

German Language and Literature

Reihe I   Série I

Deutsche Sprache und Literatur
Langue et littérature allemandes

Bd./Vol. 578

PETER LANG
Frankfurt am Main · Bern

Leonard P. Wessell, Jr.

u

The Philosophical Background to Friedrich Schiller's Aesthetics of Living Form

PETER LANG
Frankfurt am Main · Bern

CIP-Kurztitelaufnahme der Deutschen Bibliothek

Wessell, Leonard P.:

The philosophical background to Friedrich Schiller's
aesthetics of living form / Leonard P. Wessell, jr. -
Frankfurt am Main ; Bern : Lang, 1982.
  (Europäische Hochschulschriften : Reihe 1, Dt.
  Sprache u. Literatur : Bd. 578)
  ISBN 3-8204-7195-2
NE: Europäische Hochschulschriften / 01

ISSN 0721-3301
ISBN 3-8204-7195-2
© Verlag Peter Lang GmbH, Frankfurt am Main 1982

Printed by fotokop Wilhelm Weihert KG, Darmstadt

To Professor Ernst Behler,

A truly outstanding mentor

ACKNOWLEDGMENTS

I wish to thank the following groups for their support which made the researching, typing and printing of this investigation possible:

Council on Research and Creative Work of the University of Colorado, Boulder (Research)

Committee on University Scholarly Publication of the University of Colorado, Boulder (Publication)

TABLE OF CONTENTS

Chapter I

Philosophy and Aesthetics: The Structure of Theory

Introduction: Object of Investigation

"Man," says Aristotle, "is a rational animal." Man has, indeed, long prided himself on his powers of rationality. Sooner or later man seeks to penetrate rationally into the reality which surrounds him in order to render this reality intelligible to his mind. The different systematic formulations of the results of man's rational investigations constitute the various sciences by means of which he tries to comprehend existence. The term "science" in this context does not refer just to the so-called physical sciences, e.g., physics, chemistry, etc., but also to any organized body of knowledge about any aspect of being. As Jacques Maritain notes, "science is...a knowledge in which, under the compulsion of evidence, the mind points out in things their reasons for being."[1]

This concept of science involves at least two notions. First, each science must have a material object or subject matter which constitutes its selected field of investigation. "By material object of a science we understand the general object with which it occupies itself in its investigations."[2] Besides a material object, each science must have a formal object, i.e., a particular point of view from which the material object is viewed. "By formal object we understand that special phase of the general object which forms the subject matter peculiar to this science and which distinguishes it from all other sciences."[3] For instance, the material object of biology is the chemical organization of physical elements at a specific level of complexity. The formal object of biology, which distinguishes biology from the general field of chemistry, is the specific organization of elements involved in living things.

All historical evidence points to the continuous role of aesthetic experience in human life. Culture and aesthetics are intimately intertwined. However, man has not always occupied himself with aesthetic experience as the material object for reflective or theoretical activity. Aesthetic theory has, in short, a history. Although ancient, medieval and renaissance thinkers focused upon this and that aspect of aesthetics, a general science of aesthetics qua the aesthetic is primarily a product of the 18th century. Alexander Gottlieb Baumgarten (1714-1762), perhaps the most incisive of "dogmatic" philosophers in 18th century Germany, is generally accredited with the establishment of the science of aesthetics (by those impressed with Baumgarten's theorizing) or, at least, with the invention of the name "aesthetics" (by those not impressed by Baumgarten's theorizing). At any rate, in the course of the 18th century, aesthetic experience, conceived formally as aesthetics, was subjected to "scientific" investigation. The century is peppered with "Theorien der schönen Künste und schönen Wissenschaften."

A focal point, if not a watershed, in aesthetic theory in the 18th century is the theoretical reflections of Friedrich Schiller. Schiller's Über die Ästhetische Erziehung des Menschen in einer Reihe von Briefen (1794) in particular is of inestimable importance. I contend that Schiller's theory of aesthetics, rather than Immanuel Kant's Kritik der Urteilskraft (1790), constitutes a nodal point in 18th century aesthetic theory because it, more than Kant's theory,[4] points the way for the future. Richard Kroner has sought to show that Schiller's aesthetic theory influenced the development of German idealism because it secured a central role for aesthetics in the philosophical process.[5] Richard Sommer contends, furthermore, that from the point of view of psychology, Schiller rather than Kant is the culmination of 18th century aesthetics.[6] Schiller's analysis of aesthetic experience is, in my judgment, important for any attempt to comprehend the evolution of the science of aesthetics in the 18th century and, for that matter, for the first half of the 19th century. Schiller's concept of aesthetics has shown itself to be many faceted. It has implications for social, political, and sociological criticism.[7] The utopian thought of a Herbert Marcuse would be impossible without Schiller.[8] The psychological theory of Carl Jung shows the imprint of Schiller's thought.[9] However, the philosophical content of Schiller's analysis of aesthetic experience will constitute the specific aspect of Schiller's aesthetic theorizing to be investigated.

Schiller sought to understand aesthetic experience primarily under the form of beauty. Aesthetic experience is the awareness of beauty. In short, "Schönheit" is the object of aesthetic awareness. Schiller's Kallias Briefe (1973) and Über die ästhetische Erziehung des Menschen can be considered as a broad attempt to determine the structure of beauty, i.e. to specify the properties of the object of beauty. In his Ästhetische Erziehung, Schiller contends: the object of a judgment of beauty "wird also lebende Gestalt heißen können: Ein Begriff, der...dem, was man in weitester Bedeutung Schönheit nennt, zur Bezeichnung dient."[10] In a footnote Schiller goes on to explain some of the background to his concept of living form.

Zum bloßen Leben macht die Schönheit [Edmund] Burke in seinen "Philosophischen Untersuchungen über den Ursprung unserer Begriffe vom Erhabenen und Schönen" [1756]. Zur bloßen Gestalt macht sie, soweit mir bekannt ist, jeder Anhänger des dogmatischen System, der über diesen Gegenstand je sein Bekenntnis ablegte: unter den Künstlern Raphael [Anton] Mengs in seinen "Gedanken über den Geschmack in der Malerei" [1762]; andrer nicht zu gedenken. So wie in allem, hat sich in diesem Stück die kritische Philosophie [Kants] den Weg eröffnet, die Empirie auf Prinzipien and die Spekulation zur Erfahrung zurückzuführen (AEM, xv, pp. 615-616).

This footnote clearly shows (1) that Schiller consciously recognized that his concept of living form has historical antecedents (which can be designated as the aesthetics of life and of form), (2) that these antecedents have philosophical roots in empiricism (for which Burke is a representative) and in rationalsim viz. dogmatism (for which Mengs is a representative), and (3) that only Kantian philosophy contains the critical principles a theorist needs in order to be able to unite empiricistic and rationalistic theories of aesthetics. Furthermore, Schiller seems to imply that he has accomplished such a union with his notion of living form.

The above quotation contains in nuce the justification for and the determination of the theme of this study. Quite simply, the primary goal of this study will be to explain the footnote given by Schiller, i.e. to examine

Schiller's aesthetics of living form in its historical context. However, before I can proceed with any analysis of the historical background to Schiller's aesthetics and Schiller's treatment of it, I must first adumbrate further implications contained in the citations just given.

Schiller in the footnote was not so much interested in announcing the results of his theoretical labors as in calling attention to the reflective endeavor itself. In other words, the accent of this statement rests not so much upon conclusions as upon the method used to derive the conclusions. After all, it is Kantian criticism that has found a "way" to unite the empirical realm and the speculative principles into an adequate aesthetic theory. In order to call attention to a distinction implicitly made by Schiller I should like to recall the fact that a theoretical model underlies and generates the contents of any given aesthetics. In other words, a theoretical mode of analysis is and must be used by an aesthetician in order to formulate a theory formally concerned with the aesthetic qua aesthetic. Because Schiller refers to empiricism, dogmatism, and Kantian criticism in connection with the aesthetics of life, form and living form, I hold that Schiller, at least implicitly, is also claiming that an ars philosophice cogitandi underlies and generates aesthetic theory. In other words, philosophical method and aesthetic method constitute a unity, i.e. form parts of a single theoretical process.

Although Schiller suggests that there is a connection between the ars philosophice cogitandi and the method for aesthetic theory, he does not develop or specify the formal structure of such a union. It is clear, for example, that Burke's aesthetics of life is grounded in an empiricistic framework and that Schiller seems to hold that such a connection is a natural one. Differing and different aesthetic theories reflect differing and different philosophical theories. But what is the relational structure between aesthetics and philosophy -- both conceived as modes of a theoretical ars cogitandi? One will seek in vain in Schiller's writings for any discussion of the formal structure of theorizing independent of a specific system.

Any evaluation of Schiller's treatment of his historical antecedents will reflect, in my judgment, the interpreter's own conceptualization of the nature and function of theorizing. Factually, aesthetic theory in the 18th century is grounded in philosophical reflection. In my opinion, this "fact" is not fortuitous, rather the necessary outcome of the formal nature of theorizing per se. If Schiller's aesthetic theses are to be understood, particularly in context with their historical antecedents, then it is of advantage to understand the "scientific" process of theorizing. Schiller's own theories are but a species of the genus of theory formation. At any rate, my own interpretation of what Schiller accomplished in aesthetic theory is mediated by my comprehension of what if means, formally viewed, to theorize scientifically. I wish to emphasize the notion of "formality." I am consciously abstracting from any specific theory. For instance, Ernest Nagel distinguishes between probabilistic, functional, teleological, genetic, and deductive types of explanation found in different theories of natural science.[11] I would contend that, however much theories differ in contents, they nevertheless exhibit a formal similarity because they are the product of a reflective process. Thinkers theorize differently on a material level,

Schiller's aesthetics of living form in its historical context. However, before I can proceed with any analysis of the historical background to Schiller's aesthetics and Schiller's treatment of it, I must first adumbrate further implications contained in the citations just given.

Schiller in the footnote was not so much interested in announcing the results of his theoretical labors as in calling attention to the reflective endeavor itself. In other words, the accent of this statement rests not so much upon conclusions as upon the method used to derive the conclusions. After all, it is Kantian criticism that has found a "way" to unite the empirical realm and the speculative principles into an adequate aesthetic theory. In order to call attention to a distinction implicitly made by Schiller I should like to recall the fact that a theoretical model underlies and generates the contents of any given aesthetics. In other words, a theoretical mode of analysis is and must be used by an aesthetician in order to formulate a theory formally concerned with the aesthetic qua aesthetic. Because Schiller refers to empiricism, dogmatism, and Kantian criticism in connection with the aesthetics of life, form and living form, I hold that Schiller, at least implicitly, is also claiming that an ars philosophice cogitandi underlies and generates aesthetic theory. In other words, philosophical method and aesthetic method constitute a unity, i.e. form parts of a single theoretical process.

Although Schiller suggests that there is a connection between the ars philosophice cogitandi and the method for aesthetic theory, he does not develop or specify the formal structure of such a union. It is clear, for example, that Burke's aesthetics of life is grounded in an empiricistic framework and that Schiller seems to hold that such a connection is a natural one. Differing and different aesthetic theories reflect differing and different philosophical theories. But what is the relational structure between aesthetics and philosophy -- both conceived as modes of a theoretical ars cogitandi? One will seek in vain in Schiller's writings for any discussion of the formal structure of theorizing independent of a specific system.

Any evaluation of Schiller's treatment of his historical antecedents will reflect, in my judgment, the interpreter's own conceptualization of the nature and function of theorizing. Factually, aesthetic theory in the 18th century is grounded in philosophical reflection. In my opinion, this "fact" is not fortuitous, rather the necessary outcome of the formal nature of theorizing per se. If Schiller's aesthetic theses are to be understood, particularly in context with their historical antecedents, then it is of advantage to understand the "scientific" process of theorizing. Schiller's own theories are but a species of the genus of theory formation. At any rate, my own interpretation of what Schiller accomplished in aesthetic theory is mediated by my comprehension of what if means, formally viewed, to theorize scientifically. I wish to emphasize the notion of "formality." I am consciously abstracting from any specific theory. For instance, Ernest Nagel distinguishes between probabilistic, functional, teleological, genetic, and deductive types of explanation found in different theories of natural science.[11] I would contend that, however much theories differ in contents, they nevertheless exhibit a formal similarity because they are the product of a reflective process. Thinkers theorize differently on a material level, though on a formal level they can be viewed as "doing" the same kind of activity and the formal structure of this activity can be articulated.

Before I undertake in the following chapters a historical analysis of the aesthetics of life, form, and living form, I would first like to preface my investigation with a "theory" about theorizing. As Karl S. Popper has written: "The logic of scientific knowledge can therefore be described as a theory of theories."[12] Consciously or not, Schiller was theorizing scientifically and as such the specifics of his own theories fall under the formal parameters of theory formation per se. If we can grasp the nature of "scientific" theorizing and, particularly, of its relationship to philosophical theorizing, I believe, we can gain a deeper insight into Schiller's actual connection with previous theorists and the originality of his own contributions in the attempt to define the nature of the aesthetic.[13] My historical exposition of Schiller's endeavors will, in effect, be modelled on what I take to be the structure of theorizing. This structure will serve heuristically as a schema to order my presentation of the evolution of aesthetics in the 18th century.

The Structure of "Theorizing"

The fundamental feature of scientific-theoretical thinking, in my judgment (and I follow Ernst Cassirer), is the primacy of the concept of "objectivity."[14] Scientific thinking simply does not accept the empirically given at face value. The spontaneous tendency of uncritical human thinking is to "see" things from the perspective of man's immediate life needs, particularly of the human senses. Ontological status is not granted by theoretical judgment to sense perceptions in their given immediacy. They first must be critically mediated, i.e. measured against a theoretical construct based upon the principles of contradiction, consistency, and sufficient reason. As A.E. Taylor has shown, rational knowledge implies systematic wholeness.[15] The contents of an empirically given manifold are stratified and then structured according to their specific relations to the principle of objectivity. The world of scientific-theoretical perception is not a world given and complete from the outset, rather one that has been constructed and specified by theoretical acts of judgment. Such judgmental acts are only possible because of certain conceptual or theoretical constructs that order the fleeting series of sensible perceptions according to constant relations. It is the sum total of such constant relations that constitutes or, indeed, defines the notion of "objectivity." The objects of experience obtain cognitive "reality" to the degree that they exemplify the constant relations of a structural system. Cassirer has sought to articulate the meaning of "objectivity" in the following manner.

Die empirische Wirklichkeit", der feste Kern des „objektiven" Seins, im Unterschied zur Welt der bloßen Vorstellung oder Einbildung, hebt sich dadurch heraus, daß das Beharrliche gegenüber dem Fließenden, das Gleichbleibende gegenüber dem Veränderlichen, das Feste gegenüber dem Wandelbaren immer schärfer und deutlicher unterschieden wird. Der einzelne Sinneseindruck wird nicht einfach als das, was er ist und als was er sich unmittelbar gibt, hingenommen, sondern es wird an ihn die Frage gestellt, wie weit er sich im Ganzen der Erfahrung bewähren und gegenüber diesem Ganzen behaupten werde. Erst wenn er dieser Frage und dieser kritischen Probe standhält, gilt er als aufgenommen in das Reich der Wirklichkeit, der objektiven Bestimmtheit (PsF, II, 42).

In short, the various constants in empirical experience (that indeed transform an otherwise chaotic manifold of sensations into the orderly unity called empirical experience) exhibit relations between themselves. These systems of relations are often called "laws." When the interrelationship between the sum total of sub-systems has been articulated, a unity of the whole will be determined. The particular of the empirical manifold thereby "takes on" real status as a function of its relation to this totality. Cassirer states:

> So wird hier, im theoretischen Aufbau des Zusammenhangs der Erfahrungswelt, alles Besondere mittelbar oder unmittelbar auf ein Allgemeines bezogen und an ihm gemessen. Die Beziehung der Vorstellung auf einen Gegenstand" besagt zuletzt nichts anderes und ist im Grunde nichts anderes, als diese ihre Einordnung in einen übergreifenden systematischen Gesamtzusammenhang, in welchem ihr eine eindeutig bestimmte Stelle zugewiesen wird. Die Erfassung, die bloße Apprehension des Einzelnen, erfolgt somit, in dieser Form des Denkens, bereits sub specie des Gesetzesbegriffs. Das Einzelne, das besondere Sein und das konkret besondere Geschehen, ist und besteht; aber dieser sein Bestand ist ihm nur dadurch gesichert und verbürgt, daß wir es als einen Sonderfall eines allgemeinen Gesetze denken können und denken müssen. Die Objektivität dieses Weltbildes ist somit nichts anderes als der Ausdruck seiner vollständigen Geschlossenheit, als der Ausdruck der Tatsache, daß wir in und mit jedem Einzelnen die Form des Ganzen mitdenken und das Einzelne somit gleichsam nur als einen besonderen Ausdruck, als einen Repräsentanten" dieser Gesamtform ansehen (PsF, II, 42-42).

Through such a mediating process "grenzt sich so das Konstante gegen das Veränderliche, das Objektive gegen das Subjektive, die Wahrheit gegen den Schein ab: und in dieser Bewegung erst stellt sich nun für das Denken die Gewißheit des Empirischen - stellt sich sein eigentlicher logischer Charakter dar" (PsF, II, 45).

In order to unify the contents of an empirical manifold into a systematic totality, the varied contents of the manifold must first be distinguished from one another and assigned to different theoretical categories. The manifold is "broken up" or analyzed into its constituents which are not presented as sensory impressions, but rather as postulates or constructs of theoretical reason. Newton's postulation of inertia, mass, gravity, and the laws of motions are examples of such a reductive analysis. The differentiation of the otherwise fluid and non-determinate configurations of perceptions into relational categories is only the first step in the scientific-theoretical process. The phenomenal manifold can only be "explained" by being synthesized within a total context. Synthesis and analysis are correlative acts of scientific-theoretical thinking. Through synthesis otherwise haphazardly co-existing and successive sensations are integrated into an orderly system of objective relations. Indeed, objective "before", "after", and "simultaneity" are only possible because of a principal of synthesis (as Kant showed in his analysis of causality). The synthetic constants as the permanent elements in the variable flux of sense impressions distinguish between a mere subjectively experienced sequence of sensations and the "objective" temporal order pertaining between them. The application of a synthesizing category such as causality introduces into the flux of events a series of "conditions" and "effects". One event is grounded in another and the dynamic relation of grounding is not arbitrary nor dependent upon the emotional or emotive state of the observer. Causality differentiates the elements of the manifold into the typical and accidental, the determining and transient, and thereby structures experience into an orderly whole.

In the above exposition of the structure of scientific-theoretical thinking -- an exposition modelled strictly on Cassirer's own interpretation -- a very important structural element was insufficiently stressed. This element is none other than the paradigmatic or model-oriented nature of scientific thinking. This aspect has been well formulated and discussed by such diverse thinkers as Thomas Kuhn, Susanne Langer, and Stephen Pepper,[16] and will aid in understanding Schiller's references to three types of aesthetic theory.

The Function of Questioning

In what sense scientific-theoretical thinking is paradigmatic and just how such paradigms play a role in theory formation can be understood if it is recalled that there can be no theory without first there being a theoretical question. In other words, theorizing proceeds through acts of questioning. Susanne K. Langer has cast light upon the nature of a question, particularly in the context of theoretical thinking. Langer writes:

> A question is really an ambiguous proposition, the answer is its determination. There can only be a certain number of alternatives that will complete its sense. In this way, the intellectual treatment of any datum, any experience, any subject, is determined by the nature of our questions, and only carried out in the answer...[Questions] make more than the frame; they give the angle of perspective, the palette, the style in which the picture is drawn -- everything except the subject. In our questions lie our principles of analysis, and our answers may express whatever those principles are able to yield.[17]

Kuhn designates such "principles of analysis" as "paradigms". Arthur O. Lovejoy (whom Kuhn acknowledges as having influenced him) calls them "unit ideas", T. E. Hulme calls them "central attitudes",[18] and Cassirer calls them "objectivity constants".

A "paradigm", as Kuhn notes, possesses a certain priority relative to empirical fact. This priority consists in the dependency of the empirical manifold upon the paradigm for intelligibility. The paradigm enables a researcher, first of all, to conceptualize a problem, conceive relevant questions, invent necessary tests, and to interpret the results in a meaningful manner. The priority of the "paradigm" flows from the nature of theoretical questioning. A question entails certain implications. First of all, a question arises where there is hope for new knowledge. Metaphorically, a question is the act whereby a thinker casts a net of intelligibility upon the chaotic sea of events. "Theories", writes Popper, "are nets cast to catch what we call 'the world': to rationalize, to explain, and to master it. We endeavor to make the mesh even finer and finer."[19] Secondly, there can be no discovery of new knowledge without there being some sort of cognitive presupposition, i.e. a structure to the theoretical net. A question functions as a cognitive horizon or viewpoint from which to approach an inadequately understood subject matter. The term "to approach" is, of course, a physical term and refers to physical displacement. It is here being used metaphorically to refer to the thinking activity whereby a subject theorizes, i.e. envelops his subject matter in "objectivity constants". Theoretical thinking wants to "see" the singular as an example of the universal. This conceptual orientation is a formal element presupposed in the cognitive horizon of question.

How do paradigms or principles of analysis enable the theorist to be "in motion", i.e. to theorize? "Such ideas," writes Langer,"...are the terms in which theories are conceived; they give rise to specific questions, and are articulated only in the form of these questions. Therefore, one may call them generative ideas in the history of thought."[20] Theoretical movement from the side of the subject is "generative" i.e. is one of giving rise to specific questions. The subject is thereby enabled "to approach" the subject matter. The goal of theoretical motion, from the point of view of the object, is to subsume a given manifold under "objectivity constants". In short, the many is reduced to the one, or at least, ordered by the one. A question furnishes the "one" used to bring about cognitive order. Paradigms or principles of analysis offer the constants of synthesis or, better, synthetic principles. Indeed, paradigms not only function as the constants by means of which empirical facts are synthesized into a lawful whole, but they also determine what aspects of any given configuration of sense perceptions will be taken to be relevant to a problem, i.e. to be "facts" in the first place. As a principle of theory-formulation a paradigm (or objectivity constant) functions as a model which is analogously immanent to all instances of scientifically explained events. H. Gomperz writes: "To explain a phenomenon means to show that...it exhibits certain analogies with other phenomena, familiar to us from common experience. And a phenomenon functioning in this way as an explanatory analogy, may be styled a thought-pattern."[21]

Analogy is a formal feature of any principle of analysis and it is that which enables an idea to become generative. Through the act of questioning, a given manifold is progressively subsumed under the principles of analogy contained in the questions. Pepper has explained the process of theory formulation in the following manner.

The method in principle seems to be this: A man desiring to understand the world looks about for a cue to its comprehension. He pitches upon some area of commonsense fact and tries if he cannot understand other areas in terms of this one. This original area becomes then his basic analogy or root metaphor. He describes as best he can the characteristics of this area, or, if you will, discriminates its structure. A list of its structural characteristics become his basic concepts of explanation [i.e. paradigms] and description. We call them a set of categories. In terms of these categories he proceeds to study all other areas of fact whether uncriticized or previously criticized. He undertakes to interpret all facts in terms of these categories. As a result of the impact of these other facts upon his categories, he may qualify and readjust the categories, so that a set of categories commonly changes and develops.[22]

For scientific theory, the "real" is that which is measured against the permanent in the flux of perception, the constant in the variable. The particulars are linked together in accordance with law, i.e. with a systematic whole. The principle or "basic analogy" that generates the objective framework relative to which all individual events are structurally located within a theoretical whole, is accordingly, called a "root metaphor" by Pepper. A scientist views his subject matter, so to speak, through the eyes of his "root metaphors" and will "see" no more than what such paradigmatic and generative analogies allow, i.e. without bringing the validity of his accepted paradigms into doubt. In short, paradigms determine how a theorist will <u>view</u> his subject matter and thereby form questions.

Theoretical Thinking as Philosophy and Metaphysics

To theorize is to envelope a subject matter in a net of "objectivity". Insofar as all particulars of a given manifold can be referred structurally to a totality or whole, they receive theoretical status within a given paradigm system. The construction, development, and criticism of the conceptual contents of the root metaphors of empirical sciences constitute a special science of its own, i.e. it entails a certain type of questioning. This type of questioning is none other than philosophy. Philosophical theorizing is concerned with the <u>whole</u> or totality of all possible events that constitute the cosmos of a <u>given</u> science. In other words, philosophy is <u>formally</u> interested in the paradigmatic "one" that unites the contents of a <u>manifold</u> into a science. There can be philosophical considerations about biology, history, physics, aesthetic experience, etc. What distinguishes the philosophy of this or that science or, indeed, the philosophy of science <u>per se</u>, from the scientific procedure of the science concerned is that <u>the</u> <u>theorist</u> asking philosophical questions is not interested in examining any specific instance of the subject matter or, indeed, all instances taken distributively. Philosophy does not study the empirical particular as a manifestation of the universal, rather the universal <u>qua</u> its essence. What underlies philosophical theorizing is that which <u>determines</u> the total manifold of phenomena to be parts of a whole, to be unified within a common framework. Philosophy analyzes the conceptual content of the most general generative ideas, basic analogies, or principles of analysis used by a scientist to approach and comprehend a given subject matter. In short, philosophy deals with the "objectivity constants" in terms of which the "facts" of any given science are interpreted.[23]

Theoretical comprehension <u>per se</u>, is, however, essentially unlimited in scope. Any given empirical <u>science</u> is, of course, limited materially and formally to a limited subject matter. But the theoretical movement in its inner dynamics is one that seeks to envelope the entirety of the "world" in a web of intelligibility. Objectivity constants, paradigms, or metaphors used for such ambitious tasks are called by Pepper, "world hypotheses". World hypotheses are concerned with whatever may be or occurs. When philosophical questioning is not focused upon the subject matter of any specific science, but upon whatever is or can be a part of a world hypothesis, philosophy becomes what Aristotle designated as first philosophy or today is called metaphysics. Metaphysics is, accordingly, concerned with those principles of unlimited extension that determine the manner in which a theorist will view the entire scope of the world. Metaphysics is not concerned with the concrete results that flow from perceiving the world in one way or another, but with the very principles of theoretical perception qua their conceptual nature. It should be evident that "perceptual" differences on the level of first philosophy will result in enormous differences in the evaluation and interpretation of "facts" on the level of concrete and emprirical analysis. Many of a theorist's conclusions about the world derive not from the examination of things, rather from the philosophical commitments implied in the way a theorist starts his conceptual activity.

Materially, metaphysics is concerned with whatever is or can be, i.e. with that which underlies and unites various, diverse, and determinate phenomena into one universally common framework. This common denominator is the fact that they all are or can be. The unifying factor immanent in the sum total of all entities (taken distributively) is their being. Philosophy as metaphysics studies formally the ontological essence of the principles of totality of whatever is, "das Sein des Seienden überhaupt."[25] To inquire about the being of all entities is to ask about what makes such being intelligible, i.e. about the nature of "generative" paradigms that structure the being of all things. Metaphysics discusses what constitutes being and thereby enables it to function as the basic analogy of a world hypothesis, i.e. to generate the paradigmatic structure to which all particular entities must conform if they are to be granted "objective" reality. Since the metaphysical content of the root metaphors of world hypotheses serves as a generative principle shaping scientific perception, or generating objectivity constants, it can also be contended that metaphysics is concerned with the origin and causes of whatever is. Metaphysical questioning is, in short, directed towards the totality immanent in whatever is and correlatively towards the causal or intelligible origins of whatever occurs (is) within the totality of being. In Aristotle's terminology, metaphysics is formally concerned with the first causes and principles of every being merely qua its being, not qua any of its determinate and hence limiting or individualizing characteristics.

In distinguishing metaphysical theory from scientific theory, even from the philosophy of science, I do not intend to imply a necessary opposition between metaphysics and science. Professor Anthony Quinton has asserted "that the real point of constructing a metaphysical system is the recommendation of a conceptual framework, a set of concepts, that is, that can be applied to the whole of our experience and will do full justice to it."[26] Metaphysics is related to scientific theorizing regulatively and prescriptively in the sense that metaphysics furnishes the most universal set of categories, constants, or principles of objectivity that determine a scientist's analysis and interpretation of empirical events. Indeed, the ultimate meaning of a so-called empirical "fact" is a function of its relationship to a structural totality, the most universal form of which is metaphysical in nature. Alfred North Whitehead has noted: "Whenver we attempt to express the matter of immediate experience, we find that its understanding leads us beyond itself, to its contemporaries, to its past, to its future, and to the universal in terms of which its definiteness is exhibited. But such universals, by their very character of universality, embody the potentiality of other facts with variant types of definiteness. Thus the understanding of the immediate brute fact requires its metaphysical interpretation as an item in a world with some systematic relation to it."[27] The being of an empirical fact exhibits at least three levels of intelligibility. First of all, the fact is empirically presented as a brute given or immediate sensate event. For instance, a rock falls and hits the earth. Secondly, the event is interpreted as a manifestation of an empirical system of laws, i.e. the rock and earth are treated as examples of material bodies per se and hence are related together by the general law pertaining between material bodies, e.g. gravity. Therefore, the fall of the rock is viewed as an example and exemplification of an empirical-causal system of constants. Finally, the physical-causal system is embedded in and justified by the structural properties of whatever is: i.e. of a world hypothesis, e.g. Newton's mechanistic mode of explanation.[28] The root metaphors of world hypotheses constitute the metaphysical framework in terms of which the brute given of the empirical manifold is ultimately assigned objective status.

Theory Formation and Schiller's Aesthetics

The dynamics of theory formation is one of posing questions. A question enables a theorist to proceed from an indefinite cognitive background to specific empirical judgments. Theorizing can be simply designated as the method of systematic questioning. The principles directing systematic inquiry are the objectivity constants, the root metaphors, basic analogies, thought-patterns, etc. that determine a theorist's "perception" of a given subject matter. Such principles of analysis are part of the formal structure of theory formation per se. This formal feature can illuminate Schiller's tripart division of aesthetic theory in the 18th century and lends plausibility to such a division as being historically accurate.

Susanne Langer contends that a "philosophy is characterized more by the formulations of its problems than by its solution of them."[29] This thesis can be generalized to refer to any level of theory formation, to any "school" or "-ism" i.e., a specific theory (e.g. an aesthetics of form) is more accurately understood as a unity because of the questions it asks rather than because of the specific conclusions it comes to. Indeed, theorists of a given school, particularly over a long period of time, are quite likely to disagree with one another relative to many specifics, yet evince a continuity because of a shared paradigm commitment. The parameters of formulation rather than conclusions define a "school" or intellectual movement.

Langer's assertion that the unity of a philosophy lies in its formulation of problems has, in my judgment, enormous implications for the periodization or classification of intellectual movements. Indeed, it can be generalized into a criterion for cultural classification per se. However, I wish for my purposes to consider no more than its implications for theoretical movements. For instance, a movement such as the Aufklärung, particularly relative to philosophy, does not exhibit unity in the myriads of concrete assertions made by its adherents. The attempt on the part of some scholars to work out in detail, so to speak, the taxonomy of judgments (i.e. value and cognitive assertions) made by Aufklärer has lead to aberrant theses, often opposed formally. In order to find the unity of "Aufklärung" some scholars, for instance, are led to construct schematized and abstract descriptions (a common denominator) that have in effect no concrete representatives.[30] Other scholars proceed in the opposite direction and effectively equate the Aufklärung, with some individual.[31] Logically formulated, scholars often hover between constructing an ideal class without any real members or an ideal member without any real class (i.e. a class with more than one member). The reason for such inadequate periodization and classification arises because the scholar is looking for unity in the wrong place, namely in the conclusions of a conceptual movement rather than in its principles of theoretical motion.

Furthermore, if a scholar does pay too close attention to the changing opinions on the level of conclusions, he can easily lose the point of unity. For instance, Alexander von Bormann distinguishes between the interpretation of "Geschmack" in the first half of the 18th century and in the second half.[32] "Geschmack" is, of course, the faculty of aethetic judgment or of judging something to be aesthetic. To a large extent aesthetic problems were discussed in the 18th century from the point of view of "Geschmack." Bormann gives Johann Ulrich König and Johann Christoph Gottsched as examples of what he calls "der Geschmack des Verstandes."[33] Bormann connects these aestheticians with philosophers such as Christian Wolff and Alexander Baumgarten. These are theorists of the Frühaufklärung. Moses Mendelssohn and Anton Raphael Mengs among others are given as representatives of such an altered concept of taste. I am not here interested in the specifics of Bormann's analysis of types of taste. It suffices to note that Bormann applies Marxist categories and seeks to show that changes in theories of taste "reflect" different stages of bourgeois civilization in the 18th century rather than any real theoretical evolution. Bormann denigrates the validity of "ein bloßes begriffsgeschichtliches Studium" of aesthetic theory.[34] Theory is simply the function of a class's social history.

The important point is that Borman contrasts theorists chronologically separated by some years. Indeed, Bormann opposes one group to another as if they were in effect two different schools. At any rate, Bormann has focused upon concrete differences and considered them to be typifying for the two groups. I do not wish to deny differences in aesthetic theory at different times during the 18th century in Germany. However, I would contend that Bormann has falsified the historical situation. If theorists at different times hold essentially different views of the nature of taste, one should expect that the later theorists would acknowledge this difference in some manner. If theorists in the second half of the 18th century reflect in their theories the altered social history of a class, then they should on the level of theoretical discussion be aware of their opposition to theorists of the first half of the century. Yet Professor Konrad Ladrone in 1784 attempts to define beauty (=the object of taste judgments) within the framework of what Schiller called an aesthetics of form and what Bormann views as early Enlightenment.[35] Ladrone would have been classified by Schiller as a member of the "Schar der Vollkommenheitsmänner."[36]   Ladrone supports his Gestalt theory of beauty and explicitly refers to Baumgarten, Mengs, Mendelssohn and others.[37]   Indeed, Ladrone's work is based upon Mendelssohn's aesthetic principles. Ladrone simply saw no absolute opposition between theorists of the first and second half of the century. Where Bormann asserts a radical difference, Ladrone experienced a basic sameness. Schiller himself in the Kallias Briefe categorizes Mendelssohn and Baumgarten as "Vollkommenheitsmänner" and clearly designates such a school as "Wolfianer" (KB, pp 394-395). In short, contrary to what Bormann's analysis would suggest, many "late" 18th century theorists experienced a continuity with "early" 18th century theorists. If there is a fundamental and irreconcilable difference in the meaning of "Geschmack" between the two halves of the century, there were contemporary theorists, both important and unimportant, who at the time failed to notice it.

As stated above, I do not wish to deny that there are differences between the parts of the century. The point is to grasp such differences adequately and in such a manner that the contemporary experience is not falsified. Differences exist within a unity, not between unities. But where is the unity situated? I contend that the unity was seen by Schiller, Ladrone and others in the basic principles of analysis. Wolff, Baumgarten, Mendelssohn, Mengs and others were "Vollkommenheitsmänner." In other words, the philosophical and metaphysical meaning of "Vollkommenheit" played an essential role in theory formation about aesthetic experience. "Vollkommenheitsmänner" formulated similar questions with regard to the science of aesthetics (or of "Geschmack").   Relative to this mode of formulation the differences in conclusions seemed insignificant when the fundamental problems of what is the nature of beauty was discussed. This means that Schiller's critique of the aesthetics of form is not one directed against this or that conclusion, rather against the very mode of theory formulation in the dogmatic manner.

I suggest that my theoretical model, i.e. my theory of theory formation, enables an interpreter to grasp the "facts" of 18th century aesthetic theory more accurately than Bormann's sociological and Marxist reductionism. Because Bormann reduces aesthetic theorizing to a function of the social history of a class, he is simply unable to grasp the theoretical continuity that pervades more than one phase of such a social history.   Indeed, Bormann's apparent denigration of any attempt to construct a history of concepts enables him to obfuscate matters in order to make polemical points against the "bourgeoisie".   The unity of theoretical activity lies in its principles of analysis. Differences arise relative to anomalies or more specific articulations of questions. The "movement" or evolution of a school results from an innerplay between principles of analysis, attempts to articulate a comprehensive system, and anomalies. The history of such an "innerplay" of factors will yield both the unity and diversity, the constant and the changing, the structure and novelties of a theoretical school. The key point is that the root metaphors of a given mode of theorizing must be explicated and their application to a given subject matter articulated.

In the light of the above, I am now in a position to outline more accurately my intended explanation of Schiller's footnote and my exposition of 18th century aesthetics. I simply wish to explore the "innerplay" of factors that generated aesthetic theory. I am not, except for Schiller, primarily interested in individual authors, rather in the aesthetic schools of form, life, and living form. Therefore, I am concerned first and foremost with the root metaphors of each school. Pepper suggests that a theorist "pitches upon" an area of common sense in order to derive a basic analogy with which to interpret other areas of experience. Furthermore, the respective schools are grounded in philosophical positions. I shall, therefore, seek to establish the metaphysical paradigm "pitched" upon by each school. I will pay particular although by no means exclusive attention to G. W. Leibniz for the philosophy of form, to John Locke for the philosophy of life, and to Immanuel Kant for the philosophy of living form. Once the root metaphor of each school has been analyzed, I shall attempt to show how this basic analogy was articulated into the "objectivity" constants of the respective aesthetic universes.

My attention is to (re)construct an ideal system, i.e. not one theorist will be considered as paradigmatic for a whole school. On the contrary, I shall be seeking to bring to light the paradigm that united various theorists into a single broad school of aesthetics. Although my "picture" of aesthetics in the 18th century must, accordingly, be schematic, I contend that it will not constitute a class without any members. The reason for this derives from the fact that I will be focusing upon the generative principles shared by many individuals. The development, articulation, and application of such principles varies amongst theorists of the same school. Therefore, no one thinker can be said fully to represent a school in detail. But many did share a general theoretical stance. My investigation will focus upon this stance. My exposition will also be a bit more structural and static appearing than the ongoing "flow" of history was. This is because I am more interested in the underlying principles of unity, rather than in the web of generated conclusions. My intention is (1) to reveal the metaphysical universe that provides the most general system of objectivity constants, the theoretical horizon, in terms of which a school poses questions about aesthetics. (2) Secondly, I shall seek to explain the aesthetic universe, particularly in its philosophical dimension, in terms of which each school seeks to examine the empirical "facts" of aesthetics. (3) Finally, the specific manner in which the "fact" of beauty is measured in each school against the respective theoretical constants will be examined. The specific point of "measurement" will revolve around the concepts of form, life, and living form.

Footnotes - Chapter I

[1] Jacques Maritain, Distinguish to Unite or The Degrees of Knowledge, trans. Gerald B. Phelan (New York, 1959), p. 3.

[2] Celestine N. Bittle, The Domain of Being: Ontology (Milwaukee, 1939), p. 4.

[3] Ibid.

[4] For an opposing viewpoint consult Alfred Baeumler, Das Irrationalitätsproblem in der Ästhetik und Logik des 18. Jahrhunderts bis zur Kritik der Urteilskraft (Darmstadt, 1967).

[5] Richard Kroner, Von Kant bis Hegel (Tübingen, 1961), II, pp. 45-47.

[6] Richard Sommer, Grundzüge einer Geschichte der deutschen Psychologie und Aesthetik von Wolff-Baumgraten bis Kant-Schiller (Amsterdam, 1966 [reprint of 1896 edition]), pp. 425ff.

[7] In this connection see Michael J. Böhler's excellent translation of Schiller's thought into sociological theory in Soziale Rolle und Ästhetische Vermittlung. Studien zur Literatursoziologie von A.G. Baugarten bis F. Schiller (Bern/Frankfurt, 1975), pp. 239-322.

[8] Herbert Marcuse holds that Schiller's aesthetic ideas "represent one of the most advanced positions of thought." Cf. Eros and Civilization. A Philosophical Inquiry into Freud (New York, 1955), pp. 169ff.

[9] Cf. Carl Jung, Psychological Types or the Psychology of Individuation, trans. H. Godwin Baynes (New York, 1924), pp. 123-162.

[10] Über die ästhetische Erziehung in Sämtliche Werke, 4th ed., ed. Gerhard Fricke and G. Göpfert (München, 1967), V, letter xv, 614. Hereafter referred to in the text as AEM plus letter and page number.

[11] Cf. Ernest Nagel, The Structure of Science: Problems in the Logic of Scientific Explanation (New York, 1961), pp. 15-28.

[12] Karl S. Popper, The Logic of Scientific Discovery (New York/Evanston, 1968), p. 59.

[13] I should like to stress at this point that I am not now seeking to ascertain the specifics of Schiller's mode of theorizing as Ernst Cassirer has sought to do. (C.f. "Die Methodik des Idealisimus in Schiller's philosophischen Schriften," Idee und Gestalt [Darmstadt, 1971], pp. 81-112.) I am interested now simply in the general form of theorizing per se, relative to which Schiller's own method would be a sub-system.

[14] Cf. Ernst Cassirer, Philosophie der symbolischen Formen. Zweiter Teil: Das mythische Denken (Berlin, 1925), pp. 39--77. Hereafter referred to in the text as PsF, II plus page number. In these pages Cassirer contrasts "scientific" thinking with mythic thinking. In the process, Cassirer presents an excellent summary of his ideas on scientific thinking.

[15] Elements of Metaphysics (London/New York, n.d. [first printed in 1903]), pp. 18-41.

[16] Cf. Thomas Kuhn, The Structure of Scientific Revolutions, 2nd ed., (Chicago, 1970); Susanne Langer, Philosophy in a New Key. A Study in the Symbolism of Reason, Rite, and Art (New York, 1961), pp. 15-33; and Stephen Pepper, World Hypothesis. A Study in Evidence (Berkeley/Los Angeles, 1961).

[17] Philosophy in a New Key, pp. 15-16. Cf. also Felix Cohen, "What is a Question?," The Monist, XXXIX (1929), pp. 350-364. Concerning the function of questioning in the construction of metaphysics see Emerich Coreth, Metaphysics, trans. Joseph Donceel, (New York, 1968).

[18] Cf. Thomas Kuhn, The Structure of Scientific Revolutions, pp. 45-76; T.E. Hulme, Speculations, ed. Herbert Read, (New York, n.d. [first printed in 1927]), pp. 64-71; and Arthur Lovejoy, The Great Chain of Being. A Study of the History of an Idea, (New York, 1960), pp. 3-13.

[19] Logic of Scientific Discovery, p. 59.

[20] Philosophy in A New Key pp. 15-16.

[21] H. Gomperz, Philosophical Studies (Boston, 1953), p. 76.

[22] World Hypotheses, p. 91.

[23] For an interpretation of the philosophical processs as a radical form of questioning see Wilhelm Weischedel, Der Gott der Philosophen. Grundlegung einer philosophischen Theologie im Zeitalter des Nihilisus (Darmstadt, 1971), I, pp. 21-23.

[24] Cf. World Hypotheses, p. 91.

[25] Weischedel, Der Gott der Philosophen, I, p. 24.

[26] "Final Discussion," in The Nature of Metaphysics, ed. D. F. Pears (London, 1957), p. 142.

[27] Alfred North Whitehead, Process and Reality. An Essay on Cosmology (New York, 1960), p. 22.

[28] In this connection, see Pepper's exposition of the mechanistic root metaphor in World Hypotheses, pp. 186-231.

[29] Philosophy in A New Key, p. 16.

[30] Cf. M. Kronenberg's exposition of Enlightenment philosophy in "Grundcharakter der Verstandesaufklärer" in Geschichte des Deutschen Idealismus (München, 1909), I, pp. 180-234. Except for Christian Wolff, no names are mentioned. This makes it difficult to say just who the German "Verstandesaufklärer" were.

[31] Gerhard Funke attempts to treat Leibniz' philosphy as the essence of the Enlightenment. However, Funke writes: "Denn Leibniz war kein Leibnizianer - er war nicht Empirizist, night Rationalist, nicht Kritizist, er war Aufklärer." See "Einleitung," in Die Aufklärung in ausgewählten Texten dargestellt (Stuttgart, 1963), p. 45. Leibniz - the non-Leibnizian (!) - may have been the "Aufklärer," but only on Funke's narrow definition. The class of "Aufklärer" seems to have only one member, hardly a definition of a period.

[32] Cf. "Einleitung," in Vom Laienurteil zum Kunstgefühl. Texte zur deutschen Geschmacksdebatte im 18 Jahrhundert (Tübingen, 1974), pp. 1-16.

[33] In specific Bormann refers to Johann Ulrich König, Untersuchung von dem guten Geschmack in der Dicht-und Rede-Kunst (Leipzig/Berlin, 1727), and Johann Christoph Gottsched, Versuch einer kritischer Dichtkunst (Leipzig, 1730).

[34] Cf. "Einleitung," Vom Laienurteil zum Kunstgefühl, pp. 15-16.

[35] Cf. Konrad Ladrone, Uiber einfache und zusammengesetzte Schönheit nach Engels und Mendelssohn Grundsätzen (Mainz, 1784).

[36] Kallias Briefe in Sämtliche Werke, V, P. 394. Hereafter referred to in the text as KB plus page number.

[37] Uiber einfache und zusammengesetzte Schönheit, pp. 33-35.

Chapter II

Aesthetics of Form

A. Introduction

In this chapter I shall, of course, seek to elucidate the essence of the school of Vollkommensheitsmänner, whose aesthetic theories collectively were categorized by Schiller as an aesthetics of form. I wish, once again, to emphasize the fact that I am primarily interested in a "school of thought," not in a specific thinker. By nature my presentation of a school must be more schematic and "ideal" than an exposition of the thought of a single individual. The details of specific assertions, value judgments, or contentions do not in themselves interest me. Variations in details are evident in the various concrete judgments of different Vollkommenheitsmänner. What I am seeking is that which connects one thinker with another in order to constitute a "school." That which connects various individuals into one school is the "type" of questions they ask. Within the parameters set by a "type" of question various and varying answers (viz. concrete assertions) are possible. Although some answers may differ from one another, they nevertheless evince a continuity, a unity through their plausible relationship to the question-type that called them forth. In order to penetrate into the heart of the aesthetics of form we must first develop an insight into the question-type used by the Vollkommenheitsmänner.

The Metaphysical Nature of the Question-Type

The aesthetics of form rests upon definite premises, upon a definite "point of view." Interestingly, the genesis of this school coincides with the genesis of modern aesthetic theory as a philosophical discipline, at least within Germany of the 18th century. German theorists of the 17th century were, of course, interested in aesthetic matters. E.g., what are the rules for writing a beautiful poem? However, aesthetic theory was carried out within the framework of a rhetorical tradition stretching back to antiquity and revived during the Renaissance. In other words, the artist did not formally consider the "being" of the beautiful. An explicit metaphysical horizon was absent.[1] What is distinctive of 18th century aesthetic theory (and hence of the origin of aesthetics as a "science") is its explicit connection with philosophical and ontological theory. The aesthetics of the Vollkommenheitsmänner evolved out of a rationalistic ontology, specifically out of the Leibniz-Wolffian school. Looking back upon the development of aesthetic theory from late in the 18th century (ca. 1789), Andreas Heinrich Schott noted not only the connection between metaphysics and aesthetic theory, but also the "superiority" of the Germans in this matter.

> Zu den merkwürdigsten Veränderungen der Kritik [d.h. der Aesthetik] den neuesten Zeiten gehört ohne Zweifel die wissenschaftliche Bearbeitung derselben, die unter uns [Alexander Gottlieb] Baumgarten zuerst unternommen hat....Wenn irgend eine der neuern Nationen Geschicke dazu [zu Kritik] hat, so ist es gewiß die unsrige: denn wir haben in unsre nothwendigste Metaphysik mehr Deutlichkeit und Ordnung, in unsre metaphysische Sprache mehr Reichtum gebracht, und uns an das abstracte Denken mehr gewöhnt, als andere Nationen.[2]

Indeed, the philosopher, Johann Christoph Schwab, also looking back upon the 18th century, asserted that the Germans exhibited a particular penchant for metaphysics during a time when other peoples had in effect abandoned it.[3]

The connection between aesthetic and metaphysical theory informs the approach to aesthetics followed by the Vollkommenheitsmänner and hence the question-type used.[4] In the previous chapter I contended that metaphysical reflection is aimed at the totality (or paradigmatic structure) immanent in the being of all things, i.e. it establishes the most general parameters of "objectivity" and hence of reality. Once the ontological structure of this totality is ascertained, the totality can be used to generate questions about more particular areas of investigation. In short, metaphysics furnishes the most general principles for synthesizing any type of manifold into a "scientifically" known unity. Georg Friedrich Meier (1717-1777), certainly one of the "fathers" of an aesthetics of form, was very clearly aware of the function of the "totality" in influencing the parameters of the more specific sciences such as aesthetics. Meier himself wrote about the general "character" of philosophy:

Der Character der wahren Weltweisheit [Philosophie] erfodert es überhaupt, daß man dasienige, was alle schöne Künste und Wissenschaften mit einander gemein haben, deutlich, ordentlich und gründlich untersuche, und daß man also dasselbe, aus einem einzigen und allgemeinen Grundsatze, herleite. Der wahre Weltweise [Philosoph] sucht allemal, das Ganze zu übersehen. Er betrachtet die Welt im Ganzen, er untersucht ihre Vollkommenheit, die Harmonie, Symmetrie under Zusammenordnung aller ihrer Theile. Folglich sucht er die Regeln zu entdecken, nach welcher alles in der Welt auf eine so vortrefliche Art zusammengeordnet ist. Nun kan, in keinem Ganzen, eine allgemeine Ordnung angetroffen werden, wenn nicht alle Theile dersselben nach einer einzigen allgemeinen Regel zusammengeordnet sind, aus welcher alle überigen Regeln fliessen, nach welchen diese oder iene Theile noch insbesondere zusammengefügt sind. Es erfodert es demnach die Natur der wahren Weltweisheit, daß man überall die ersten Gründe der Dinge, und die ersten Grundsätze aufsuche, aus denen alle Wahrheit, alle Regeln der Vollkommenheiten und der mannifaltigen Ordnungen, fliessen....Es wäre demnach zu wünschen, daß man die allererste Regel in dieser Welt finden könnte. Aus derselben würden, als aus dem allerersten Grundsatze, alle Regeln der Bewegung, alle moralische Gesetze, alle Regeln der Erkentnis, alle Regeln der Vernunftlehre und der schönen Künste und Wissenschaften, kurz alle wahre Regeln, die irgendswo in dieser Welt beobachtet werden, erkant und hergeleitet werden können.[5]

This passage by Meier exhibits in nuce what may be called the mind-set or intellectual disposition of Vollkommenheitsmänner qua philosophers. As a philosophical aesthetician, Meier was seeking to comprehend that which is common to all the various fields of artistic endeavor. That which is common to the various art forms is, of course, their aesthetic quality. In other words, aesthetics is that science which deals with the being constituitive of all art forms (viz. art works). Meier himself writes about the science of aesthetics: "Denn wenn man diesen ersten Grundsatz [aller Regeln der Schönheit] ausführlich und philosophisch abhandelt, so bekomt man eine Wissenschaft, welche auf alle schöne Künste und Wissenschaften angewendet werden kan, und welche als ihre gemeinschaftliche Quelle kan angesehen werden, und das soll eben die Aesthetik seyn" (BEG, p. 19, §8). Almost thirty years later, Johann Joachim Eschenburg could concoct a similar definition of aesthetics. "Aesthetik, im allgemeinstn Verstande genommen, ist die vollständige Theorie aller schönen Wissenschaften und Künste."[6] And Michael Hißmann simply defined aesthetics in the following manner: "Das Geschäfte der Aesthetik besteht in der Aufsuchung des Wesens der Schönheit."[7]

As a science, aesthetic theory orders its manifold according to specific rules (= principles). This is, however, formally true for all sciences, e.g. morality, epistemology, logic, etc. The synthesizing process in each science requires a grounding in the nature of things. In other words, the general rules proper to each science must be seen as derivative of a single foundational principle (Grundsatz). Such a principle will yield "alle wahre Regeln" that structure any possible science "irgendwo in dieser Welt." Such a Grundsatz, entails "die ersten Gründe der Dinge, und die ersten Grundsätze, aus denen alle Wahrheit, alle Regeln...der mannifgaltigen Ordnungen fliessen." "Die ersten Gründe der Dinge" are, however, the most general objects of metaphysical inquiry. Meier writes: "[Die Metaphysik] giebt uns solche Merkmale und Prädicate der Dinge an die Hand, welche von allen, was wir denken und denken können, gesagt werden müssen...[Die Metaphysik] ist wie eine Sonne, welche um sich herum alle Wissneschaften, und alle Arten der menschlichen Erkenntniß, als Planeten erleuchtet, erwärmt, befruchtet und in Bewegung setzt" (M, I, 17 and 19, §9).[8] In specific, the first principles of things, scientifically known, constitute ontological theory. Meier writes: "Man versteht durch die Ontologie, oder durch die Lehre von den Dingen, diejenige Wissenschaft welche die allgemeinern Prädicate eines Dinges abhandelt" (M, I, 32) . Heinrich Adam Meißner in his Philosophisches Lexicon (1737) writes about ontology: "Ontologia, Ontologie, Grund Wissenschaft, ist derjenige Theil der Welt-Weischeit, darin die allgemeine Erkenntniß der Dinge abgehandelt wird. Diese Wissenschaft soll diejenigen Lehren abhandeln, welche den Grund zu den übrigen legen."[9]

Meier quite correctly refers to the "Grundsatz" inherent in all things as "das Ganze." "Der wahre Weltweise sucht allemal das Ganze zu übersehen." A metaphysical view of things is, indeed, a view of the "Welt im Ganzen." Not surprisingly, Meier contends in his Metaphysik: "Die Metaphysik ist demnach als eine Quelle zu betrachten, aus welcher alle Wissenschaften, alle Künste und selbst die richtige Erkenntniß des gemeinen Lebens, als so viele Ströme, herausfliessen. Sie ist die Wurtzel aller Arten der Erkenntniß, und sie wird also mit Recht die Hauptwissenschaft genannt" (M, I, 6, §3). In other words, in order to grasp "dasienige, was allen schönen Wissenschaften mit einander gemein haben," the philosopher must first establish an adequate "Grundsatz" for the aesthetic totality. The totality which grounds aesthetic theory must in turn have its foundation in the totality of the world, i.e. in the being of things. Aesthetic theory is, therefore, necessarily a function of metaphysical theory. No understanding of the question-type underlying the aesthetics of form can be adequate without some insight into the metaphysical "Grundsatz" of the Vollkommenheitsmänner.

The immediate task is, consequently, to explicate the Grundsatz or generative paradigm underlying the metaphysics of an aesthetics of form. In
this way I shall accomplish the first of my tasks, namely to explain the
metaphysical universe which furnishes the most general system of constants in
terms of which the Vollkommenheitsmänner posed questions about aesthetic
matters. My exposition of such a metaphysical Grundsatz will be divided into
two aspects. I shall distinguish between the object of metaphysics (i.e.,
doctrine of being), and the manner in which metaphysical knowledge is
achieved (i.e. the process of cognition). The content of metaphysics shall
be designated as the substantive aspect and the epistemological side will be
called the methodological aspect. These two aspects require a brief
explanation as they are two sides to the same philosophical coin.

The Substantive and the Methodological

The substantive Grundsatz that is of importance for establishing a
rationalistic aesthetics is the metaphysical principle constituting the
"real" in opposition to the non-real, or, in other words, the ontological
criterion whereby a rationalist can distinguish between reality and illusion. As A. E. Taylor has noted, ordinary experience abounds with the distinction between what is and what appears.[10] This contrast is prompted by
what is given by sense experience. When empirical perceptions given in the
immediacy of experience contradict each other, the mind (particularly the
theoretical one) cannot accept both perceptions as equally "real" or "true."
Immediate empirical experience cannot, accordingly, be accepted without criticism of what it often appears to be. The apparent stability of the earth
in contrast with its "real" motion would be an example. Consistency requires
that empirical experience be sorted out and evaluated according to some
scheme of "objectivity constants."

Vollkommenheitsmänner evince many examples of such a distinction, even
in the field of aesthetic interpretation. Johann Christoph Gottsched, for
instance, was well aware that different individuals judge differently about
the beauty of an object based upon immediate sense experience. What is beautiful for one person may not be beautiful for another. In no way would Gottsched allow both judgments to be "true." The result would be an infringement
upon the principle of contradiction. "Haben denn da beyde Urtheile wahre
Schönheiten oder Ungereimtheiten zum Grunde? So müßte ja ein Ding zugleich
schön und häßlich, zugleich wahr und falsch, zugleich weiß und schwartz seyn
können?"[11] In order to save himself from such an apparent aesthetic chaos,
Gottsched distinguished between "true" and "false" judgments about beauty.
The immediate empirical experience of beauty is not sufficient proof that the
object is really beautiful. The object could constitute "nur eine Scheinschönheit an sich" (VCD, p. 134, §23), rather than be "eine Schönheit an
sich" (VCD, p. 130, §16). Similarly, Meißner concluded, because judgments of
beauty depended upon (sensate) pleasure: "...so können wir für schöne halten, was in der That nicht schöne ist, und im Gegentheil entweder Schönheit
nicht mercken, oder gar einen Ubelstand daraus machen. Und daher ist es möglich, daß einer etwas für schöne hält, der andere nicht" (PL, pp. 528-529).
Meier too spoke of "Scheinschönheit" (BEG, p. 28, §12). Vollkommenheitsmänner
sought to develop a criterion for distinguishing between real and seeming
beauty and hence to establish a criterion for "true" aesthetic judgments.
This criterion has a metaphysical root. "Die Schönheit eines künstlichen
Werkes," writes Gottsched, "beruht nicht auf einem leeren Dünkel; sondern sie

hat ihren festen und nothwendigen Grund in der Natur der Dinge" (VCD, p. 132, §20). At this point, I do not wish to attempt to explain this criterion. I have only sought to illustrate the fact that Vollkommenheitsmänner tended to believe in an objective "Schönheit an sich" which is open to theoretical analysis and that this analysis has its roots in a metaphysical point of view.[12]

The distinction made between real and seeming beauty is formally the same distinction that lies at the origin of "modern" philosophy. This distinction arose in context of the application of mathematical thinking to the physical sciences. Harry Prosch has described the scientific treatment of motion (particularly in astronomy) from Copernicus through Newton.[13] Prosch did this in order to illustrate the widening chasm between the senses and reality that evolved during this period. In other words, the Copernican universe implied that the senses in their immediacy do not furnish "true" information. According to the senses the sun revolves around a stationary earth. In "reality," the earth revolves around a stationary sun -- so the Copernican universe. Commenting upon this development, Prosch writes: "If this view [i.e., the Copernican view] were accepted it would mean that man must always correct the obvious deliverances of his senses -- that things, even in the heavens, are not as they seem to man's perceptions....For the state of affairs which this theory supposed meant that men were not naturally in a favorable position to view things as they really were..."[14] The contrast between seeming and being referred to by Prosch is at the basis of modern philosophy. If things are not as they empirically seem to be, how is man cognitively to discover the nature of real being? The "Father" of modern philosophy, René Descartes, developed in effect his philosophy as an attempt to overcome the real -- seeming opposition. Descartes, as is well known, sought to doubt everything possible. That which can be doubted, cannot be taken as a certain index of reality. Descartes concluded that he could not doubt his very doubting. However much Descartes could think things as doubtful, he could not doubt his very thinking. Cogito, ergo sum! This thesis became the foundation of Descartes' philosophy and grounds the methodological aspect of modern (at least 18th century German) philosophy.[15]

Of particular interest is the significance of Descartes' universal doubt. By doubting all "objective" reality (particularly empirical "data"), Descartes radicalized the opposition between is and seems. The objective world was thereby relegated to mere "appearance." However, Descartes doubted things, not in order to produce scepticism, but rather to find a certain way (methodology) of discovering the true being of things. In other words, Descartes was looking for a method of ascertaining a criterion between real and seems. This criterion was found by Descartes to be located in the very rational subjectivity of the human self as revealed in the cogito, ergo sum. The essential nature of subjectivity was, of course, reason. In so far as the self (viz. the sum) is beyond doubt and in so far as this self implies rationality (viz. the cogito), then man possesses a means for constructing the rational structure of being or the root constants in terms of which "objectivity" is measured. In other words, man can discover being through the "pure" (= a priori) use of this rational faculty. Pure reason projects out of itself the outline of reality, i.e. the criterion that distinguishes between is and seeming. I shall explain the epistemological significance of "pure reason" in subsequent sections. At this point, I only wish to indicate the peculiar cognitive methodology of "modern" (particularly German) rationalism. Problems in epistemology revolve in the 18th century around the use and validity of pure reason in the construction of an ontological criterion for real being. The search for this criterion was simultaneously a search of the rational structure of the self, of pure reason. Epistemological and ontological, methodological and substantive problems eventually culminated in Kants' Kritik der reinen Vernunft (1781). This most famous work by Kant only has full meaning within the context of the rationalistic interest in pure reason as the foundation for determining "real" being. And Kant's critique of pure reason gave Schiller the necessary principles for constructing his own aesthetics of living form. In the ensuing two sections I shall deal schematically with the substantive and methodological aspects of the "real" universe of the aesthetics of form.

B. The Ontological Universe of the Aesthetics of Form

The Real: The Rationalistic Criterion

A major, substantive problem facing the Vollkommenheitsmänner as philosophers was the need to resolve the is-seeming opposition. As noted above, the is-seeming opposition was exacerbated by the emergence of the modern physical sciences. Descartes, as a philosopher, had sought to overcome the problem, by finding an indubitable criterion for truth. G. W. Leibniz, who may, in conjunction with Christian Wolff, be designated as the "philosophical" father of German rationalism,[16] followed Descartes in this manner. Leibniz asserted: "Il ne faut reconnoître pour vrai que ce qui est si manifesté qu'on ne puisse trouver aucun sujet de doute."[17] It is quite obvious that, if a proposition is only accepted as certain when it is "manifestly indubitable," there must be a very firm foundation for why this is true. The only type of truth that could fulfill the requirement of indubitableness was called by Leibniz a truth of identity. Any other proposition could only be true by virtue of the fact that it could be resolved into and reduced to a truth of identity. Concerning such primary truths Leibniz writes:

Primae veritates sunt quae idem se ipso enuntiant aut oppositum de ipso opposito negant. Ut A est A, vel A non est A. Si verum est A esse B, falsum est A non esse B vel A esse non B. Item unumquodque est quale est. Unumquodque sibi simile aut aequale est. Nihil est majus aut minus se ipso, aliaque id genus,....omnia tamen uno nomine identicorum comprehendi possunt.
Omnes autem reliquae veritates deducuntur ad primas ope definitionum, seu per resolutionem notionum, in qua consistit probatio a priori, independens ab experimento.[18]

Identities are "truths" by virtue of the fact that the predicate of the proposition is contained in or flows from the subject of the same proposition. The reason why identities can be indubitable derives from the immediate and necessary identity between the subject and the predicate. A proposition of identity contains or, rather, is its own indubitable self-justification. It cannot be doubted without accepting a contradiction, i.e., a thing would be what it is (principle of identity) and not what it is (the assumption presupposed by doubt). In short, identities are their own "sufficient reason" for their truth. Indeed, truth conceived as identity is in effect the logical form that structures Descartes' famous cogito, ergo sum. Descartes' foundational truth is a truth of identity. Leibniz enunciated the principle of identity in the following manner:

> Semper igitur praedicatum seu consequens inest subjecto seu ante-
> cedenti; et in hoc ipso consistit natura vertatis in universum seu
> connexio inter terminos enuntiationis, ut etiam Aristoteles obser-
> vavit. Et in identicis quidem connexio illa atque comprehensio
> praedicati in subjecto est expressa in reliquis omnibus implicita,
> ac per analysis notionum ostendenda, in qua demonstratio a priori
> sita est....Statim enim hinc nascitur axioma receptum, nihil esse
> sine ratione, seu nullum effectum esse absque causa. Alioqui veri-
> tas daretur, quae non potest probari a priori, seu quae non resol-
> veretur in identicas, quod est contra naturam veritatis, quae sem-
> per vel expresse vel implicite identica est (Cout, pp. 518-519).

Leibniz formulated this same thesis in a more pointed manner: "...praedica-
tum inest subjecto; ou je ne sais ce que c'est la vérité."[19]

This thesis, praedicatum inest subjecto, has been viewed by many scholars as the foundational principle of Leibniz' system. At any rate, the thesis offers an excellent starting point from which to derive the primary nature of reality for German Vollkommenheitsmänner. This criterion lies hidden
in the use of the verb in-esse. Leibniz intended the verb not only to refer
to a logical relationship, but also to an ontological one. True propositions
are "identical" because in some sense being itself is self-identical, is
one. Such oneness does not exclude diversity, differences, or variety. The
praedicati are identical (viz. one) in the subject, not, or course, taken in
isolation from each other. The principle of identity does not deny a manifold of differences, rather it only states how those differences are related
together in order to be real, or in short, simply to be. In other words, the
principle refers to the common element constituting all being. And this element is one of inhering, being together, in short, of inesse. The notion of
inesse must be more fully examined.

The inesse as the ontological basis for the principium identitatis implies that to be real for any given thing is above all to be that which it
is, to be self-identical. Since self-identity is the premise and index of
reality, being is accordingly characterized as oneness. The unum is prior to
being, or, more accurately, it is that element (and hence criterion) that
makes something to be. Leibniz summarized things in his letter of April 30,
1687, to Arnauld:

> Pour trancher court, je tiens pour un axiome cette proposition
> identique qui n'est pas deversifiee que par l'accent, sçavoir que
> ce qui n'est pas véritablement un estre n'est pas non plus
> veritablement un estre. On a toujours crû que l'un et l'estre sont
> chose reciproques. Autre chose est l'estre, autre chose est des
> estres; mais le pluriel suppose le singulier, et là où il n'y a pas
> un estre, il y aura encore moins plusiers estres. Que peut-on de
> plus clair? (PS, II, 97)

Being is to the degree that it is one. Leibniz writes "que je ne conçois
nulle realite sans une veritable unité" (PS, II, 97).

An analysis of this concept will reveal the ontological constant that constitutes the objectivity of the universe of German rationalism. In other words, the concept of identity (or oneness) generates the primal Grundsatz that rationalists such as Meier were seeking in order to determine "die ersten Gründe der Dinge." Paradoxically, the principle of oneness, functioning as a Grundsatz, can be designated as the "Satz vom Grunde." Many 20th century scholars are of the opinion that the "Satz vom Grunde" is the common source from which Leibniz' philosophy flows.[20] Interestingly, various rationalists of the 18th century also came upon the idea and the term. Meier, for instance, sought to ground his own metaphysics upon the "Satz vom Grunde" which he explained as: "Alles was möglich ist hat einen Grund; oder wo etwas ist, muß auch etwas seyn, warum es ist, warum es eben so und nicht anders ist....Wir behaupten diese Wahrheit ganz allgemein. Wir schliessen Nichts aus, und sagen: alles hat einen Grund" (M, I, 55, §32). This Grundsatz of the Vollkommenheitsmänner, directly expressive on an ontology of oneness, entails two basic features which will now be examined.

Feature One (1): All things are in principle universally intelligible, i. e. contain a sufficient reason. "Things" are intelligible because they are a function of oneness. The principle of identity implies that all truth, all reality, and all things are grounded in oneness in order to be. This entails radical intelligibility, since the cognitive grasping of oneness (unity) is possible for all things (if not for man, then at least for God). Leibniz himself maintains that "[ce Grand Principe] de la Raison suffisante, qui porte qu'il n'y a point d'enonciation veritable dont celuy qui auroit toute la connoissance necessaire pour l'entendre parfaitmenent, ne pourroit voir la raison."[21] Leibniz (and he was repeatedly echoed throughout the 18th century) formulated his belief in the intelligibility of things in the following manner: "Nihil potest simul esse et non esse, sed quodlibet est vel non est: Nihil [potest esse] est sine ratione" (Cout, p. 515).[22] "[Le Principe] de la Raison suffisante, en vertu duquel nous considerons qu'aucun fait ne saurait se trouver vray ou existant, aucune enonciation veritable sans qu'il y ait une raison suffisante pourquoy il en soit ainsi et non pas autrement" (PS, VI, 612).[23]

This doctrine has often been either misunderstood or inadequately understood. Wolff, Baumgarten, Meier and other Vollkommenheitsmänner, did, to be sure, seek to establish this principle through logical argumentation based upon the principle of contradiction. This argumentation is open to serious criticism insofar as it is taken purely as an argument of logic. The logical aspect of the argument has obscured other aspects, proto-idealistic aspects, of its meaning. Leibniz and his rationalistic followers were not only interested in a logical thesis, but in the possibility of consciousness per se. In other words, for there to be consciouness of some-thing (ens chose, Ding), there must be present to consciousness a discernible content or positivity. Without such a positive content there can be no awareness. That which constitutes the content (positivity) of that which is (or can be) present to consciousness is called the ratio, raison or Grund. Baumgarten formulates the proposition: "RATIO (conditio, hypothesis,) est id, ex quo cognoscible est, cur aliquid fit."[24] In Meier's German translation of Baumgarten's Metaphysica it reads: "Der Grund ist dasjenige, woraus erkannt werden kan, warum Etwas sey."[25] Without this content viz. Grund there can be no cognition (in the sense of awareness of something). Accordingly, Meier writes:

[Es ist] einerley, ob man sagt: es sey etwas möglich, oder es sey
vorstellbar und könne erkannt werden, so verstehen wir durch den
Grund einer Sache, alles dasjenige, warum sie ist, warum sie würklich ist, warum wie ebenso und nicht anders beschaffen ist, warum
sie erkannt wird, und zwar warum sie so und nicht anders erkannt
wird. Die Gründe verhalten sich wie die Wasserquellen. Gleichwie
das Wasser aus diesen fließt, also ist der Grund einer Sache dasjenige, woraus sie her fließt oder woher es komt, daß sie möglich
ist, das sie würklich ist, daß sie handelt, leidet, verändert wird,
erkannt wird, und daß sie überhaupt ihre Prädicate hat und keine
andere (M, I, 45-46, §27).

Meier's notion of a Grund as a Wasserquelle out of which all the predicates
of a thing flow is derivative from Leibniz' thesis, praedicatum inest subjecto. A Grund is simply the ontological form of this root inherence or oneness of being. In other words, the thesis: nihil sine ratione means that
aliquid has a cognizible content called a ratio in order to be an ens (i.e.
object of awareness).

We can now specify the nature of this content. Oneness as a Grund has
the structure of a Warum. This Warum is not that of a question, but rather
that of an answer (weil). In a letter to Nikolaus Hartsoeker of December 7,
1711, Leibniz speaks of "le grand principe du pourquoy,"[26] and explains that
"rien n'arrive sans un pourquoy suffisante, ou bien sans une raison determin-
ante" (PS, III, 529). Once again, Leibniz' fundamental principle is praedicatum inest subjecto. The bond or link between subject and predicate is one
of identity in the sense that all predicates are contained in an anlysis of
the subject. The subject contains the principle of unity (and hence of intelligibility) that relates together the varied manifold of predicates into
one systematic whole, into a logically ordered chain. This being-ordered of
the predicative manifold to the oneness of the subject enters consciousness
as a Warum. The Warum lends to the Grund a conceptual and intelligible
meaning and is accordingly a principle of determination, i.e. it determines
all the predicates by ordering them together. In other words, that which
makes a possible content into some-thing is the Grund (ratio) which binds,
unites, brings together, or, in short, determines a manifold into a oneness.
As an object of cognition, this Grund manifests itself as a Warum. The basis
of being is not atomistic, rather always relational.

Feature Two (2): Reality is connexial. This characteristic follows
logically from "Feature One." That content of consciousness that
distinguishes between be-ing (ens) and appearance (nihil) is the "Satz vom
Grunde." As a determining principle, the "Satz vom Grunde" implies a
"Folge." Meier writes: "Eben so wohl, als man behaupten muß, daß alles
seinen Grund habe, muß man auch behaupten: daß alles seine Folgen habe....-
Nichts ist ohne alle Folge" (M, I, 63, §36). In other words, the elements
or contents of being are related together as the determining and the determined, as Grund and Folge. And that which establishes the link between Grund
and Folge is the intelligible Zusammenhang (or nexus). Baumgarten writes:
"Quod rationem habet, seu, cuius aliquid est ratio, RATIONATUM eius dicitur,
et ab eo DEPENDENS. Praedicatum, quo aliquid vel ratio, vel rationatum est,
vel ultrumque, NEXUS est" (M, 5, §5).

We are now in a position to formulate in the most general manner the criterion for reality and truth for the Vollkommenheitsmänner. The difference between ens and nihil, truth and falsity, reality and appearance is oneness (unitas or unum) insofar as it can unite diversity into a chain of nexus. There can be no being that is absolutely outside of a connexial context. To be is to-be-related as Grund and Folge, i.e. to evince a Grund-Folge-Struktur. In short, as Baumgarten wrote: "Alles Mögliche ist ein Grund, Nichts ist ohne Folge, Nichts ist gantz unfruchtbar, und, so bald Etwas gesetzt wird, so bald wird auch Etwas gesetzt, welches in ihm gegründet ist" (Meta, p. 8, §21). An aliquid (Etwas) can lay claim to being only to the degree that its internal structure entails reference, both as Grund and Folge, to a contextual whole. This nexial order is the metaphysical truth of being. Meier, for instance, writes: "Folglich besteht die metaphysiche Wahrheit einer Sache darin: wenn das Mannigfaltige in derselben einander nicht widerspricht, und in einander gegründet ist; oder darin: wenn die Bestimmungen [praedicati] einer Sache beysammen möglich und mit einander verknüpftsind" (M, I, 156, §89). Baumgarten expresses the same idea in a more pointed manner: "VERITAS METAPHYSICA (realis, obiectiva, materialis) est ordo plurium in uno, VERITAS in essentialibus et attributis entis, TRANSCENDENTALIS" (M, pp. 24-25, §89).[27]

The order that relates the many to a oneness is the veritas, metaphysica seu objectiva. Such an ordo plurium in uno is the general criterion of objectivity. it is the ontological "objectivity constant" that grounds any possible world, any kind of being - including, as shall be shown, aesthetic being. Whatever the manifold may be, it gains ontological and hence objective status insofar as it manifests metaphysical truth. And the manifestation of metaphysical truth is precisely the criterion that distinguishes between is and seeming. A cardinal example that was repeatedly discussed in the 18th century was the problem of a dream. How can one distinguish betwen a series of phenomena called empirical "reality" and a series called a "dream" (illusion)? The distinction resides in the "ordo plurium in uno." In other words, rationalists held that dreams contain within themselves less order than experience during wakefulness. Also, the contents of a dream as plura have little or no nexus with the ongoing ordo plurium in uno of normal phenomena. Gottsched tersely summarized the argument.

So bemerke man, daß man die Wahrheit von einem Traume nicht würde unterscheiden können, wenn dieser Satz des zureichenden Grundes nicht zum Propierstein angenommen würde. Im Traume geschieht fast alles ohne zureichenden Grund. Man ist bald hier, bald da; und man weis nicht warum? wie man hin, oder weggekommen? Im Wachen aber, oder in der Wahrheit, hat alles seine Urasachen. Wer da kommt, weis, warum er kommt; und so weiter. Dieser Satz [vom Grunde] kan also ein sicheres Merkmal der Wahreit abgeben.[28]

The "Principium Perfectionis"

Thus far the rationalistic criterion for distinguishing between is and seems has been discussed. However, an adequate comprehension of the metaphysical Grudsatz for an aesthetics of form requires that one more derivative principle be briefly elucidated. The veritas metaphysica in itself is not sufficient to cause possible being to become existent being. For this, the principium perfectionis is needed. The reasons for this must now be discussed.

Whatever can be or whatever contains possibility (and the two formulations are equivalent) must contain a Grund, i.e. an intelligible determination (Merkmal). Such a positive determination qua its intelligible structure is a "Realität." Meier, for instance, writes: "Eine bejahende Bestimmung, die nicht bloß bejahend zu seyn scheint, sondern es auch in der That ist, heißt eine Realität, oder eine reelle Bestimmung....Eine Realität ist also ein wahrer Zusatz zu einer Sache, wodurch sie in der That etwas bekomt, und vergrösserert oder vermehrt wird" (M, I, 83, §48). Every predicate, then is a "reality" insofar as it contains a ratio. But this is simply to say that the "reality" of being consists in being an essence. In other words, the thesis, nihil sine ratione, means that all being is essential being. The complexity of intelligible Gründe which constitute the determining ordo plurium in uno of being is simply essence. Baumgarten writes: "Complexus essentialium in possibli, seu possibilitas eius interna est ESSENTIA" (M, p. 13, §40). But essentia as a Grund does not constitute existence. In other words, it is obvious that there are essentiae which exhibit no existentia. Therefore, to be essential is first and foremost to be possible, and conversely, to be possible is to be essential reality. But to be essential is not per se to exist.

What, then, is existentia? In his German metaphysics Christian Wolff defined existence in the following manner: "Es muß also ausser der Möglichkeit noch was mehreres dazu kommen / wenn etwas syen soll / wodurch das mögliche seine Erfüllung erhält. Und diese Erfüllung des möglichen ist eben dasjenige / was wir Würklichkeit nennen."[29] In his Ontologia Wolff gives a similar definition. "Hinc Existentiam definio per complementum possibilitatis...Dicitur existentia etiam Actualitas" (Ontologia, p. 143, §174). Wolff himself did not adequately explain what he meant by "complementum." However, it is not hard to grasp what Wolff (and other Vollkommenheitsmänner) were after. Existence is not a dimension of being distinct from essence (i.e. from the connexial Grund-Folge-Struktur of things). To acknowledge existence as something beyond or other than essence would be to destroy the universal validity of oneness as the heart of the real. To be would entail more than a ratio. Instead, as Wolff and many others contended, existence is a mode of essence.[30] In what sense is this so?

Every subject contains within itself all its possible predicates. This, of course, was an important element in Leibniz' doctrine of monads. When a being is totally determined (i.e., has all its Bestimmungen or determinationes) it can be said to have "actualized" all its possible Gründe and Folgen. It is completed or erfüllt. Possibility as essence entails existence insofar as its essentiality is unfolded to completion (Erfüllung). Whenever the Grund (or complex of Gründe) of any given being has all its consequences "drawn" and is accordingly fulfilled, it exists. Just as a logical argument is (completed) the moment all its premises and conclusions are carried out, so too will possibilia exist the moment their essential structure is totally determined in regard to the connexial structure of ordo plurium in uno that constitutes Realität.

Why, then, do not all possibilia immediately exist? The reason is simple. The logical and ontological Folgen of a given possible being (Grund) can contradict the Folgen of other possibilia. And that which is a contradiction is nihil, is accordingly sine ratione and hence without Realität. In short, connexial incompatibility frustrates the determinationes of some essential possibilia. Leibniz himself wrote: "Sed quia alia aliis incompatibilia sunt, sequitur quaedam possibilia non pervenire ad existendum..."(Cout, p. 534). "Si omnia possibilia existerent, nulla opus esset existendi ratione, et sufficeret sola possibilitas" (Cout, p. 530). Similarly, if an argument contains premises whose conclusions would be contradictory, the argument can never be (a completed argument).

What, then, overcomes this ontological frustration? Leibniz writes: "Interim ex conflictu omnium possibilium existentiam exigentiam hoc saltem sequitur, ut Existat ea rerum series, per quam plurium existit, seu series omnium possibilium maxima" (Cot, p.534). Not all the varying series of compossibilia represent the same amount of ordo plurium in uno. The greater the manifold and the greater its ordering unity, the more perfect a set of compossibilia is. Perfectio or Vollkommenheit is accordingly a higher grade of essence and hence that which makes essence real. Leibniz held: "...perfectionem esse gradum realitatis seu essentiae."[31] And in the same letter: "Perfectio mihi est quantitas seu gradus realitatis" (PS, I, 225). The greater the essential reality, the more a being will tend to exist. The most perfect ordering of essentiality - which is called perfection - does, and indeed, must exist. Existentia as the complementum possibilitatis is simply perfectio.

Baumgarten succinctly defined perfection as: "Si plura simul sumpta unius rationem sufficientem constituunt, CONSENTIUNT, consensus ipse est PERFECTIO, et unum, in quod consentitur, RATIO PERFECTIONIS DETERMINANS (focus perfectionis)" (M p. 26, §94). It is obvious that perfection is simply an intensification of the principle of veritas metaphysica and ultimately of the doctrine of oneness. Perfection is the manner in which the unum becomes maximally actual in the plura. It is, therefore, one of the most important metaphysical principles of rationalism.

Schiller designated the aestheticians of form as Vollkommenheitsmänner because in one way or another such theoreticians sought to ground and explain aesthetics, particularly beauty, in terms of the concept of perfectio. How this was done, will be shown presently. It suffices at this point to note that perfectio is one of the most important ontological constants that determine the objectivity and hence reality of any possible order of being.

Methodo Scientifica

In the previous section I sought to analyze the structure of metaphysical truth for German Rationalism. Truth expressed as a judgment is possible because metaphysical truth constitutes the essence of being. Truth is in things, as Wolff maintained: "Vertitas adeo, quae transendentialis apellatur & rebus ipsis inesse intelligitur, est ordo in varietate eorum, quae simul sunt ac se invicem consequuntur, aut, si mavis, ordo eorum, quae enti conveniunt" (Ontologia, p. 383, §495). The truth which inheres in things is that which is ultimately grasped by the intellect. It is the unknown which the intellect makes known. The discovery procedure entails a philosophical methodology.   Concerning philosophical knowing Baumgarten writes, "Philosophia est scientia qualitatum in rebus sine fide cognoscendarum.   Scientia est cognitio ex certis certa; ergo philosophia ex certis cognoscenda est."[32] "Scientific" knowledge derives from certainly known premises.   For this reason, philosophy as a metaphysical procedure is always a demonstrative process.   As Wolff writes: : "In philosophia prima [sive ontologia] utendum est methodo demonstrative" (Ontologia, p. 2, §4).

In order to grasp the origins of aesthetic theory in terms of German rationalism it is necessary to pay some attention to the metaphysical method used, i.e., to the theoretical process by means of which metaphysical truth in things is grasped as truth through assertions.   Baumgarten himself conceived the science of aesthetics as a metaphysics of beauty.   Baumgarten wrote in the Handschrift for his Kollegium on aesthetics (probably held in 1750): "Will man... in Methapern reden, und liebt man die Mythologie der Alten, so nenne man [die Aesthetik] die Philosophie der Musen und der Grazien. Noch mehr da die Metaphysik das Allgemeine der Wissenschaften enthält, so könnte man die Aesthetik nach einiger Ähnlichkeit die Metaphysik des Schönen nennen."[33]   Meier himself is even more assertive: "Weil nun die Metaphysik die ersten Gründe der ganzen menschlichen Erkenntnis enthält, so kan man sagen, daß die Aesthetick sich gegen alle schönen Künste und Wissenschaften eben so verhalte, als die Metaphysick gegen die ganze menschliche Erkenntnis, und daß sie daher mit Recht die Metaphysick aller schönen Wissenschaften und Künste könne genant werden."[34]   Meier's formulation is of particular interest.   First of all, aesthetics is related to its subject matter as metaphysics is to its subject matter.   Furthermore, this relationship grounds the metaphysical procedure that is paradigmatic for aesthetic theorizing.   We must grasp the nature of this procedure itself.

Let us first examine the definition of metaphysics.   Baumgarten, with his usual terseness, defines metaphysics: "METAPHYSICA est scientia primorum in humana cogitione principiorum.   Ad metaphysicam referuntur ontologia, cosmologia, psychologia, et theologia naturalis" (M, p. 1, §§1 and 2).   And Meier with unusual brevity constructs a similar definition.   "Die Metaphysik ist...die Wissenschaften, welche die ersten Gründe, oder die ersten Grund-Wahrheiten der gantzen menschlichen Erkenntniß enthält" (M, I, 5, §3). These definitions evince a peculiarity proper to rationalism.   The strangeness in such definitions resides in the fact that the above conceptions of metaphysics say nothing about being.   Traditionally, metaphysics is the science of being qua being.   But being is not even mentioned!   To be sure, ontology, which is the first metaphysical science, is,as Baumgarten wrote, the "scientia praedicatorum entis generaliorum" (M, p.2 §4).   But these predicates of being are not the first object of the metaphysician's intellectual vision.   The principles of being are somehow a function of the princples of human knowledge (or knowing).   Again Baumgarten: "Entis praedicata generaliora sunt prima cognitionis humanae principia, ergo ontologia refertur, cum ratione ad metaphysicam" (M, p.2, §5).   In order to reach the truth in things the metaphysician does not first focus upon the res themselves, rather upon the process of thinking (or knowing) itself.   In this very process there resides the ratio for the praedicata generaliora of being. We must now attend to the reason for this metaphysical peculiarity of the Vollkommenheitsmänner.

The historical origins for the rationalistic methodo scientivica lies in Descartes' cogito, ergo sum. As noted above, Descartes developed this thesis as an answer to scepticism. Methodologically, Descartes consciously severed the human mind from objective reality by means of his universal doubt. However, Descartes could not doubt the doubting and thereby the reality of the subjectum that does the doubting. Reality is given in the cogito's own reflexive act. The cogito, ergo sum as an assertion of truth expresses or posits that which lies within the subjectum (=I-principle). That which is asserted cannot oppose or contadict the subjectum as being. The criteria for objective reality or for being are not present immediately as objectivity, rather are articulated as the implicit principa cogitandi that make the cogito, ergo sum assertion possible. Since the cogito reaches real being, namely the sum, whatever is posited with this thinking process, is posited also for being (objectivity) per se. Now this cognitive power (Denkkraft or Vorstellungskraft) is simply der menschliche Verstand.

It is fascinating to follow Christian Wolff in his German metaphysics as he takes up Descartes' cogito, ergo sum and develops out of it a demonstrative method (cf. VG, pp. 1-6, §§1-9). This method is formally the same as that of mathematics (as the science of quantity) "Man siehet also / daß die Geometrischen Wahrheiten so gewiß erwiesen werden, / als daß wir selber sind und folgendes alles / was auf geometrische Art erwiesen wird/ so gewiß sey/ als daß wir selber sind" (VG, p. 5, §9)[35] In other words, the absolute certainty of the cogito, ergo sum is a material truth which contains implicitly the methodological form found in mathematics. And it is precisely through this form that an individual can intellectually grasp the certainty of self-existence. Mathematics as a science, however, is not grounded in sense experience, rather it is the product of the understanding's a priori development of its own concepts. Mathematical truth is certain because the subject and predicates can be shown necessarily to form an identity. Mathematics functions, therefore, as a formal model for metaphysical knowing per se and is grounded in the cogito, ergo sum.

Once Wolff establishes how the demonstrative method is grounded in the very cognitive process of the subject as it grasps itself as real, Wolff then turns to the cognitive process itself in the next sections in order to articulate just what principles this process entails. Wolff very quickly "demonstrates" that this process entails the principles of contradiction and of sufficient reason. In other words, without these cognitive principles there could be no grasping of the self as being. Consequently, these principles constitute and reveal essential truths of being. As Wolff wrote in his Ontologia: "...principium contraditionis & principium rationis sufficientis sunt fons omnis, quae datur in rebus, veritatis, hoc es, datus in ente veritas, quaetenus ea, quae insunt, per ista principia determinantur" (Ontologia, p. 385, §498). The principles of human cognition thus show themseleves also to the principles of being.

In short, the ontological outline of reality or objectivity is projected out of the structural principles of the self as a self-thinking subjectum. As Moses Mendelssohn wrote: "Der Mensch ist sich selbst die erste Quelle seines Wissens; er muss also von sich selbst ausgehen, wenn er sich von dem, was er weiss, und was er nicht weiss, Rachenschaft geben will."[36] This thinking self is, of course, "pure reason," i.e. reason freed from any empirical content and functioning a priori according to its own principles. Reason spins, so to speak, out of itself the outline of the real.

Ordo plurium in uno is posited as a criterion for reality because such a unum constitutes the form of self-identity. The self as the objectum cogitatum must be thought as one, as self-identical. The principles of human knowing are the first principles of human knowing. Meier, as shown, defines metaphysical truth as order in variety. Meier also conceives metaphysical truth as agreement of being with the principles of human knowing. "Worin besteht die metaphysiche Wahreit einer Sache? Wir sagen, in der Uebereinstimmung der Sache mit den allgemeinen Grundsätzen der menschlichen Erkenntniβ "(M, I, 155, §89). Similarly Baumgarten: "Hinc VERITAS METAPHYSICA potest definiri per convenientiam entis cum principiis catholcis" (M, p. 25, §92) And, of course, the most catholic (i.e., universal) principles of human cognition are the principles of contradiction and of sufficient reason!

In the course of this study the rationalistic conception of the metaphysical analysis will be further considered. For the moment it suffices to note that objectivity and subjectivity are two sides of the same mataphysical coin. The constants that constitute objectivity are a function of the structure of subjectivity or of that which subjectivity posits out of itself. Correlatively, subjectivity is in itself oriented towards objectivity. Paradoxically, the metaphysics (and aesthetics) of form is objective because it is subjective. Objectivity is grounded in subjectivity, in "pure reason." Neither Baumgarten nor Meier discussed in any detail the purely methodological side of the science of aesthetics. Instead, they concentrated upon the praedicata generaliora of aesthetic being. However, a provisional methodological definition can be constructed. Aesthetics for Vollkommenheitsmänner is, in effect, grounded upon the principia pulchre cogitandi or, more accurately, upon the first principles of aesthetic consciousness (=cognitio aesthetica). Baumgarten defined metaphysics as the "scientia primoum in humana cognitione principiorum." Provisionally, I contend, aesthetics, as a metaphysical science, was for Baumgarten (and for Meier) the "scientia primorum in humana cognitione sensitiva principiorum."[37] In the next few sections I shall seek to explain this contention.

C. The Aesthetic Universe

The Generative Principles of Aesthetic Theory

In the previous sections I have outlined the metaphysical universe that provides the system of objectivity constants for the Vollkommenheitsmänner. In the next few sections I shall concentrate upon the aesthetic universe in terms of which the Vollkommenheitsmänner analyzed the phenomenon of beauty. Again I stress the fact that I am expositing the dynamics of a school of thought. This procedure enables me to avoid certain problems in the secondary literature as a problem. Limiting attention to Baumgarten and Meier as founders of the aesthetics of form, one finds many contradictory positions amongst interpreters. Baumgarten, for example, is variously viewed as an originator of aesthetics, the last representative of a metaphysical or rhetorical tradition (Meier thereby becomes the father of aesthetics) or as in effect a proto-Kantian. Sometimes Meier and Baumgarten are equated (Meier being a populizer of Baumgarten), sometimes they are opposed as having

varying theories. Meier's aesthetics is variously judged as
metaphysical-objective or psychological-subjective. Such are but a few of
the disagreements among scholars.[38] The focal point of most studies,
however, has been the individual theorist and his specific system. Scholars
have accordingly and rightly been interested in distinguishing one theorist
from another. My view point is that of a school of thought. As long as the
theses of different theorists are plausible extensions of a specific
question-type and hence illustrative of a given school, problems of
consistency, agreement or disagreement between theorists relative to specific
theses, are not a necessary subject for discussion and debate in this study.
My view point renders much disagreement between scholars as meaningless
(i.e. for problems of school categorization). Only an assertion that a
"total" opposition exists between thinkers is of interest to me. In other
words, when a scholar asserts differences between, say Baumgarten and Meier
are so great that one should classify the men in different schools, I must,
of course, note if not defend my position. Fortunately, this is seldom
done. The result is that I will avoid any real discussions of secondary
literature, as tempting as it is to do so.

Perhaps a great deal of difference amongst interpreters arises from
their failure to grasp adequately the relationship between subject (or
subjectivity) and object (or objectivity) in the metaphysical process of
rationalistic theorizing. To think scientifically is, for Rationalism,
procedurally, to establish "die ersten Gründe" of a given science.
Methodologically, however, the rationes in rebus are cognitively discoverable
as a function of the thinking self (i.e. the principia cognitionis). This
peculiar unity between subjectivity and objectivity in rationalistic
philosophy is evinced by Meier. Meier writes about aesthetics as a science:

> Die Aesthetick sol eine Wissenschaft seyn. Da nun eine Wissenschaft
> eine Erkenntnis ist, welche aus ganz unumstößlichen Gründen herge-
> leitet wird, so mus auch die ganze Aesthetick auf dergleichen
> Gründe gebauet werden....Es ensteht hier von selbst die Frage,
> woher man die Gründe nehmen können, aus welchen die aesthetischen
> Regeln hergeteitet werden müssen. Ich werde nicht die Ausschwei-
> fung begehen, und aller der Gründe erwehnung thun, welche die Aes-
> thetick mit allen Wissenschaften gemein hat; sondern ich wil nur
> diejenigen anführen, die ihr besonders eigen sind. Ich rechne
> dahin 1) die Regeln der Vollkommenheiten und Schönheiten über-
> haupt. Die aesthetischen Schönheiten sind eine Art der Vollkommen-
> heiten. Da nun die Arten der Dinge dasjenige voraus setzen, was
> ihren Gattungen zukömt, (ab universali ad particulare valet conse-
> quentia) so fliessen die Regeln der Aesthetick aus den algemeinen
> Regeln aller Vollkommenheiten, 2) Die Lehre von der Seele, und in-
> sonderheit von der Natur der untern sinlichen Erkentnisvermögen
> derselben. Wie die Ursach beschaffen ist, so ist auch die Würckung
> beschaffen. Die schöne Erkentnis und der Vortrag derselben ist
> eine Würckung der untern Erkenntniskräfte...(Anf, I, 5-6, §3).[39]

It is clear that "die ersten Gründe" of the science of aesthetics are
derived from two sources. Aesthetic experience is clearly a function of the
objectivity constant "Vollkommenheit." This fact, of course, led Schiller to
designate the aestheticians of form as Vollkommenheitsmänner. The rules of
the arts flow from the notion of "Vollkommenheit." Consequently, aesthetic

theory is concerned with "objectivity." But aesthetic theory must also focus upon the "soul" (viz. subject) that produces and experiences beauty. Aesthetics is also a function of psychology, of subjectivity. Psychology is concerned with the ontological structure of the "self." As Baumgarten wrote: "PSYCHOLOGIA est scientia praedicatorum animae generalium" (M, p. 173, §502). That which can enter as an object into consciousness is determined by the structure of the thinking subject. Aesthetic rules flow from the notion of "Vollkommenheit." But as we have seen that "Vollkommenheit" itself is derived from the "Prinzip vom Grunde." This principle in things is simultaneously grounded in the principia cognitionis humanae prima. The same thinking self that projects out of itself the outline of ontological objectivity, also projects out of itself the outline of aesthetic objectivity, namely aesthetic perfection. It is, accordingly, not surprising that Meier seeks the first principles of aesthetic theory in a Seelenlehre.[40] This tendency does not, however, make Meier's aesthetics "subjective" in the sense of being cut off from objectivity.

What, moreover, belongs to the essence of the soul? Baumgarten writes: "...anima mea est vis repraestentativa" (M, p. 174, §506). For Meier and others the soul is a "Vorstellungskraft." The soul is a vis representativa in that it re-presents reality to the self from the vantage point of the self within the totality of being. This view of the soul is, of course, rooted in Leibniz' monadology and doctrine of pre-established harmony.[41] The important thing is that the outline of objectivity (as far as man is concerned) is a function of consciousness or, more accurately, of the activity of becoming conscious (=ars cogitandi). Consicousness entails, consequently, a twofold structure, namely the object cognized (cogitatum) and the cognizing subject (actus cogitandi). This duality finds mediation and unity in the notion of cognitio (sometimes the term cogitatio is used). In other words, the cognitio, as the effect of the vis repraesentativa in act, unites both objectivity and subjectivity. In his Acroasis Logica Baumgarten defines cognition: "COGNITIO* est complexus repraesentationum, sue perceptionum...*eine Erkenntnis" (AL, pp. 1-2, §3). Cognitio evinces objective contents (i.e. repraesentationes) and the very act of awareness of such contents (namely the perceptiones). In other words, the very structure of consciousness that makes the cogito possible generates simultaneously the structure (=ordo, ratio, unum) of the cogitatum. The structure of knowing and the structure of the known are aspects of the form of cognition.

A further analysis of the nature of cognitio in the human soul will reveal how the Vollkommenheitsmänner constructed the aesthetic universe, whose crowning perfection is beauty. Concerning the object of aesthetic theory Meier writes: "Die Aesthetick handelt von den schönen Erkentnis" (Anf, I, 7, §4). "Schöne Erkentnis" is a species of the "Erkentnis" per se. The nature of "Erkentnis" in general grounds aesthetic cognitio. We shall see that the metaphysical category of Vollkommenheit refers to both the subjective and the objective poles of aesthetic cognition and that Vollkommenheit is accordingly the principium rationis of "schöne Erkentnis." But first, the nature of cognitio must be further analyzed.

Gradus Cognitionis

To be is to be a connexial part within a totally determined and determinate system of "Gründe" and "Folgen." Perfect knowledge of being would encompass an awareness (perceptio) of all the notae (Merkmale) that constitute the essential contents of all things and their connexial relationality (the unum in pluribus) uniting the notae. What would be known is ontological reality in itself. Such perfect knowledge is possessed only by God (as an infinite mind). Such cognitio would be called distincta, adequata, and perfectissima or in German deutlich, ausführlich, and vollständig. In other words, the plura, the unum, and their nexus would be totally present to consciousness as a connexial whole.

Such perfect knowledge is, of course, only fully possible for God. Reality, totally intelligible in itself, transcends man's Erkenntnis-Kräfte. As a result, human cognitio frequently cannot grasp the full intelligibility in things. Human cognitio is often confusa or verworren. In other words, knowledge is "confused" because the human anima cannot discern the objective unum (principium rationis sufficientis) relating the plura into the ordo realitatis. The limited human mind can be clearly aware of notae and of the differences between the notae without having a distinct awareness of the unity between them. The result is a cognitio clara et confusa. Although there is a ratio in the order of things, it, as the object of awareness, remains obscura or dunkel to the mind. Finally, if the contents of consciousness become ever more blurry to the point of disappearing, the cognitio is progressively obscura. Meißner briefly presented the Leibniz-Wolffian grades of cognition in his lexicon. Although thinkers would sometimes modify the terminology somewhat, Meißner's schematic presentation is typical for the rationalistic school (cf. PL, p. 59).

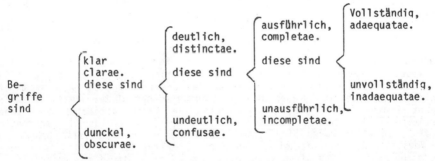

It must be stressed that the categories of deutlich, klar, verworren, and dunkel do not refer per se to specific contents of experience (e.g. intellectual versus empirical contents). The categories refer first of all to the mode of perception, to the subjective aspect of cognitio. They represent the limits of man's cognitive powers, not the limits of what really is. Just because a repraesentatio "appears" to the mind as confusa, it does not follow that the res itself is confusa. Indeed, to an infinite mind all is klar, deutlich, and vollständig (i.e. Grund and Folge). Consequently, such cognitive categories are relative. A scientist, for instance, can have a clear and rational concept of parts of an abstract problem and yet have a "confused" notion of the logical unity between the parts. Indeed, because man is limited, he possesses very little if any pure and totally distinct knowledge. Even man's most distinct viz. rational notions are to a degree verworren.[42]

However, although such categories are relative, there does exist two kinds of contents that most often are either verworren or deutlich. Empirical or sensate notae are klar, and verworren. Mathematical notae are klar, deutlich and often also vollständig. In other words, deutliche Erkenntnis is logico-intellectual in nature, whereas klare, aber verworrene Erkenntnis is sinnlich in nature. The grades of cognitio can be schematically represented in the following manner:[43]

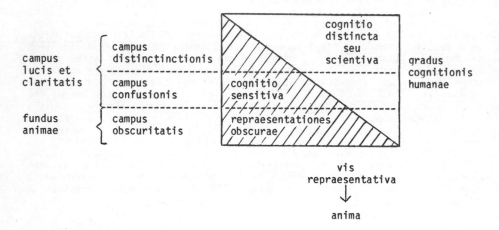

$$\text{campus lucis et claritatis}\ \left\{ \begin{array}{l}\text{campus distinctinctionis}\\ \text{campus confusionis}\end{array}\right.$$

fundus animae { campus obscuritatis

cognitio distincta seu scientiva

cognitio sensitiva

repraesentationes obscurae

gradus cognitionis humanae

vis repraesentativa
↓
anima

Materia Universi Aesthetici Prima

Aesthetic experience is a species of cognitio.. Therefore, the "stuff", so to speak, out of which it arises and is constituted must be a grade of cognitio. Although the grades of cognition arise out of the limits of man's Erkenntiskräfte, they are, as contents, de facto ultimates in human experience. The campus confusionis et claritatis yields the aesthetic "stuff." In other words Sinnlichkeit is a formal characteristic proper to the Vorstellungen of aesthetic cognition. Aesthetic cognition must be understood as a species of sensate cognition. This is the first principle of the aesthetic universe of the Vollkommenheitsmanner. Meier, it will be recalled, sought a starting point, a Grundsatz, for aesthetic theory. He found this Grundsatz is the notion of senstate cognition. Meier writes:

> Nunmehr will ich es versuchen, einen Grundsatz fest zu setzen, von dem erweisen werden kan, daß der alle Eigenschaften an sich habe, die ein Satz haben muß, wenn er der erste Grundsatz aller schönen Künste und Wissenschaften seyn soll. Ich nehme nemlich diese Regel an: Die sinnliche Erkenntniß sey so schön als möglich. Oder wenn man die Regel sich in einem einzigen Begriffe vorstellen will, so kan man, die gröste Schönheit der sinnlichen Erkenntiß, als den ersten und allgemeinen Begriff ansehen, worunter alle Regeln aller schönen Künste und Wissenschaften begriffen sind, und also enthält dieser Begrif in der That den allerersten Grundsatz aller dieser Künste und Wissenschaften (BEG, p.43, §20).

In his Kollegium on aesthetic theory (ca. 1750) Baumgarten specified the area of aesthetic experience:

> Wir kommen zuerest auf die schönen Erfindungen...[und] wir
> verstehen darunter, ein Ding sich zum ertsen Male so vorstellen,
> daß es in die Sinne fällt und rührt. Sie enthält die Regeln schön
> und rührend von Dingen zu denken, davor man bisher noch nicht so
> gedacht. Die Erfindung gehört für die Äesthetik, denn die
> Schönheit der Erkenntnis ist der Zweck derselben. Alles was schön
> ist, gehöret es nicht hierher....
>
> Wir nennen...die Äesthetik eine Wissenschaft von der
> sinnlichen Erkenntnis..., weil die Hauptbegriffe sinnlich bleiben,
> so wie man das einen deutlichen und scientifischen Vortraq nennt,
> wo die Hauptbegriffe deutlich sind....Die Schönheit wird hier nicht
> in die Verwirrung gesetzet, sondern es wird gezeigt, wie verworrene
> Vorstellungen schön werden sollen (H, pp. 80-81, §§14 and 17).

And finally, Johann Georg Sulzer, much later in the century, delineated the object of aesthetic theory in the following manner:

> Die Hauptabsicht der schönen Künste geht auf die Erwekung eines
> lebhaften Geflühls des Wahren und des Guten, also mus die Theorie
> derselben [d.h. die Aesthetik] auf die Theorie der undeutlichen
> [bez. sinnlichen] Erkenntnis und der Empfindungen gegründet seyn.[44]

From the above citations it is clear that representationes sensitativae are the matter, so to speak, the materia prima of an aesthetic universe. This aesthetic universe does not per se exclude all "deutliche Erkenntnis. The main thing is that Sinnlichkeit predominates. As soon as the dominant sensate content has been "cleared up" to the level of rational or distinct clarity, the aesthetic experience (and hence the aesthetic universe) disappears. Aesthetic cognitio entails, consequently, a sensate content as the manifold (plura) of its possibility and hence reality. Aesthetic experience emerges when the sensate manifold has been ordered or transformed in such a way that it becomes beautiful. Aethetic theory has its theoretical task to explain the order of this transformed sensate experience.

I have now specified the plura of the aesthetic universe of the Vollkommenheitsmänner. But reality is just not a manifold, rather an ordo plurium in uno. How are the plura sensitiva to be ordered into an aesthetic unum? We shall see that perfectio is precisely their integrative factor. For the moment I will continue to follow the methodological procedure of rationalistic metaphysics. In other words, the principle of unity in things is ascertainable as an extension of how (ordo) the soul thinks its contents. The next question to answer is, accordingly, how does the soul represent the unum in order to produce a cognitio aesthetica?

Logic and Aesthetics

There are two basic types of cognition, namely distinct and confused. The content of knowledge for each field is respectively rational-intellectual and sensate-empirical. But cognition is not simply the awareness of a plura. For there to be cognitio, there must be always a cognizable note of unity that makes an object possible for consciousness. Meier himself writes: "Ein Merkmal, ein Kennzeichen der Erkenntniβ und der Sachen (nota, character cognitionis et rei) ist dasjenige in der Erkenntniβ oder den Sachen, welches, wenn es erkant wird, der Grund ist, weswegen wir uns ihrer bewuβt sind..."[45] Without some sort of Grund there can be no reality, no possibility of consciousness. An awareness of the Grund in things is, of course, the awareness of the truth of things and the propositional formulation of such an awareness constitutes logical truth. The very nature of the soul is to represent being or that which can be (possibility). There are, of course, different levels and kinds of being. The various sciences (e.g. physics, psychology, cosmology, ontology, etc.) are the products of knowing different modes of being. There is, however, only one cogitating process. This process, conceived as an Erkenntniskraft, is the activity of the soul and has its own rules as has been noted above. Although there are many different kinds of objects to know, there are only two basic properties possessed by objects. That is, objects are either distinct or sensate (or some sort of mixture). The soul represents to itself notae distinctae and notae confusae. Accordingly, the soul possesses two basic faculties of knowing, respectively the facultas cognoscitiva superior or das obere Erkenntnisvermögen and the facultas cognoscitiva inferior or das untere Erkenntnisvermögen. Each faculty of the soul has its subclass of rules which enable it to function most perfectly, i.e., to produce a perfection of cognition of being. Meier writes: "Alle unsere Erkentnis ist entweder deutlich vernünftig philosophisch, oder undeutlich und sinlich. Mit der ersten beschäftiget sich die Vernunftlehre, und mit der letzten die Aesthetick...Weil nun die Aesthetick sich gegen die sinliche Erkentnis eben so verhält, als die Vernunftlehre gegen die vernünftige; so kan man sie die Logic der untern Erkentniskraft nennen, (Gnoseologiam inferiorem)" (Anf, I, 8-9, §5).

Both logic and aesthetics have as their respective goals the perfection of their respective forms of cognition. The rules for thinking truth (be it distinct or empirical truth) have, of course, their origin in the one single power of the soul. This single power is simply specified by the kind of object towards which it is directed.[46] Acordingly, similiarities pertain between logic and aesthetics, though specified in different manners. This is reflected in their definition. Baumgarten defines each science in the following manner:

> LOGICA (dialectica, ars rationis, analytica, sensus veri et falsi, scientia scientiarum, medicina mentis, organon, pharus intellectus,) ARTIFICIALIS est philosophia cognitionis intellectualis perficiendae.. (AL, p.5, §9)

> AESTHETICA (theoria liberalium artium, gnoseologia inferior, ars pulchre cognitandi, ars analogi rationis,) est scientia cognitionis sensitivae.[47]

> Aesthetices finis est perfectio cognitionis sensitivae, qua talis, §1. Haec autem est pulcritudo...(A, p.6, §14)

The various definitions given in apposition are of interest as they represent different ways of viewing the same process. However, the main point for my analysis at this stage is the juxtaposition of logic as an ars rationis and aesthetics as an ars analogi rationis. Logic is in effect an ars logice cogitandi whereas aesthetics is an ars pulchre cogitandi. The general principle that orders both types of thinking is the ratio. A ratio is the unum that determines the soul's ordering of the plura into a connexial totality. In other words, the cognitive process itself has a ratio that functions as its rule of order. The result is that every cognitio possess certain formal features. The nature of these formal features consitutes the perfection of cognitio. The notion of the perfectio cognitionis must be further detailed.

The Structure of the "Perfectio Cognitionis"

Let us recall the definition of perfection as given by Baumgarten. "Si plura simul sumta unius rationem sufficientem constituunt, CONSENTIUNT, consensus ipse est PERFECTIO, et unum, in quod consentitur, RATIO PERFECTIONIS DETERMINANS (focus perfectionis)" (M, p. 26, §94). This definition holds formally for all cognitio. In other words, cognitio entails a manifold, a unity, and a relationship of the manifold to unity. The greater the manifold, the unity, and the connexial interrelationship, the greater is the cognitive perfection. Accordingly, Meier writes about intellectual knowledge.

> Wenn das Mannifaltige in einer Erkenntniβ zu einer Absicht übereinstimt, oder den hinreichenden Grund von derselben enthält; so besteht darin die Vollkommenheit der Erkentniβ (perfectio cognitionis)....

> Die gelehrte [philosophische] Erkentniβ muβ mit den Vollkomme-nheiten der Erkentiniβ auesgeschmückt seyn....(AaV, p. 7, §§22, 24)

A cognition that is "ausgeschmückt" with perfection is one grounded in unity. In intellectual knowledge all representations are seen as integrated into a connexial focus (sufficient reason). Individual representations lose their isolation, opaqueness, and atomisticity in perfected intellectual knowledge and, instead, manifest the determining and ordering power of the nexus of unity. This rational unum, because it determines the ordering process of the manifold and is that in which the manifold agrees (constituunt), is clearly a perfectio. The unity of cognition is, therefore, a formal feature of perfected cognition per se.

The principle of cognitive unity has further articulations. There are various specified ways of ordering the manifold and ultimately relating it as part of cognition to the object allegedly known. Baumgarten lists certain formal features of rational knowledge:

> Die wahre Erkenntniβ ist eine Realität...Der Grad der Erkenntniβ, welcher ihr zukommt, weil sie mehrere Gegenstände vorstelt, ist die Weitläuftigkeit (ubertas, copia extensio, divitiae, vastitas cognitionis)...Ihre Wichtigkeit (dignitas, nobilitas, magnitude, gravitas, maiestas), weil sie grössere vorstelt....Je richtere Sachen eine Erkenntniβ vorstelt, und je ordenlicher, desto richtiger ist sie, folglich auch desto grösser. Eine genaue Erkenntniβ (exacta, exasciata) stelt richtigere Gegenstände vor...Eine grössere Ordnung in der Erkenntniβ ist das Methodische derselben (acroamaticum, disciplinale), ...Die

Vorstellungen in einer Seele sind entweder grössere, oder kleinere, und in so ferne sie Gründe sind, wird ihnen eine Kraft beygelegt...Die grössere Kraft derselben heißt ihre Stärke (robur) ...(Meta, pp. 161-162, §379).

Meier in his Vernunftlehre adds the formal properties of truth (agreement of the cognition with the object referred to), of practicality (the use of intellectual knowledge to guide praxis), and certainty. The structure of perfected intellectual cognition can be in part schematically represented:

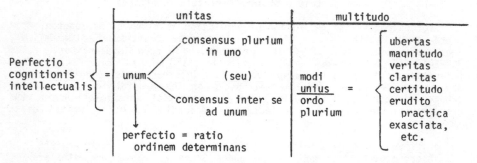

The features listed above are by no means exhaustive. Ubertas, magnitudo, etc. are different ways which the unum as a formal ratio determinans is united with (or, better, unites) the multitudo (manifold) of cognition. The more a given intellectual cognition exhibits such formal modes of unity, the more perfect it is, i.e. the more the ars rationis dominates the ars logice cogitandi. Cognition thereby comes to perfected logical form. Baumgarten's definition of perfection can be further specified as a principle of perfected knowledge in the following manner: "Si plura cognitionis intelletualis simul sumta unius rationem sufficientem constituunt, consentiunt logice, consensus ipse est perfectio cognitionis intellectualis." This formulation is, of course, mine, not Baumgarten's.

Perfectio Cognitionis Sensitivae

The matter or material of intellectual cognition is clear and distinct representations. The principle ordering the intellectual manifold is the ars rationis. A rationally ordered intellectual manifold evinces formally certain logical features. Some of these were briefly examined in the preceding section. The manifold of sensate cognition consists, of course, of notae confusae, i.e. empirical contents. These contents too must be ordered if sensate cognition is to be generated and perfected. The principle of order is the ars analogi rationis. Concerning this ordering power, Baumgarten writes:

Nexum quorundam confuse, quorundam distincte percipio. Ergo habeo intellectum nexum rerum perspicientem, i.e. RATIONEM, & facultates nexus confusius cognoscentes, quales 1) inferior facultas identitates rerum diversitates rerum cognoscendi, quo ingenium sensitivm, 2) inferior facultas diversitates, quo acumen sensitivum pertinet, memoria sensitiva, facultas fingendi, facultas diiudicandi, quo iudicum sensitivum, & sensum, expectatio casuum similium, facultas characteristica sensitiva, Hae omnes, quantenus in repraesentando rerum nexu rationi similes sunt, constituunt ANALOGON RATIONIS, complexum facultatem animae nexum confuse repraesentantium (M, pp. 235-236, §640).

Meier himself makes no real use of the term analogon rationis. In his translation of Baumgarten's Metaphysica Meier does render the term as "das Vernunftähnliche."[48] In his Anfangsgründe aller schönen Wissenschaften Meier refers to "die schöne Vernunft" and defines it: "Die schöne Vernunft ist das Vermögen, den Zusammenhang der Dinge, folglich auch den Zusammenhang der Wahrheiten, auf eine aesthetisch deuliche Art zu erkennen."[49] The "aesthetisch deutliche Art zu erkennen" is simply the perfection of sensate cognition. In other words, Meier's "schöne Vernunft" has the same basic function as Baumgarten's analogon rationis. Also Meier's discussion of the "das sinnliche Beurtheilungsvermögen" as the power to judge sensate perfection and his analysis of "der sinnliche Witz" as the sensate perception of unity parallels Baumgarten's discussions (and may, indeed, be influenced by them). Furthermore, as is evident from the quotation above, Baumgarten discusses the analogon rationis in the terms of cognitive faculties in much the same manner Meier understood them. "Das Vernünftähnliche" is, in short, part of Meier's "Seelenlehre."

It should be first of all noted that, with the expection of the Dichtungsvermögen, the analogon rationis entails the same faculties as does the ratio. Indeed, this is to be expected. There is only one Vorstellungkraft in the human soul. This one power is specified by the objects it considers. The nature of the soul remains constant, i.e. its nature is to represent reality as the one ordering the many. As an intellectual power, the soul can perceive intellectual (distinct) notes and thereby represent intellectual nexus. The selfsame synthetic power is, however, limited, i.e. it often can only represent to itself "verworrene Vorstellungen." "Verworrene Vorstellungen" constitute, of course, the plura, the "stuff" out of which the aesthetic representation is constructed and hence, by means of which the aesthetic experience (= cognitio aesthetica) is generated. The problem for an aesthetics of form is, as Baumgarten noted: "Die Schönheit wird hier nicht in die Verwirrung gesetzet, sondern es wird gezeigt, wie verworrene Vorstellungen schön werden sollen" (H, p. 81, §17). The solution is that the Vorstellungskraft must order the plura under a formal principle of unity. Being, including aesthetic being, always entails an ordo plurium in uno.

It is at this point that Baumgarten and Meier (singularly or collectively) have been least understood. The human soul can only order a plura by means of a unum. Such an ordering constitutes, of course, perfectio (= consensus plurium in uno). The unum as a ratio ordinem determinans is a constitutive feature of the cognitio and of the repraesentationes that make up the object of the cognitio. This aesthetic ratio or unum evinces a unity specific to its own aesthetic nature. In other words, the aesthetic ordo plurium in uno has its own peculiar structure, similar to, but distinct from the intellectual unum. This is because the unum itself is an analogon rationis. It is similar to an intellectual ratio in that it supplies the sufficient reason (Grund) for a manifold. It differs from the intellectual unum in that its very perfection entails sensate notes. The aesthetic unum itself must be "undeutlich," not just the plura. Meier writes: "Die ganze sinliche Erkentnis [der aesthetischen Vorstellung] wird von uns undeutlich erkant. Folglich müssen alle Volkommenheiten derselben, in so ferne sie eine sinliche Erkentnis ist, solche Volkommenheiten seyn, die undeutlich erkant werden. Dergliechen Volkommenheiten nent man aber Schönheiten. Folglich besteht, die Schönheit der Erkentnis, in derjenigen Uebereinstimmung des Mannigfaltigen in derselben, welches sinlich erkant werden kan" (Anf, II, 46, §28). In short, the sensate principle of unity, i.e. the aesthetic "Vollkommenheit," cannot be reduced on principle to logical or intellectual structures. The principle of unity itself must partake of Sinnlichkeit!

Above it was shown that the perfectio becomes the form of cognition insofar as the representations exhibit a consensus plurium in uno. Such a consensus, as a formal feature of cognition per se, also constitutes the perfectio cognitionis sensitivae. Meier succinctly describes the analogous structure of aesthetic cognition:

> Wenn wir eine Schönheit gewahr werden wollen, so müssen wir in eine Sache 1) viel mannigfaltiges entdecken; 2) den Brennpunct der Schönheit, oder einen Zweck; 3) die Uebereinstimmung des mannigfaltigen zu diesem Zweck.[50]

As noted, the unity of aesthetic cognition is similar to that of intellectual cognition in that it orders the many to the one. This consensus inter se ad unum is the perfection of sensate cognition that transforms such cognition into aesthetic experience. However, this aesthetic unity differs from the unum of intellectual cognition in that it must partake in "Verworrenheit," i.e. in "sinnliche Vorstellungen."[51] In other words, the sensate representation of unity must possess in itself a sensate power of determination. In imitation of Baumgarten, Meier designated such a unifying representation formally as a "Hauptvorstellung" or a "Thema." Meier writes:

> In einer aesthetischen Ausführung müssen alle Gedanken, woraus zusammengesetzt ist, dergestalt genau mit einander verbunden seyn, daß kein einziger überflüßig sey, sondern daß sie alle aufs festeste mit einander verknüpft sind. Es mus sich also ein jeder zu dem Ganzen, wie ein unentbehrlicher Theil, verhalten, welcher nicht ohne Verletzung des Ganzen von den übrigen abgesondert werden kan....Diejenige Vorstellung, oder derjenige in und unter welchem alle übrigen Gedanken, die in einer [aesthetischen] Ausführung vorkommen, enthalten sind, wollen wir die Hauptvorstellung (thema) nennen, und es ist ohne mein Erinnern klar, daß alle aesthetische Ausführungen eine Hauptvorstellung enthalten müssen....Weil in allen aesthetischen Ausführungen eine Einheit angetroffen werden mus, so mus man jedesmal nur eine Hauptvorstellung abhandeln" (Anf, III, 294-295, §684).

In a much more terse manner Baumgarten made the same definition in his early work on the nature of poetry. "Nexus repraesentationum poeticarum debet facere ad cognitionem sensitivam, ergo debet esse poeticus....Id, cuius repraesentatio aliarum in oratione adhibitarum rationem sufficientem continet, suam vero non habet in aliis est THEMA."[52] Meier's definition of a "Hauptvorstellung" is simply an extension of the definition of a poetic theme to a general aesthetic category of unity. The unum of a work of art (at least, the verbal arts) is a theme. The various sensate images, metaphors, examples, representations, etc., obtain perfection when they consent (agree) in the theme and function as its articulation. The "Hauptvorstellung" is the nexus sensitivus or the ratio sensitiva.[53] The cognition of a sensate manifold, of a theme, and of their interrelationship constitutes the aesthetic consensus plurium in uno and thereby the perfectio cognitionis sensitivae. The result is, of course, "schöne Erkenntnis," which reveals itself to be "das Vernunftähnliche."

Not only is there an analogy between the logical and the sensate unum, but there is also one between the modi unius of each cognitive faculty. In other words, aesthetic cognition, precisely because it entails perfection, too must be "ausgeschmückt" with the features of cognitive unity and the relationship of this unity to the manifold. The perfection of aesthetic cognition is a subclass of the nature of cognitive perfection per se. As Phillip Gäng reminds his readers: "Vollkommenheit is also ein Oberbegriff, der auch den Begriff von Schönheit unter sich enthält."[54] In his Kollegium Baumgarten maintained:

> Die Ästhetik wird die Vollkommenheit haben müssen, die Erkenntnis überhaupt haben muß, wann sie vollkommen sein soll. Die Metaphysik hat uns schon gelehrt, daß die Kenntnis um so viel besser ist, je reicher, edler, richtiger, klarer, gewissenhafter und lebhafter sie ist. Diese 6 Kennzeichen geben ihr ihre Vorzüge. Die ästhetische Kenntnis muß eben dieselben haben, sie muß reich, edel, wahr, voll Licht, gewiß aund lebthaft sein.... (H, 83, §22)

And in his Aesthetica Baumgarten writes in the corresponding paragraph:

> Ubertas, magnitudo, veritas, claritas, certitudo, et vita cognitionis, quatenus consentiunt in una perceptione, et inter se...dant omnis cognitionis perfectionem, phaenomena sensitivae pulchritudinem, universalem, praesertim rerum et cogitationum, in quibus juvat
> Copia, nobilitas, veri lux certa moventis. (A, 9, §22)

Meier too constructs a parallel between logical and aesthetic categories. Indeed, the vast majority of both Meier and Baumgarten's respective aesthetic theories are taken up with the problem of what I have called the aesthetic modi unius. In other words, such categories are specifications of the unum aestheticum insofar as it constitutes the pure form of aesthetic cognition. The various "Theorien der schönen Künste and Wissenschaften" that dot the historical landscape of 18th century aesthetic theory repeatedly made use of such categories.[55] Each author, of course, made his own modifications. I shall not delineate the meaning of Baumgarten's six categories. Such an analysis would, for instance, show that each category, whose model lies in logic, contains a specific sensate form of unity. The ubertas (vastitas) refers, for instance, to the "richness" of the manifold, the greater the unitive powers of the unum and hence the greater the perfectio. The main point to hold in mind is that the categories of the modi unius "consentiunt in una perceptione" and hence constitute articulations of the aesthetic principle of sufficient reason. They are derivatives of the aesthetic ratio determinans. Indeed, they constitute the formal ordo of such a ratio.

D. Beauty as the Perfection of the Aesthetic Universe

Perfection as the Principle of Aesthetic Objectivity

Thus far I have briefly outlined the ontological universe of the Vollkommenheitsmänner. The objective heart (= the objectivity constant par excellence) is the Prinzip vom Grunde. The real is a function of the unum. The plura are real to the degree that they participate in the unum. Conversely, the unum becomes actualized ("erfült") when it is articulated as the ordo plurium. When the unum manifests itself as the maximum variety unified by the maximum order, it becomes perfectio. Perfectio thereby becomes the "really real" of the rationalistic universe. The ontological universe of rationalism is the reality out of which aesthetic being arises and is constructed. Aesthetic being entails a limitation or specification of ontological being. As a class of being, aesthetic being must and does exemplify the structure of ontological being. Therefore, the principles of ontological being, including the principle of perfection, hold for the formal structure of aesthetic being. The ontological universe of the Vollkommenheitsmänner functions as the paradigm model out of which the general question-types were generated for limited areas of being such as aesthetic reality.

Besides examining the ontological universe I also examined the material ingredients of the aesthetic universe and the cognitive mode of awareness of this universe. In other words, the first major problem facing the aestheticians of form was to determine the nature of that which specifies ontological being into aesthetic being. What, so to speak, is the "material" of the aesthetic manifold? This question only had sense and only could be answered in the terms of the ontology of form. All reality is an sich intelligible. However, the human mind is limited and as a result it can often only represent being as appearance (phenomena), i.e., as sensate contents.[56] The sensate constitutes the "stuff" of aesthetic being. Therefore, aesthetic consciousness is limited to and arises out of sensate contents. Having determined the "stuff" of the aesthetic universe, I next focused upon the structure of the aesthetic awareness of this universe. Since consciousness per se entails cognition, any awareness of any kind of being must also be conceived as a mode of cognition. The result is that aesthetic awareness entails sensate cognition. But cognition itself is a kind of being and hence it exemplifies the formal principle of being. In other words, cognition per se must partake in perfectio, if it is to be real. Real cognition is perfected cognition. Since the "stuff" of the aesthetic universe consists of sensate representations, aesthetic cognition must entail a perfectio cognitionis sensitivae. And as Baumgarten wrote: "Haec [perfectio] autem est pulchritudo" (A, p.6, §14). In other words, the perfection of sensate cognition transforms the sensate awareness into aesthetic awareness.

I have so far purposely refrained from analyzing the nature of this transformation. Instead I have concentrated upon some of the structural properties pertaining to the form of aesthetic awareness (=cognitio aesthetica). Accordingly, the emphasis has been upon the subjective meaning of the doctrine. After all, cognitio requires a cogito. The subjectum cogitans must have its sensate cognition so structured so as to become aware of beauty. I have not discussed all the ramifications of this doctrine and will not do so. I will, nevertheless, focus upon one further and important aspect of the doctrine. I must do this in order to complete my exposition of the aesthetic universe of form and to show how beauty constitutes the perfection of this universe.

The best way to proceed is to follow the rationalistic methodology to its fruition. I have repeatedly noted that the aesthetics of form is objective because it is subjective. In other words, the manner in which a subjectum cogitans thinks (i.e.. represents) its objectum is constitutive of what the objectum is. The outline of being resides in the structural principles of pure reason. "Pure" in this case refers to the "one" vis repraesentativa of the human soul insofar as this power furnishes consciousness with notae distinctae. The term "pure" intends in effect "Deutlichkeit" as the constitutive property of reason's ontological concepts (and hence of the contents of logical cognition). For reasons leading back to Descartes' cogito, ergo sum, reason functioning in its purity can and does project out of itself the reason in things. The veritas metaphysica is simultaneously the veritas in rebus, i.e. the conformity of things to the universal principles of human cognition. "Objectivity" as a system of constants exists because such constants are constitutive of the power that thinks being as objective.

The selfsame vis representativa is, however, not always able to function as a "pure" power, i.e. it cannot always represent to itself "deutliche Vorstellungen." Instead, this single "Erkenntniskraft" functions "impurely," i.e. it represents to itself "verworrene Vorstellungen" which, to all intents and purposes, constitute the de facto material of human cognition. Positively expressed, the subjectum cogitans often "thinks" sensately, i.e. produces "sinnliche Vorstellungen." These very representations are the content of the human mind's "impure" perceptions. Together the repraesentationes sensitivae and the perceptiones sensitivae constitute the cognitio sensitiva. In other words, cognitio sensitivae entails for Baumgarten a "complexus repraesentationum infra distinctionem subsistentium" (A, p.7 §17). In his Acroasis Logica, Baumgarten added the notion of perceptio in the definition. The important point is that cognitio does not only refer to the form of awareness but also to the contents of awareness, be they material or formal. More precisely, the form of awareness can only be insofar as the contents of awareness (more accurately, the complexus of such contents) are so formed. For example, ubertas (Reichtum) is a formal property of perfected cognition because such cognition encompasses richly the manifold perceptiones of an object. The necessary interconnection between subjectivity and objectivity, form and content, or the manner of knowing and the known is a plausible extension of the cogito, ergo sum thesis or the doctrine of being as oneness. In the cogito, ergo sum subject and object are one, only modally distinct. The principles of thinking the object are simultaneously those of the object thought. These principles, either subjectively or objectively taken, evince the form of oneness (or oneness as form).

The same relationship that pertains between pure reason and ontological being also pertains between "impure" reason (=sensate consciousness) and sensate being. That which generates this similarity is the fact that there is only one representative power in the soul. The rules governing the activity of this power hold formally for all its kinds of content. As an intellectual faculty this one power produces a manifold of repraesentationes distinctae. Similarly, this same power as a sensate faculty produces repraesentationes infra distinctionem subsistentiae (i.e., sensitivae). However, the nature of this power is not just to represent manifoldness. It is, instead, primarily directed towards oneness, albeit as the order of the manifold. In this general sense, the vis repraesentativa is correctly called "reason." This faculty conceived as a positing viz representing power is governed by general rules which are most abstractly formulated in logic (Vernunftlehre). Concerning the main synthetic rules of the human mind Hermann Samuel Reimarus writes: "Alle Kräfte haben ihre Regel," wodurch ihr Bemühen etwas gewisses zu verrichten bestimmt ist....Weil nun die Kraft zu reflectieren in einem Bemühen zur Einsicht der Einstimmung und des Widerspruchs besteht: so kann die Kraft zu reflectieren keine andere Regeln, als die Regeln der Einstimmung und des Widerspruchs, haben."[57] These rules are, of course, in effect the two principles of human cognition discussed above. They ground both the truth in cognitive judgment and the truth in things. Once again, Reimarus:

> Eben diese Regeln der Vernunft sind der Grund aller Wahrheit ....Wenn sich nun zeigen läßt, daß sich die wesentliche Wahrheit der Dinge nach eben den Regeln der Einstimmung und des Widerspruchs richtet, wornach wir auch denken: so muß auch zwischen der logischen und wesentlichen Wahrheit eine Einstimmung seyn; d.i., wenn wir nach den Regeln der Einstimmung und des Widerspruchs denken: so müssen auch unsere Gedanken mit den Dingen selbst übereinstimmen, oder wahr gedacht seyn (V, pp. 33-34 §17).

The fruits of the rationalistic methodology are that the ars rationis is simultaneously the ratio in rebus. A similar relationship pertains between the ars analogi rationis (or "die schöne Vernunft") and ratio aesthetica in rebus. In other words, the principle of unity of perfected sensate cognition exists also in rebus pulchris either as a beautiful object or as an object beautifully represented. The ars pulchre cogitandi entails a res pulchra as its cogitatum. This cogitatum, as the ordo plurium in uno produced by the ars analogi rationis, is the general "objectivity constant" of aesthetic being. In other words, "Schönheit an sich" is nothing less than "die sinnlich erkannte Einheit des Mannichfaltigen"[58] or the observabilitas perfectionis[59] or "die Vollkommenheit insofern sie eine Erscheinung ist."[60] Such formulations are but a few of the different expressions for the objective correlative to the perfectio cognitionis sensitivae. Just as perfectio in things is the objective correlative to the rules of "pure" ratio, so is "Schönheit" the objective correlative to the rules of the analogon rationis. This thesis must be further examined as it will reveal the heart of the aesthetics of form.

"Vollkommenheit" as the "Grund" of Beauty

The definition of beauty given above makes sense in the context of rationalistic ontology of aesthetics. Aesthetic being is a type of being and as such it incorporates into its reality ontological principles. It thereby constitutes a type of world. Similarly, aesthetic being too must possess a truth proper to its being, i.e. a veritas aesthetica. Baumgarten defines such truth.

> Veritas aesthetica postulat obiectorum elegantur cogitandorum 1) possibilitatem, absolutam, quatenus sensitive cognoscenda est...
>
> Veritas aesthetica poscit possibilitatem obiectorum suorum, 2) hypotheticam...quatenus ab analogo rationis diiudicari potest (AP, p. 274, §431, §432)

And in his Kollegium Baumgarten maintained: "[Der schöne Geist] stellt sich die Gegenstände dieser und anderer möglichen Welten vor, und beides macht die ästhetische Wahrheit im weitläufigen Verstande" (HP, p. 219, §441)

Aesthetic being qua being must, accordingly, possess possibility and hence entails a metaphysical dimension. As shown above possibility is that which possesses a "Grund," or, simply that which can be thought. Concerning the nature of any possible world Meier writes: "Ein iedwedes mögliches Ding...hat eine metaphysische Wahrheit...Da nun die Welt überhaupt möglich, und diese Welt noch dazu würklich ist, so hat eine iedwede Welt, und also auch diese, eine Wahreit und Gewißheit."[61] We have seen that for both Meier and Baumgarten that metaphysical truth is an agreement of being with the first principles of human cognition. In other words, the "Anfangsgründe" of things (of any possible world) correspond to the "Anfangsgründe" of thinking. And what are the principles of thinking? I quoted Reimarus above to the effect that the "Regeln der Einstimmung und des Widerspruchs" direct the act of thinking. These principles are, of course, simply the principium rationis sufficientis and the principium contradictionis (discussed above). Consequently, any possible world must possess such principles: Meier writes:

> Ueberdis ist in einer ieweden Welt ein allgemeiner Zusammenhang, und es ist demnach ein iedweder Theil entweder ein Grund aller übrigen, oder eine Folge der übrigen, oder beydes zugleich. Mithin ist durchgehends, in der Verknüpfung der Theile der Welt, der Satz des hinreichenden Grundes beobachtet, und es ist demnach klar, daß eine iedwede mögliche Welt, alle Kennzeichen der Wahrheit eines Dinges, an sich habe. Eine Welt, in welcher keine Wahrheit, ist eine fabelhafte Welt, und als ein Traum zu betrachten, oder als ein Unding, welchen den Namen einer Welt nicht verdient (M, II, 107, §341).

The aesthetic truth of aesthetic being, too, must manifest ontological truth. Thus Meier writes:

> Eine ganze aesthetische Ausführung ist ein Inbegrif vieler Gedanken, und folglich kan man sie, im Ganzen betrachtet, als einen Begrif, als eine Vorstellung annehmen. Soll sie schön seyn, so mus sie notwendig wahr seyn. Nun beweißt man in der Metaphysik, und es ist auch vor sich klar, daß alle Wahrheit einer Sache in der Ordnung des Mannigfaltigen bestehe, oder wenn das Mannigfaltige in einer Sache einander nicht widerspricht, und einen zulänglichen Grund hat, oder nach dem Satze des Widerspruchs und zureichenden Grundes mit einander verbunden ist (Anf, III, 271, §673).

To claim that the being of aesthetic reality is structured by the principle of sufficient reason is to say that its reality is constituted by perfectio. As Meier writes: "Die Vollkommenheit besteht nun, in der Zusammenstimmung vieler Dinge zu Einer Realität. Wenn daher das

Mannigfaltige in einer Sache, oder die verscheidenen Bestimmungen derselben, den hinreichenden Grund von Einer Realität enthalten, so besitzt die Sache Vollkommenheit" (M, I, 165, §94). Perfection is not only the form of "schöne Erkenntnis," but it also constitutes the objectivity constant of that which is perfectly "erkannt." Indeed, "schöne Erkenntnis" (="Vollkommenheit der sinnlichen Erkenntnis") is perfected cognition because its contents (repraesentationes) exist in a connexial order whose highest principle is perfectio. Aesthetic experience is always an awareness of a ratio determinans informing the sensate contents of sensate consciousness. Indeed, this ratio determinans (=perfectio) constitutes the very possibility of aesthetic being, ultimately gives form to the cognition of such being, and is the object which aesthetic consciousness focuses upon as the beautiful. There can only be a perfectio cognitionis because of the perfectio in rebus. And this perfectio is precisely the aesthetic possibility and hence aesthetic truth of a beautiful art work.

It is not enough, however, simply to state that aesthetic being entails perfectio. This ontological property is formally present in all kinds or levels of being. The perfectio of aesthetic being must be specified if an aesthetic universe is to be and if the veritas aesthetica is to entail more than the veritas metaphysica. Many scholars, perhaps Benedetto Croce is the most notable, have failed to understand the Vollkommenheitsmänner on this point.[62] Concerning the aesthetic cognition of perfection Mendelssohn writes: "Ist nun die Erkenntnis dieser Vollkommenheit sinnlich, so wird sie Schönheit gennannt."[63] Critics assert that the Vollkommenheitsmänner are contending in effect that aesthetic awareness is simply a blurry intellectual awareness of that which is in itself not blurry (=logical order). There is some truth in this accusation if Gottsched is here intended. In his Critische Dichtkunst and Erste Gründe Gottsched does seem to contend that aesthetic perfection can be reduced to intellectual perfection.[64] However, this is not true for most of the Vollkommenheitsmänner. The "stuff" of the aesthetic universe is, to be sure, "verworrene Vorstellungen" of intelligible being. Given the ontological premises of rationalism, sensate experience could not be metaphysically interpreted in any other way. Sensate reality is derivative! However, the perfection proper to sensate contents is not intellectual perfection per se, i.e. it does not consist of the order proper to notae distinctae. The unifying factor is not the ars rationis, rather the ars analogi rationis. The principle of unity and thereby the aesthetic perfection is analogous to rational perfection. Rational perfection entails notae distinctae. Consequently, the ratio determinans is distincta. The result is intellectual cognition--deutliche Erkenntnis. But Vollkommenheitsmänner explicitly rejected "Deutlichkeit" as a property proper to aesthetic cognition. In other words, that which specifies ontological being into aesthetic being is "Verworrenheit" viz. "Sinnlichkeit." That which evinces intellectuality must cease to be beautiful. Meier writes: "Es wird nicht nur gar leicht erhellen, daß [der Sachen] Schönheit in einer Volkommenheit bestehe, sondern daß dieselbe auch augenblicklich verschwindet, so bald man die Volkommenheit deutlich erkent, ob gleich diese Voldommenheit unverändert fortdauert" (Anf, I, 38-39, §23). "Verworrene Vorstellungen" of aesthetic experience are not to be united (and thereby intellectualized) by "ein deutlicher Grund." Conversely, Baumgarten contends: "Die Schönheit wird hier nicht in die Verwirrung gesetzet, sondern es wird gezeigt, wie verworrene Vorstellungen schön werden sollen" (H, p. 81, §17). And that which transforms "verworrene Vorstellungen" into an aesthetic whole is

precisely a "Vollkommenheit" that in itself "sinnlich." The consensus
cogitationum that constitutes the aesthetic perfectio must remain sensate,
remain a phenomenon. "Pulcritudo cognitionis sensitivae," writes Baumgarten,
"erit universalis, consensus cogitationum, quatenus adhuc ab earum ordine et
signis abstrahimus, inter se ad unum, qui phaenomenon sit (A, p. 7, §18).
Above I noted that for both Baumgarten and Meier the theme is the aesthetic
principle of unity of a poem. A perceived theme is similar to intellectual
perfection in that it unites the many into an order. It differs in that its
properties remain sensate. The unity is properly "felt," rather than
"understood." The perfectio aesthetica stands in analogy to the perfectio
rationalis.

Once again, what is beauty? It is the "appearing" of the perfetio
aesthetica to the sensate consciousness of man. In other words, beauty is
the appearance or observability of perfection insofar as perfection is
sensately cognizable. Baumgarten contends: "Perfectio phaenomenon, s.
gustui latius dicto observabilis, est PULCRITUDO..." (M, p. 248, §662).
Meier writes: "Daß die Schönheit überhaupt eine Vollkommenheit sey, in so
ferne sie undeutlich oder sinlich erkand wird, ist, unter allen gründlichen
Kennern der Schönheit, heute zu Tage eine so ausgemachte Sache, da es unnötig
zu seyn scheint, davor einen weitläuftigen Beweis zu fuhren" (Anf, I, 39,
§23). Despite Meier's assurance I will give some "proof" of his thesis.
Christian Gottfried Schütz contends: "Schönheit ist Vollkommenheit in der
Verbindung des Mannigfaltigen, in so fern sie dem Verstande anschauend
[=sinnlich] vorgestallt, oder sinnlich deutlich erkannt werden kann."[65]
Eschenburg maintains, "daß [die schönen Künste] durch diese Vereinigung ihren
gemeinsamen Endzweck, die Darstellung sinnlicher Vollkommenheit auf eine weit
mannifaltigere und würksamere Art erreichen."[66] Eberhard, writing about
beauty as the object of art, contends: "...so ist die lebhafte [=sinnliche]
Vorstellung der Vollkommenheit das höchste Gesetz aller schönen Künste und
Wissenschaften; die Werke der sch. K. und W. müssen ästhetisch vollkommen
seyn."[67] Schott maintains a similar position: "Das Schöne oder die
Schönheit im eigenlichsten und vollesten Sinne des Wortes findet sich nur in
zusammengesetzten Gegenständen....wenn die Zusammenstimmung des
mannichfaltigen (Vollkommenheit) sinnlich oder undeutlich erkannt wird; denn
eben dadurch unterscheidet sich die Schönheit von der bloßen
Vollkommenheit...Das Schöne im allgemeinsten Verstand besteht also in der
sinnlich vorgestellten Vollkommenheit."[68] Mendelssohn himself writes: "Die
Gleichheit, das Einerlei im Mannigfältigen ist ein Eigenthum der schönen
Gegenstände. Sie müssen eine Ordnung oder sonst eine Vollkommenheit
darbieten, die in die Sinne fällt, und zwar ohne Mühe in die Sinne fällt."[69]
In 1790 Karl Heinrich Heydenreich maintained, and I believe correctly, that
the Vollkommenheitsmänner had not progressed any whatsoever since Baumgarten
in their definition of beauty.[70]

Some scholars have distinguished between such formulations as: (1)
"Schönheit ist sinnlich erkannte Vollkommenheit" and (2) "Schönheit ist die
Vollkommenheit der sinnlichen Erkenntnis." Menzel, for instance, has
convincingly shown that the second formulation does more upon the subject and
upon the process of producing a work of art.[71] The two formulations are
distinct and allow for different articulations of the problem of beauty. But
Nivelle goes too far when he concludes that the formulations are
fundamentally different.[72] Both formulations treat the same problem, both
reflect the integral relationship between subject and object in rationalistic

metaphysics. Both formulations should be read as plausibly related theses derived from the metaphysical paradigm of form. Formulation one compliments formulation two and formulation two is only possible because of formulation one. It is not unusual to find a thinker more or less using both formulations or similar variants in a given text. For instance, Eschenburg can contend that the arts have as their object "die Darstellung sinnlicher Vollkommenheit" and that the arts obtain their goal "durch sinnlich vollkommene Darstellung."[73] Eberhard asserts: "[Die schönen oder freyen Künste] sollen also eine sinnlich vollkommene Erkenntniß hervorbringen. Die Wissenschaft der Regeln der Vollkommenheit der sinnlichen Erkenntniß und der Bezeichnung derselben ist die Aesthetick."[74] And the beauty presented is, of course, "die lebhafte [sinnliche] Vorstellung der Vollkommenheit" or simply "[eine] sinnlich vorgestellte Vollkommenheit."[75]

Conclusion: Speculations on the Meaning of Form

The term "form" or "Gestalt" was a code name that Schiller gave to aestheticians who tried to explain beauty in terms of "Vollkommenheit." "Vollkommenheit is quite simply the oneness of being (=that which constitutes being) insofar as this unum "forms" the many into connexial whole. This connexial unity is "form" or "Gestalt." Beauty arises when this unum is perceived sensately. Although Vollkommenheitsmänner consciously sought to distinguish aesthetic being from ontological being, the fact remains that the model for aesthetic reality resides in the intelligible being of oneness. The French priest, Yves André summed up the meaning of form when he quoted St. Augustin's definition of beauty. "Omnis porro pulchritudinis forma unitas est."[76] Again citing St. Augustin, André maintained "daß die Einheit sey, welches so zu sagen die Gestalt und das Wesen des Schönen, in jeder Gattung der Schönheit, ausmachet und fest stellet."[77] Insofar as sensate manifold is perceived sensately as evincing oneness, it will be experienced as beautiful or, conversely, as Eberhard contends, it is "die Einheit, die das Mannichfaltige schön macht."[78] A oneness that informs a manifold is a Gestalt or form. And it is precisely the Gestalt that constitutes the perfection of aesthetic awareness and hence the reality of beauty.

The primacy of intelligibility is quite clear in the aesthetics of Anton Raphael Mengs. It will be recalled that Schiller gave Mengs as an example of an aesthetician of form. Schiller explicitly referred to Mengs' Ueber die Schönheit und guten Geschmack in der Malerei (1762). Mengs is somewhat ambiguous as a "typical" representative of the Vollkommenheitsmänner. Such aestheticians were generally members of the Leibniz-Wolffian school. Mengs does show the influence of this school. But he also exhibits Platonic and Descartian elements. This is particularly so in Mengs' separation of the sensate from the intelligible. For example, Mengs contends that beauty can be the object of divine awareness. Moses Mendelssohn, on the other hand, denied that God could be aware of beauty.[79] Both thinkers agreed that God's consciousness is perfect, i.e. God is aware of the total structure and hence perfection of things. For Mendelssohn, beauty is always a function of sensate things. Since God's mind is infinite, God cannot have "verworre Vorstellungen" and, consequently, God cannot be aware of beauty. For Mengs beauty resides foremost in the intelligible. Consequently, human awareness of beauty is secondary, whereas God's awareness must be perfect. The differences between Mengs and Mendelssohn is a familial difference, i.e. an argument within a "school of thought." Both agree that the divine consciousness is occupied with intelligible perfection. The difference hovers around the primacy ascribed to perfection in the constitution of beauty. Mengs, in effect, fastened upon one aspect of Leibniz-Wolffian philosophy and theology and developed his notion of beauty in terms of this aspect. Mendelssohn did not do the same. I shall now examine this aspect.

The criterion that distinguishes between reality and appearance is variously oneness, order, or perfection. The universe is real because it evinces perfection in its overall order. The perfection of the universe reflects the perfection in God. To be one and to be a reflection of God are one and the same thing. The manifold of finite things is real to the degree that it manifests and is informed by connexial unity. And this unity is simply perfectio. God is referred to in Leibniz-Wolffian philosophy as a perfectissimum. Grammatically, the superlative is used. The use of the superlative suggests that the reality of God is an intensification of finite perfection. In other words, finite perfection is being used as a model for discussion of divine perfection. The limitation of the human mind forces philosophers to speak in such a manner. But in reality, God's being is the model for the structure of finite being. God is the absolute exemplar for perfection. The universe of finite things is in some sense a limitation, diminution, or restriction of divine being. God's perfection is the real model, relative to which the finite perfection is a reflection.

The perfection in God is qualitatively other than that of the world. In order to illustrate this, let us look at the ontological proof of God's existence as given by rationalists. Above it was shown that the problem for Leibniz was not to prove the existence of a perfection, but to show why it does not exist. To be, to be real, is to be an essence. Every essence is a realitas because it is a positivity (=positive determination of being). Why, then, does not every essence exist? The answer lies in the fact that some essences qua being Gründe exclude the Folgen of other essences. Co-possibility limits the reality of the finite universe by introducing negation into being. It is precisely this negativity that is absent from divine perfection. Existence conceived as the Erfüllung of all the Folgen contained in Gründe is simply the maximum reality viz. positivity. A reality will be, unless there is a negativity that would render its existence contradictory. Now, in the case of God, there is infinite essentiality with no possibility of negation. Therefore, God must exist as God's non-existence would go against the principle of contradiction. Baumgarten writes: "Si deus non actualis esset, falsum esset principium contradictionis, primum formae & materiae principum in omnibus demonstrationibus nostris" (M, p. 236, §824). Because God necessarily possesses all the possible predicates of his infinite essence, God must possess existence. For this reason God is most perfect. Baumgarten contends: "DEUS est ens perfectissimum. Ergo Deus actualis est" (M, p. 332, §811).

As already noted, God is the model for finite perfection. The designation of God as a perfectissimum derives from using finite being as the prime analogue. In reality, things are reversed. God is perfectio that entails infinite reality and hence existence. All negatio is excluded. Consequently, finite perfection is derivative from divine perfection. Divine perfection is the standard relative to which finite perfections are analogates. If the divine exemplar is terminologically taken as the model for perfection, then finite perfections are in reality not perfection per se,

rather they are in some sense imitations of perfection. Also, the perception
of this imitative perfection can be conceived as an indirect awareness of the
divine exemplar. At any rate, such a line of reasoning underlies Mengs'
treatment of beauty as <u>Gestalt</u>.

Mengs defines beauty:

> Da die Vollkommenheit nicht im Menschen, sondern nur in der
> Gottheit allein zu finden ist, der Mensch aber zunächst nur
> begreifen kann, was unmittelbar in die Sinne fällt, so hat ihm der
> Allweise auch bloss für den Begriff von der Vollkommenheit, die
> ausser ihm ist, ein Anschauungsvermögen verliehen und in dieser
> Vollkommenheit ist eben das, was wir Schönheit nennen, zu suchen.[80]

In the above citation the term "Vollkommenheit" refers to the divine
perfection insofar as divine perfection in itself functions as the model for
all finite perfections. Since God is infinite, divine perfection of
necessity transcends human cognitive powers. Man's <u>Erkenntniskräfte</u> are
basically directed and limited to sensate experience. However, man can
intuit in some way perfection in sensate things and thereby develop a concept
of perfection. Mengs illustrates his thesis. A pure mathematical point is
non-divisible. Man cannot represent pure non-divisibility to this mind.
Consequently, "weil wir uns aber einen anschaulichen Begriff von einem Punkte
müssen machen können, so nennen wir Punkt den kleinen Theil, bei welchem
keine weitere Trennung mehr bewerkstelligt werden kann,..." (<u>HS</u>, I, 199).
The point thereby becomes "sichtbar," i.e. an object of sensate
consciousness. A similar relationship holds for divine perfection. That
which is beyond all flaw, limitations, materiality becomes open to human
awareness as beauty. Mengs writes: "Man kann daher die Schönheit eine
sichtbare Vollkommenheit nennen, wie man einen von den beiden Punkten einen
sichtbaren Punkt nennt" (<u>HS</u>, I, 200). Beauty is accordingly a function of
the unity of perfection. Indeed, Mengs conceived the circle as the most
beautiful shape because it represents the simplest and hence most perfect
extension of a point. "Die runde Gestalt ist deshalb unter allen die
vollkommenste, wegen ihrer Einfachheit, denn ihre einzige Grundursache ist
die Ausdehnung ihres Mittelpunktes" (<u>HS</u>, I, 201).

Summarizing, beauty is simply "sichtbare Vollkommenheit," i.e. oneness
that is "felt." Feeling (=sensate awareness) is a derivative form of
consciousness. However, it is an ultimate for man. Ontologically, the unum
of aesthetic consciousness is derivative. Practically, it is constitutive of
human consciousness. The oneness of being is the model for reality. The
"real" in a manifold is that which makes the manifold into a unity. The
highest level of unity is called perfection. Perfection is the principle
that <u>forms</u> the many into a connexial whole. Insofar as perfection enters
human consciousness as sensate content, it will be experienced as beauty.
"Schönheit an sich" is a sensate analogue to intelligibility in itself, to
the <u>Ding an sich</u>. This is the key to the aesthetics of form. Form that has
become sensately manifest becomes <u>aesthetic</u> being. The perfect cognition of
such a sensate manifold is aesthetic cognition. For Mengs the perfection
manifested in beauty is an imitation and reminder of absolute divine
perfection. As Mengs writes: "Plato nennt das Gefühl der Schönheit eine
Erinnerung an die göttlichen Vollkommenheiten..." (<u>HS</u>, I, 200). Baumgarten,
Meier, Mendelssohn, and others distinguished the sensate and hence beauty

more distinctly from divine perfection than Mengs did. They all, nevertheless, conceived beauty as a oneness that orders a manifold, i.e. as Gestalt. And this form is in some way an imitation of the cosmic and hence divine order.

Footnotes - Chapter II

[1] Hans Peter Hermann writes: "Die Poesie von 1670 bis 1725 ist publikumsgerichtet, nicht seinsgerichtet. Sie wird nicht primär zur Realität in Beziehung gestzt, sondern zur affektiven, intellektuellen und moralischen Existenz dessen, der sie aufnehmen soll. Mit anderen Worten: sie ist in ihrem Kern rhetorisch," Cf. Naturnachahumnung und Einbildungskraft. Zur Entwicklung der deutschen Poetik von 1670 bis 1740. (Homberg Berlin Zürich, 1970), p.33.

[2] Theorie der schönen Wissenschaften. Erster Theil. (Tübingen, 1789), xix-xx.

[3] Cf. Preisschriften über die Frage: Welche Forschritte hat die Metaphysik seit Leibnitzens und Wolffs Zeiten in Deutschland gemacht? (Berlin, 1796), p.3.

[4] For histories of 18th century German philosophy from Leibniz (or Wolff) up to Kant see: Lewis White Beck, Early German Philsophy: Kant and His Predecessors (Cambridge, 1969), pp. 243-501; Ernst Cassirer, Das Erkenntnisproblem in der Philosophie und Wissenschaft der neueren Zeit (Berlin, 1922), Bd. II, 521-647; Frederick Copleston, S. J., A History of Philosophy, Vol. 6: Modern Philosophy, Part I: The French Enlightenment to Kant (Garden City, 1964), pp. 121 -172; Emerich Coreth, Einführung in die Philosophie der Neuzeit; Band I: Rationalismus, Empirismus, Aufklärung (Freiburg, 1972) pp. 136-150; Kuno Fischer, Geschichte der Philosophie, Band II: Leibniz und seine Schule, 2nd ed. (Heidelberg, 1867), pp. 743-884; Heinz Heimsoeth, Metaphysik der Neuzeit (München, 1967), pp. 79-98; John Herman Randall, Jr., The Career of Philosophy. Vol 2.: From the Enlightenment to the Age of Darwin (New York/London, 1970), pp. 50-127; Max Wundt, Die Schulphilosophie im Zeitalter der Aufklärung (Hildensheim, 1964), pp. 122-341; and Edward Zeller, Geschichte der deutschen Philosophie seit Leibniz (München, 1873), pp. 211-421.

[5] Betrachtungern über den ersten Grundsatz aller schönen Künste und Wissenschaften (Halle, 1757), pp. 23-24, §11. Hereafter referred to the text as BEG plus page and paragraph number.

[6] Entwurf einer Theorie und Literatur der schönen Wissenschaften. Zur Grundlage bey Vorlesungen (Berlin/Stuttgart, 1783), p. 3, §1).

[7] Anleitung zur Kenntniß der auserlesenen Literatur in allen Theilen der Philosophie (Göttingen/Lemgo, 1778), p. 101.

[8] Cf. Metaphysik. Erster Theil (Halle, 1755), p. 17, 19, §9. Hereafter referred to in the text as M, I plus page and paragraph number.

[9] Philosophisches Lexicon. Darinnen die Erklarungen und Beschereibungen aus des solu. tit. tot. Hochberühmten Welt-Weisen, Herrn Christian Wolffens sämmtlichen teutschen Schriften seiner Philosophischen Systematis sorgfältig zusammen getragen [worden] (Bayreuth/Hof, 1737), pp. 416-417. Hereafter referred to in the text as PL plus page number.

[10] Elements of Metaphysics (London/New York, n.d. [originally published in 1903]), PL, 1-17.

[11] Versuch einer Critischen Dichtkunst durchgenhends mit den Exempeln unserer besten Dichter erläutert, Vierte sehr vermehrte Auflage (Leipzig, 1751), p. 134, §23. Herefater referred to in the text as VCD plus page and paragraph number.

[12] Concerning the function of metaphysics in Gottsched's aesthetic and literary theory see Joachim Birke, Christian Wolffs Metaphysik und die zeitgenössiche Literatur-und Musiktheorie (Gottsched, Scheibe, Mizler), (Berlin, 1966), pp 1-48.

[13] The Genesis of Twentieth Century Philosophy. The Evolution of Thought form Copernicus to the Present (Garden City, 1966), pp. 9-82.

[14] Ibid., p.19.

[15] Cf. Martin Heidegger, Die Frage nach dem Ding. Zu Kants Lehre von den transzendentalen Grundsätzen (Tübingen, 1962), pp. 42-91.

[16] The secondary literature on Leibniz is enormous. I shall note only three works I found to be especially helpful. Cf. C. D. Broad, Leibniz. An Introduction, ed. C. Lewy (London, 1975); Otto A. Saame, Der Satz vom Grund bei Leibniz. Ein konstitutives Element seiner Philosophie und ihrer Einheit (Mainz, 1961); and Arnin Wildermuth, Wahrheit und Schöpfung. Ein Grundriss der Metaphysik des Gottfried Wilhelm Leibniz (Winterthur, 1960). For an excellent overall presentation of Wolff's philosophy see Anton Bissinger, Die Struktur der Gotteserkenntnis: Studien zur Philosophie Christian Wolffs (Bonn, 1969). Also concerning Wolff see Richard Blackwell, "Christian Wolffs Doctrine of the Soul," Journal of the History of Ideas, XXII (1961), 339-354; and "The Structure of Wolffian Philosophy," The Modern Schoolman. XXXVII (1961), 203-218; and Hans Lüthje, "Christian Wolffs Philosophiebegriff," Kant-Studien, XXX (1925), 39-66.

[17] De la sagesse (ca. 1693) in Opera Philosophica quae exstant latina, gallica, germanica omnia, ed. J. E. Erdmann (Aalen, 1959 [reprint of 1840 edition]), p. 674.

[18] Primae veritates in Opuscules et fragments inédits de Leibniz, ed. Louis Couturat (Paris, 1903), p. 518. Hereafter referred to in the text as Cout plus page number.

[19] Cf. Leibniz' July 15, 1686 letter to Antoine Arnould in Die philosophischen Schriften von Gottfried Wilhelm Leibniz, ed. C. J. Gerbardt (Hildesheim, 1960 [reprint of the 1879 edition]), II, 56. Hereinafter referred to in the txt as PS, II plus page number.

[20] Cf. Satz vom Grund bei Leibniz, pp. 13-41.

[21] Essais de Théodicée sur la bonté de Dieu, la liberté de l'homme et l'origine du mal (ca. 1710) in Die philosophischen Schriften (Hildesheim, 1961 [reprint of 1885 edition]), VI, 413. Herafter referred to in the text as PS, VI plus page number.

22 From Introductio ad encyclopaediam arcanam.

23 From La Monadologie (1714).

24 Metaphysica, editio VII. (Halle, 1779), p. 5 §14. Hereafter referred to in the text as M plus page number.

25 Metaphysik (Hall, 1766), p. 5, §14. Hereafter referred to as Meta plus page and paragraph number.

26 Die philosopischen Schriften (Hildesheim, 1960 [reprint of 1887 edition]), III, 530). Hereafter referred to in the text as PS, III plus page number.

27 Similarly Christian Wolff contends: "Veritas adeo, quae transcendentalis appellatur & rebus ipsis inesse intelligitur, est ordo in varietate eorum, quae simul sunt ac se invicem consequuntur, aut, si mavis, ordo eorum, quae enti conveniunt." Cf. Philosophia prima sive ontologia, methodo scientifica pertractata, qua omnis cogitionis humanae principia continentur, editio nova (Francofurti et Lipsiae, 1736), p. 383, §495. Hereafter referred to in the text as Ontologia plus page and paragrah number.

28 Cf. Erste Gründe der gesamten Weltweisheit, Darin alle philosophische Wissenshaften in ihrer natürlichen Verknüpfung abgehandelt werden, Zum Gebrauch Academischer Lectionen entworfen. Erster, Theoretischer Theil (Leipzig, 1733), p. 119, §218. Similar arguments were often repeated relative to the distinction between "reality" and a "dream." Cf. Christian Wolff's Ausführliche Nachricht von seinen eigenen Schriften, die er in deutscher Sprache von den verscheidenen Theilen der Welt-Weißheit heraus gegeben auf Verlangen ans Licht gestellt (Franckfurt/M., 1735), p. 227. Also see Wolff's longer argument in Ontologia, pp. 379-383, §§493-494.

29 Vernünfftige Gedancken von Gott / der Welt und der Seele des Menschen/Auch allen Dingen überhaupt / den Liebhabern der Wahrheit mitgetheilet, Vierte Auflage (Franckfurt/Leipzig, 1729), p. 9, §14. Hereafter referred to in the text as VG plus page and paragraph number.

30 Cf. Ontologia, p. 143, §174. For an excellent exposition of Wolff's theory of essential being see Etienne Gilson, Being and Some Philsophers, 2nd ed. (Toronto, 1952), pp. 112-121.

31 Cf. letter (not dated, ca. 1677) from Arnold Eckhard to Leibniz in Die philosophischen Schriften (Hildesheim, 1960 [reprint from 1875 edition]), I, 228. Leibniz annotated the letter with comments which I have quoted. Hereafter referred to in the text as PS, I plus page number.

32 Acroasis Logica in Christanum L.B. de Wolff (Helae, 1761), P. 1, §§1-2. Hereafter referred to in the text as A plus page and paragraph number.

33 Printed in Bernard Poppe, Alexander Gottlieb Baumgarten. Seine Bedeutung und Stellung in der Leibniz-Wolffischen Philosophie und seine Beziehung zu Kant. Nebst Veröffentlichung einer bisher unbekannten

Handschrift Baumgartens (Borna/Leibzig, 1907), p.66, §1. Hereafter referred
to in the text as H, plus page number.

[34] Anfangsgründe aller schönen Wissenschaften (Erster Theil) (Halle,
1748), pp. 7-8, §4. Hereafter referred to in the text as Anf, plug page
and paragraph number.

[35] It is informative to read the opening section of VG in conjunction
with Wolff's German explantion of mathematical thinking. Cf. Der
Anfangs-Gründe aller Mthematischen Wissenchaften Erster Theil, Welcher einen
Unterricht von der Mathematischen Lehr-Art, die Rechen-Kunst, Geometrie,
Trigonometrie und Bau-Kunst in sich enthält, Zu meherem Aufnehmen der
Mathematik so wohl auf hohen als auf niedrigen Schulen aufgesetzt worden
(Franckfurt/Leipzig, 1750), pp. 5-32, §§1-53.

[36] Morgenstunden, oder Vorlesungen über das Dasein Gottes (1785) in
Schriften zur Philosophie, Aesthetik und Apologetik, ed. Moritz Brasch
(Hildesheim, 1967 [reprint of 1880 edition]), I, 306.

[37] Cf. Eschenburg, Entwurf einer Theorie und Literatur der schönen
Wissenschaften, p. 4, §2.

[38] For secondary sources on Baumgarten and/or Meier see: Alfred
Baeumler, Das Irrationalitätsproblem in der Ästhetik und Logik des 18.
Jahrhunderts bis zur Kritik der Urteilskraft (Darmstadt, 1967 [reprint of the
1926 edition]); Ernst Bergmann, Die Begründung der deutschen Ästhetik durch
A.G. Baumgarten und G. Fr. Meier (Leipzig, 1911); Hans Böhm, "Das
Schönheitsproblem bei G. F. Meier, "Archiv für die gesamte Psychologie, LVI
(1926), 117-252; Frederick Copleston, S. J., A History of Philosophy. Vol.
6: Modern Philosophy Part I: The French Enlightenment to Kant (Garden City,
1964), pp. 136-140; Benedetto Croce, Aesthetic as Science of Expression and
General Linguistic, trans. Douglas Ainslie (New York, 1956 [first edition
1909]), pp. 239-250; Max Dessoir, Geschichte der neueren deutschen
Psychologie, 2nd ed, (Berlin, 1902), I, 90ff. and 559ff; Ursula Franke, Kunst
als Erkenntnis. Die Rolle der Sinnlichkeit in der Ästhetik des Alexander
Gottlieb Baumgarten (Wiesbaden, 1972; Friedrich Gaede, Poetik und Logik. Zu
den Grundlagen der literarischen Entwicklung im 17. und 18. Jahrhundert
(Bern/München, 1978), pp. 106-119: K. E. Gilbert and H. A. Kuhn, A History
of Esthetics (Bloomington, 1954), pp. 289-295; Marie-Luise Linn, "A. G.
Baumgarten's 'Aesthetica' und die antike Rhetorik" Deutsche
Vierteljahrsschrift für Literaturwissenschaft und Geistesgeschichte, XLI
(1967), 424-443: Hermann Lotze, Geschichte der Ästhetik in Deutschland
(München, 1868), p. 4-23; Norbert Menzel, Der anthropologische Charakter des
Schönen bei Baumgarten, diss. Pontifica Universitas Gregoriana Facultas
Philosophica (Wanne-Eickel, 1969); Paul Menzer, "Zur Entstehung von A. G.
Baumgartens Ästhetik," Zeitschrift für Deutsche Kulturphilosophie Logos, N.
F., IV (1938), 288-295; Hans Georg Meyer, Leibniz und Baumgarten als
Begründer der deutschen Ästhetik (Halle, 1874; Armand Nivelle, Kunst- und
Dichtungstheorien zwischen Aufklärung und Klassik (Berlin, 1960), pp. 7-46;
Hans Georg Peters, Studien über die Ästhetik des A. G. Baumgarten unter bes.
Berücksichtigung ihrer Beziehungen zum Ethischen (Berlin, 1934); Bernhard
Poppe, "Einleitung." A. G. Baumgarten. Seine Bedeutung und Stellung in der
Leibniz-Wolffischen Philosophie und seine Beziehungen zu Kant. Nebst einer
bisher unbekannten Handschrift der Ästhetik Baumgartens (Borna-Leipzig,

1907), pp. 1-57; Albert Riemann, Die Ästhetick A. G. Baumgartens unter bes. Berücksichtigung der "Meditationes", nebst einer Übersetzung dieser Schrift (Halle, 1928); Georg Saintsbury, A History of Criticism and Literary Taste in Europe. Vol. 3. Modern Criticism (London, 1906), pp. 148-150; Max Schlasler, Kritische Geschichte der Aesthetik. Grundlegung für die Aesthetik als Philosophie des Schönen und der Kunst. Erste Abtheilung. Von Plato bis zum 19. Jahrhundert (Berlin, 1872), pp. 347-354; Johannes Schmidt, Leibniz und Baumgarten. Ein Beitrag zur Geschichte der deutschen Aesthetik (Halle, 1875); Hans Rudolf Schweizer, Ästhetik als Philosophie der sinnlichen Erkenntnis. EineInterpretation der' Aesthetica' A. G. Baumgartens mit teilweiser Wiedergabe des lateinischen Textes und deutscher Übersetzung (Basel/Stuttgart, 1973), pp. 9-102; Heinz Schwitzke, Die Beziehungen zwischen Aesthetik und Metaphysik in der deutschen Philosophie vor Kant (Berlin, 1930); Robert Sommer, Grundzüge einer Geschichte der deutschen Psychologie und Aesthetik (Amsterdam, 1966 [reprint of 1892 edition]), pp. 24-58; Karl Heinrich von Stein, Die Entstehung der neueren Aesthetik [Hildesheim, 1964 [reprint of 1886 edition]), pp. 336-367; Rene Wellek, A History of Modern Criticism: 1750-1950. Vol. I, The Later Eighteenth Century (New Haven, 1955), pp. 144-146; Leonard P. Wessell, Jr., "Alexander Baumgarten's Contribution to the Development of Aesthetics," The Journal of Aesthetics and Art Criticism, XXX (1972), 333-342; F. Wiebecke, Die Poetik Georg Friedrich Meiers. Diss. Göttingen, 1967; and Robert Zimmermann, Geschichte der Aesthetik als philosophischer Wissenschaft (Wien, 1858), pp. 166ff.

[39] Similarly Johann Gottlieb Buhle writes: "Wenn die Aesthetik als die Metaphysik der schönen Wissenschaften und Künste betrachtet wird, abgesondert von den speciellern Regeln dieser selbst, so muß sie von der Natur der Seele, insoweit diese das empfängliche Subject für die Gefühle des schönen, Wahren und Guten ist, und dem Wesen der schönen Wissenschaften und Künste, insofern sie als Objecte diese Gefühle erregen sollen, ausgehen, nach beyden die allgemeinen Regeln des Schönen, Wahren und Guten bestimmen, und zugleich die Mittel zur Darstellung desselben im Allgemeinen charakterisiren." Cf. Grundzüge einer allgemeinen Encyklopädie der Wissenschaften (Lemgo, 1790), p. 46, §35.

[40] Cf. Mendelssohn's famous statement: "In den Regeln der Schönheit, die das Genie des Künstlers empfindet und der Kunstrichter in Vernunftschlüsse auflöst, liegen die tiefsten Geheimnisse unserer Seele verborgen. Jede Regel der Schönheit ist zugleich eine Entdeckung in der Seelenlehre." Cf. Über die Hauptgrundsätze der schönen Künste und Wissenschaften (1757) in Schriften. II, 143.

[41] In this connection see Johann August Eberhard's discussion of the soul as a "Vorstellungskraft" in his Allgemeine Theorie des Denkens und Empfindens (Berlin, 1776), pp. 31ff. Also concerning the soul as a vis representativa see Georg Friedrich Meier, Beweis der vorherbestimmten Uebereinstimmung (Halle, 1743).

[42] Cf. Meier, Anf, I, 20-21, §13.

[43] My diagram is similar to one constructed by Menzel. Cf. Der anthropologische Character, p. 30.

[44] Allgemeine Theorie der Schönen Künste in einzeln, nach alphabetischer Ordnung der Kunstwörter auf einander folgenden Artikeln abgehandelt. Erster Theil. Neue vermehrte zweyte Auflage (Leipzig, 1792), p. 47.

[45] Auszug aus der Vernunftlehre (Halle, 1752), p. 29, §115. Hereafter referred to in the text as AaV plus page and paragraph number.

[46] Carl Friedrich Flögel, a follower of Baumgarten and Meier, conceived aesthetic cognition as a subclass of cognition per se. The science of cognition per se was designated as "Allgemeine Logik" and deals with all possible kinds of cognition, e. g. mathematics, history, probable knowledge, and aesthetics. Each kind of limited cognition has further specified rules of order that pertain to the subject matter concerned. Cf. Einleitung in die Erfindungskunst (Breßlau/Leipzig, 1760), pp. 181-185, §§ 188-194.

[47] Aesthetica (Erster Theil) (Frankfurt/O), 1750), p. 1, §1. Hereafter referred to in the text as A plus page and paragraph number.

[48] Cf. Meta, pp. 413-414, §468.

[49] Anfangsgründe aller schönen Wissenschaften. Dritter Theil (Halle, 1750), p. 276, §675. Hereafter referred to in the text as Anf, III plus page and paragraph number.

[50] Anfangsgründe aller schönen Wissenschafter. Zweyter Theil (Halle, 1749), p. 506, §468. Hereafter referred to in the text as Anf, II plus page and paragraph number.

[51] Critics such as Croce have totally failed to note this fact and have consequently accused Baumgarten of simply reducing beauty to unclear or hazy intellectuality. Cf. Aesthetic, pp. 213ff.

[52] Meditationes philsophicae de nonnullis ad poema pertinentibus quas amplissimi philosophorum ordinis consensu (Halle, 1735), p. 25, §§65-66. Cf. also Meier's defense of Baumgarten's work, Vertheidigung der Baumgartischen Erklärung eines Gedichts, wider das 5 Stück des I Bandes des neuen Büchersaals der schönen Wissenschaften und freyen Künste (Halle, 1746).

[53] Anton Friedrich Büsching transformed in effect the aesthetic ordo plurium in uno, i.e. the ratio sensitiva, into a general formal requirement that all parts of an art work must agree in a totality. Büsching writes: "Mich dünkt, man nenne ein Ding schön, wenn man empfindet und erkennt, daß das Verschiedene in demselben mit besonderer Vollkommenheit zu einem Ganzen vereiniget sey....Je vollkommener die verbundenen einzelnen Dinge, je mehr derselben, je besser ihre Ordnung sowohl als Verhältniß gegen einander, und je größer ihre Uebereinstiummung zu dem Ganzen, welches sie ausmachen, desto schöner ist etwas." Cf. Geschichte und Grundsätze der schönen Künste und Wissenschaften im Grudriß. Erstes Stück (Berlin, 1772), pp. 10-11, §19.

[55] Cf. Johann Christoph Dommerich, Entwurf einer Deutschen Dichtkunst zum Gebrauch der Schulen abgefasset (Braunschweig, 1758), pp. 21ff, §§48ff; Johann August Eberhard, Theorie der schönen Wissenschaften (Halle, 1783), pp. 44-97, §§32-69; Phillip Gäng, Aesthetik, pp. 211-229, §§85-109; Andreas Heinrich Schott, Theorie der schönen Wissenschaften (1786), I, 132-194,

§§128-215; and Christian Gottfried Schütz, Lehrbuch zur Bildung des Verstandes und des Geschmacks (Halle, 1776), I, 79f., §45.

[56] Mendelssohn, for instance, maintained, "daß das Vergnügen an der sinnlichen Schönheit, an der Einheit im Mannigfaltigen, bloß unserem Unvermögen zuzuschreiben sei." Cf. Briefe ueber die Empfindungen (1775), in Schriften, II, 29.

[57] Die Vernunftlehre, als eine Anweisung zum richtigen Gebrauche der Vernunft in dem Erkenntniß der Wahrheit, aus zwoen ganz natürlichen Regeln der Einstimmung und des Widerspruchs hergeleitet. Vierte Auflage (Hamburg/Kiel, 1782), p. 31, §14. Hereafter referred to in the text as V, plus page and paragraph number.

[58] Eschenburg, Entwurf einer Theorie und Literatur der schönen Wissenschaften, p. 22, §35.

[59] Wolff, Psychologia empirica, methodo scientifica pertractata, qua ea, quae de anima indubia humana experientiae fide constant, continentur... (Francofurti & Lipziae, 1738), p. 421, §545.

[60] Baumgarten, Meta, p. 227, §488.

[61] Metaphysik. Zweyter Theil (Halle, 1756), p. 106, §341. Hereafter referred to in the text as M, II plus page and paragraph number.

[62] See Footnote 51.

[63] Ueber die Hauptgrundsätze der schönen Künste und Wissenschaften in Schriften, II, 146.

[64] Cf. Erste Gründe der gesamten Weltweischeit, I, 132-133, §249. In his Versuch einer Critischen Dichtkunst Gottsched seems to think that a critic can reduce aesthetic judgments to that which is "deutlich begriffen." Cf. CD, pp. 124-125, §10. The reason for Gottsched's reductionism lies in the fact that Gottsched ascribed "Geschmack" to the "Verstand" which can ultimately judge things with concepts (cf. CD, p. 123f, §9). Before Meier and Baumgarten the ascription of "Geschmack" and "Verstand" was typical. Cf., for example, Johan Ulrich König, Eine Untersuchung von dem guten Geschmack in der Dicht-und Rede-Kunst (Leipzig/Berlin, 1727). For Meier's trenchant critique of Gotttsched see his Beurtheilung der Gottschedischen Dichtkunst (Halle, 1747), pp. 63-82. Meier clearly connect "Geschmack" with man's lower or sansate mental processes.

[65] Lehrbuch zur Bildung des Verstandes und des Geschmacks, I, 63, §41.

[66] Entwurf zur einer Theorie und Literatur der schönen Wissenschaften, p. 7, §7.

[67] Theorie der schönen Wissenschaften, p. 9, §8.

[68] Theorie der schönen Wissenschaften, I, 14, §9.

[69] Briefe über die Empfindungen in Schriften, II, 29. Concerning Mendelssohn's aesthetic theory and its relationship to the thought of Meier and Baumgarten see Alexander Altman, Moses Mendelssohns Frühschriften zur Metaphysik (Tübingen, 1969), pp. 11-126.

[70] System der Aesthetik (Leipzig, 1760), I, 70-71. Flögel invented a felicitous variant. For Flögel the object of "die schöne Erkentniß" was "der sinliche Ausdruck der Vollkommenheit." Cf. Einleitung in die Erfindungskunst, p. 183, §190.

[71] Der anthropologische Charakter, pp. 13ff.

[72] Kunst-und Dichtungstheorien, p. 41.

[73] Entwurf einer Theorie und Literatur der schönen Wissenschaften, p. 7, §7 and p. 8, §8.

[74] Theorie der schönen Wissenschaften, pp. 4-5, §5.

[75] Ibid., p. 9, §8 and P, 11, §10.

[76] Versuch über das Schöne, da man untersucht worinnen eigentlich das Schöne in der Naturlehre, in der Sittenlehre, in den Werken des Witzes und in der Musik bestehe. trans. Ernst Gottlieb Baron (Altenburg, 1757), p. 12. André's work appeared anonymously in 1741 under the title Essai sur le beau, ou l'on examine en quoi consiste precisement le beau dans le physique, dans le morale....Baron did not give or did not know the author's name. For some brief comments on Andre see Francis X. Coleman, The Aesthetic Thought of the French Enlightenment (n.p., 1971), pp. 28-31.

Eberhard defines beauty as "die Zusammenstimmung des Mannichfaltigen zu Einem in der Erscheinung [=sinnlich vorgestellte Vollkommenheit]" and explicitly relates this definition to St. Augustin's thesis which Eberhard translates as: "Die Form aller Schönheit ist die Einheit." Cf. Handbuch der Aesthetick für gebildete Leser aus allen Ständen (Halle, 1807), pp. 59-60.

Baumgarten also makes reference to St. Augustin in his (Baumgartens) insistence upon the necessity of aesthetic unity for a work of art. Baumgarten writes: "Erit haec objectorum UNITAS, quatenus phaenomenon sit, AESTHETICA....Sit, quod vis, simplex duntaxat et unum, et placentem simul rotundam illam brevitatem et pulcram obtinebis cohaerentiam. Hinc Augustino placuit adeo unitas, ut eam omnis pulcritudinis formam diceret (A, pp. 279-280, §439).

[77] Versuch über das Schöne, p. 12. In 1762 Seran de la Tour still utilized André in his own explanation of beauty. Cf. L'art de sentir et de juger en matiere de goût (Paris, 1762), I, 9ff.

[78] Handbuch der Aesthetik, p. 60.

[79] Cf. Briefe über die Empfindungen in Schriften, II. 29f.

[80] Ueber Schönheit und guten Geschmack in der Mahlerei (1762) in *Sämmtliche hinterlassene Schriften*, ed. G. Schilling (Bonn, 1843), I, 199. Hereafter referred to in the text as HS, I plus page number. For a secondary source on Mengs see Monika Sutter, *Die kunsttheoretischen Begriffe des Malerphilosophen Anton Raphael Mengs. Versuch einer Begriffserläuterung im Zussammenhang mit der geistegeschichtlichen Situation Europas bis hin zu Kant* (n.p., 1968).

Chapter III

Aesthetics of Life

A. Introduction

In this chapter I shall, of course, seek to elucidate the essence of that school of thinkers, whose aesthetic theories were collectively designated by Schiller as the aesthetics of life. Unfortunately Schiller gave to the members of this school no epithet as he did for the aestheticians of form. I shall, therefore, stipulatively call such thinkers the theorists of life. This appellation is intended to compliment Schiller's designation of Vollkommenheitsmänner. Schiller himself suggested Edmund Burke (1730-1797) as a prime example of a theorist of life and clearly connected Burke with empiricism. For the sake of clarity and simplification of expositon, I shall focus my attention upon the British theorists of life, leaving representatives of other nations not mentioned.

Burke was, of course, one of the leading statesmen of England in the eighteenth century. Burke's Reflections on the French Revolution (1790) was a very influential political tract and is said to have retarded the influence of the French revolutionary thought in England more than any other work. Burke, however, first gained fame not from his political ideas but from his early work on aesthetic theory, namely from his A Philosophical Enquiry into the Origin of Our Ideas of the Sublime and Beautiful (1756).[1] Burke's aesthetic methodology is similar to that of many of his contemporary countrymen. Just as aesthetic thought on the continent was greatly influenced by philosophy, so too was British thought. "Die englische Aesthetik steht," writes Robert Zimmerman, "in enger Beziehung mit dem Charakter der englischen Philosophie."[2] Philosophy in England during the eighteenth century was of the empiricistic-sensualist type. Because English aesthetics stood in such close connection with English philosophy, the limitation of my discussion of the philosophy and aesthetics of life to Britain seems justified. I do not mean to imply that there were no theorists of life in other countries, e.g. in France or in Germany. There were! Nevertheless, British theorists exercised a steady and extensive influence upon German thinkers. In particular, British aesthetics was continually reinterpreted by Germans in rationalistic terms (or terminology). The result was the development in Germany of anomalies and theoretical contradictions.

In seeking to explain the philosophical background to the aesthetics of life, I will concentrate at first upon the thought of John Locke (1632-1704). What Leibniz and Wolff were for German rationalism, Locke certainly was for British empiricism. Locke's thought will be used as an example of the empiricistic trend in England.[3] Although Locke was not always consistent, his thought contains the essential doctrines of British empiricism and furnishes the metaphysical constants in terms of which the aesthetician of life constructed his aesthetic world and hence his interpretation of beauty. Locke is generally acknowledged to have influenced all the aestheticians of life. Burke, for instance, explicitly refers to Locke four times in his Enquiry. I shall occasionally compliment my discussion of Locke's empiricism with references to David Hume (1711-1776). Hume was, in my judgment, far more radical and far more consistent in his empiricism than Locke. In many ways Hume simply makes explicit what is implicit in Locke.

Before beginning my exposition I wish once again to stress the fact that I am not seeking to present the thought of a single thinker such as Locke, however much my exposition might focus upon a single individual. Nor am I seeking to analyze empiricism in a comprehensive manner. What is of interest is the general framework in terms of which theoreticians construct the ontological universe. Such a universe supplied in turn the analytical principles used in order to formulate questions concerning the aesthetic universe of life. In specific, I shall seek to establish the empiricistic principle for distinguishing between the real and the seeming. In the process of examining this criterion I shall briefly exposit (1) the empiricistic analysis of the contents of consciousness into its ultimate constituents and (2) the empiricistic theory that explains how these elements are connected together to form a unity. The criterion distinguishing between real and seeming receives its content from the synthetic principle of unity.

B. The Ontological Universe of the Aesthetics of Life

The Empiricistic Manifold

In the previous chapter I sought to show that rationalistic metaphysics and methodology are grounded in Descartes' cogito, ergo sum. Descartes' ego, from which he (and the rationalists) derived the ontological outline of reality, was a mathematical "self." In other words, rationalists in imitation of Descartes articulated formally the reality-criterion contained in the cogito, ergo sum in terms of mathematics. The axiomatic and deductive structure of mathematics was seen as paradigmatic for ontological reality. The result was, as shown in the previous chapter, the construction of a connexial reality in which the elements of the manifold are related to each other as "Grund" and "Folge", i.e. as aspects of the One.

Locke himself set as high a standard of truth as did Descartes. Truth must be universal, instructive, real, and above all else certain. Just as Descartes found certainty in self-intuition, so too did Locke find certainty there. But Locke differs from Descartes in that he does not try to use the intuition of the self as a starting point for a deductive interpretation of reality. In reading Locke, writes Jay William Hudson, "we immediately become aware that the certainty of the self is not a primary certainty in the sense of a logical first principle - a source principle from which other certainties shall receive their valid derivation. In this we see a contrast between Locke and Descartes."[4] The reason why Locke does not try to deduce ontological knowledge about reality from the intuition of the self is that Locke does not view the contents of consciousness as homogeneous in nature. Oneness is not the prime feature of being for Locke. The objects of the mind are not just homogeneous intelligibles, parts of a connexial whole, but rather sensations.[5] Sensations are real (at least as far as man is concerned) and are not reducible to anything more basic. The rationalist's dream of the homogeneity of knowledge is broken. Knowledge must begin with the empirical experience of sensations. Furthermore, since sensations cannot be reduced to intelligible notions, theory must follow sensations and be determined by them. At this point Locke has reversed the procedural method of rationalism. Rationalism would allow to the particular a claim to reality

only as long as it could be given a niche in a deductive system. Locke, on
the other hand, would grant reality to a theory only so long as it was in
accord with the empirical "facts." Hence, Locke demanded close observation
of facts.

Locke's rejection of a deductive method for a descriptive and inductive
model opened the way for an empirical investigation of the self and hence for
an empirical psychology - one that went far beyond Locke. Sensation was now
no longer derivative and, for that matter, neither were the self's
non-rational reactions to sensations. The study of these non-rational (if not
irrational) reactions is a proper study of psychology.[6] Indeed, Locke is in
many ways the father of empirical psychology. With Locke there begins in
European thought the gradual interpretation of the life of the self from a
psychological point of view.[7]

With this general introduction to Locke in mind, it is now possible to
examine in more detail Locke's empirical interpretation of reality. Locke,
as shown above, conceived sensations as the primary "given" in human
experience. Whereas rationalists viewed sensible experience as derivative,
Locke viewed it as a practical ultimate. Experience involves, to use
Kantian terminology, a unity of a manifold, i.e. there is a variety of
particulars connected together to form the synthetic whole that constitutes
the objectivity of experience. Locke sought to analyze this experience by
means of a method involving two essential steps. First, Locke sought to find
the non-reducible units that constitute the manifold of experience.
Secondly, he sought to discover the nature of the formal or structural
connectors that bind the manifold together to create the unity of
experience. In the exposition of Locke I will follow his procedure and hence
I will first examine Locke's conception of the nature of the contents of
experience.

Locke rejected the notion that man brings anything a priori with him in
his contact with reality. Hence, Locke quite properly rejected the notion of
innate ideas and innate senses. Instead, Locke visualized man as a white
sheet of paper upon which reality writes, i.e. furnishes the materials of
knowledge. Locke's first question was: "How comes [the mind] to be
furnished [with contents]?"[8] Locke's answer is that man receives the
materials of knowledge "from EXPERIENCE" (Essay, II, 1:2). And that which
causes experience are the "external objects [which] furnish the mind with the
ideas of sensible qualities..." (Essay, II, 1:5). Furthermore, the mind can
also turn inward upon itself and perceive itself operating "as it is employed
about the ideas it has got" (Essay, II, 1:4). This type of experience is
called reflection. Besides the mere reception of sensations and the
reflection upon such acts of reception, the mind also feels pain or pleasure
in each experience (Essay, II, 7ff). It is readily apparent that the first
part of the cognitive process is essentially asymmetrical. An external
object impresses sensations upon a passive mind. The mind reacts
reflectively and emotionally to these impressions.

What is the nature of the sensible qualities produced by the external
object? Firstly, such sensations are called by Locke ideas. The term idea
"serves best to stand for whatsoever is the object of the understanding when
a man thinks" (Essay, I, 1:8). When Locke writes "thinks" here, he means
simply "being aware" of some content of consciousness. Ideas are

representations in the mind of external objects that caused them. Therefore, for Locke, "it is evident the mind knows not things immediately, but only by intervention of the ideas it has of them" (Essay, IV, 4:3). Hume, it should be noted, was dissatisfied with Locke's terminology. Hume considered Locke's use of the term idea as referring to that which is originally and vividly present to the mind to be a perversion. Hume designated Locke's "ideas" as "impressions" and reserved the term "idea" for the faint images of impressions.[9] Despite terminological differences, both thinkers agreed that thinking starts with sensations.

Secondly, all the ideas viz. contents of human consciousness can be grouped in accordance with two categories. Ideas are either simple or complex. Simple ideas are the basic constituents or originals of human experience. They are ultimate and irreducible sensations or reflections. Examples of such simple ideas are "the coldness and hardness which a man feels in a piece of ice being as distinct ideas in the mind as the smell and whiteness of a lily; or as the taste of sugar, and smell of a rose" (Essay, II, 2:1). All the different varieties of sensations or simple ideas have two basic characteristics in common. Each simple idea "contains in it nothing but one uniform appearance or conception in the mind and is not distinguishable into different ideas" (Essay, II, 2:1). Hume similarly defines simple impressions as contents "such as admit of no distinction nor separation" (Treatise, I, 1:1). Each simple idea contains a content that is totally homogeneous in itself, and simultaneously exclusive of the content of any other simple idea. Consequently, simple ideas are the ultimate, isolated, and separate atoms of experience.

It is most important to understand that simple ideas or impressions have a quality of "brute giveness" about them. They are not the "simple notions" of Descartes nor the "primae veritates" of Leibniz. The ultimate units of rationalism were like axiomatic premises (Grund) from which all the particulars of reality were to be deduced (Folge). The connections which unite the manifold of reality in rationalism are intrinsic to the "simple notions" and flow from them (to borrow Meier's metaphor). But Locke's "simple ideas" are uniform in appearance, indistinguishable into other ideas, and hence they are the ultimate given of experience. This means that there is no logical or sufficient reason why one simple idea should imply another one. This constitutes a total rejection of the rationalistic concept of the real as connexial. Locke writes that "the simple ideas whereof our complex ideas of Substance are made up are, for the most part, such as carry with them, in their own nature, no visible necessary connection or inconsistency with other simple ideas, whose co-existence with them we would inform ourselves about" (Essay, IV, 3:10). Consequently, the simple ideas are, as Etienne Gilson has written, "the isolated atoms of consciousness (Locke himself uses the term), a kind of stable building blocks out of which...Locke will build the edifice of consciousness."[10]

In summary, I wish to stress how radically empiricistic reality is opposed to that of rationalism. Rationalism conceived reality as connexially one. Every "particular" is conceived as a part of an axiomatic and deductive whole. To be a particular element for rationalism is to be a function of an axiomatic totality. The very intrinsic nature of the particular contains reference to other particulars. The individual is defined as a Bestimmung in a web-like series of Gründe and Folgen. Individuality itself is but the most determinate Bestimmung or Folge within the connexial totality. In this sense the individual is intelligible through and through. Should there be a "particular" whose being does not entail participation in a connexial oneness, this particular would, indeed, be an unwelcomed and anomalous guest in rationalistic reality. Indeed, such an anomaly would cause the world to lose its systematic viz. mathematical intelligibility and the human mind would be faced with an atomistically given fact. As Moses Mendelssohn wrote: "Gesetzt, es könnte etwas ohne allen Grund vorhanden sein, so wäre das Dasein desselben eine Wahrheit, die mit keiner anderen Wahrheit verknüpft ist, eine isolierte Insel im Reich der Wahrheiten, zu welcher auf keinerlei Weise zu gelangen ist."[11] However, as a "child" of rationalism Mendelssohn conceived individuality as a concrete Bestimmung for which it is possible to give a sufficient reason why it is predicated of a subject. Mendelssohn notes: "Es ist schlechterdings unmöglich, dass eine Bestimmung wahr und unbegreiflich sein sollte."[12] But it is precisely this thesis that empiricism asserted. From a rationalistic point of view, the empiricistic world consists of Bestimmungen (particulars) that do not exhibit the mathematical features of Grund and Folge and are, therefore, quite unbegreiflich. In a sense, for empiricism a Bestimmung is "wahr" precisely because it is "unbegreiflich," i.e. atomistic.

"Life" as the Principle of Unity

Locke was faced with a very serious problem. Reality is not merely a chaotic collation of random sensations. Hume poignantly formulated the empiricistic problem. "Were ideas entirely loose and unconnected, chance alone would join them..." (Treatise, I, 1:4). But chance is not the de facto principle of unity. A Newtonian order rules. Such an order implies oneness and connection between the particulars. Again Hume formulated the situation for empiricism, "... and 'tis impossible the same simple ideas should fall regularly into complex [ones] (as they commonly do) without some bond of union among them, some associating quality, by which one idea naturally introduces another" (Treatise, I, 1:4). Just what is the nature of this "bond of union" that naturally connects viz. introduces one atom of consciousness with another in order to generate the "objective" world?

Each simple idea (or impression) is a closed entity unto itself. Its very being excludes the being of other atoms of consciousness. It is not the function of an axiomatic oneness. How, then, can such closed-off ideas enter into a unity with other similarly uniform ideas? Locke suggested a solution. "Though the Mind be wholly passive, in respect to its simple Ideas: Yet, I think, we may say, it is not so, in respect of its complex Ideas; For those being Combinations of simple Ideas, put together, and united under one general Name; 'tis plain, that the Mind of Man use some kind of Liberty, in forming those complex Ideas..." (Essay, II, 30:3). In his solution Locke reverses the assymetrical nature of the first part of the cognitive process. The mind is in a sense a synthetic force, i.e it is the active source of the "bond" between simple ideas. The mind combines "simple ideas into a compound one, and thus all complex ideas are made" (Essay, II, 12:1). Complex ideas are, therefore, "made up of Collections of simple ideas" (Essay, II, 29:13).

In interest of historical accuracy, however, it must be noted that the composition theory of complex ideas is not the whole of Locke's thought, at least not in the minds of many of his interpreters. R. I. Aaron thinks, for

instance, that the composition-theory is a misinterpretation of Locke.[13] It
is quite "obvious" from any examination of Locke's theories about abstraction
and substance that Locke allows ideas in the mind that are not readily
divisible into simple ones. Locke, the thesis goes, gives a second meaning to
the terms of simple and complex. According to Gibson, "it appears... that
the distinction that Locke has in mind, throughout his discussion of ideas,
is one between ideas which are 'primary' or 'original' and those which we may
call secondary or derivative ideas, rather than between the simple and the
complex, the two principles of division being identified under the influence
of the compositional theory."[14] This second meaning is conceived as
inconsistent with the literal meaning of the terms of simple and complex.

I should like to note that I do not agree with this critique of the
compositional interpretation. I agree that Locke's notion of "substance"
cannot easily be brought into harmony with his empiricistic doctrine of
simple ideas. Certainly Hume exercised a devastating critique of the
notion.[15] However, I do not see how such a possible inconsistency negates
the thesis that the composition theory is one of the primary empiricistic
features of Locke's thought. Also, the interpretation of the relationship of
simple and complex ideas entailing a relationship of the "original" and
"derivative" does not, in my judgment, necessarily contradict the
compositional interpretation. Indeed, the two interpretations seem to me to
be complimentary. A "simple" idea is primary not only because it evinces a
"uniform appearance," but also because it strikes the mind as "original",
i.e. as "forcibly vivid." The notion of "simple" refers to the ontological
atomicity of an idea, whereas the notion of "original" refers to its
presentational intensity. Hume certainly made copious use of these two
aspects without evincing a contradiction. I think the same holds basically
for Locke. Furthermore, the "original-derivative" interpretation does not
alter the fact that the "bond" between simple ideas is basically an
imposition of unity from without by the mind as it "connects" simple ideas
into complex ones. This "compounding" activity of the mind is the
philosophical legacy bequeathed by Locke to the empiricistic tradition. Hume
formulated this empiricistic position when he contended that the "creative
power of the mind amounts to no more than the faculty of compounding,
transposing, augmenting, or diminishing the materials afforded us by the
senses and experience....In short, all the materials of thinking are derived
either from our outward or inward sentiment: The mixture and composition of
these belongs alone the mind and will."[16]

According to Locke there are three fundamental kinds of complex ideas,
namely modes, relations, and substances. The notion of "substance" alone is
of interest for understanding the problem of "objectivity" for British
empiricism (at least insofar as Locke influenced the tradition).[17] According
to Locke, ideas, be they simple or complex, are "Either real, or fantastical...[and] true, or false. First, by real Ideas I mean such as have a
Foundation in Nature; such as have a Conformity with the real Being, and
Existence of Things, or with their Archetypes. Fantastical or Chimerical, I
call such as have no Foundation in Nature, nor have any Conformity with that
reality, to which they are tacitly referr'd, as to their Archetypes" (Essay,
II, 30:1). Justified or not, Locke (and in effect also Hume) believed that
sensations are the product of "things" or "objects" existing independent of
the (perceiving) mind. Locke in effect was a "realist" in the sense proposed
by Josiah Royce. According to Royce, "the one mark of the realistic type of

Being... [is] the indifference of any real being to what you may, as the knower, think about it... [The object] is a realistic being so long as it is supposed to be quite independent of your knowledge, and so undetermined by your knowledge."[18] Locke located "reality" in the independence of objects from the knowing mind. Truth thereby becomes the conformity of the mind's knowledge (ideas) to external archetypes. Locke states his philosophical "faith" in the of objectivity in the following way:

> The Mind, being as I have declared, furnished with a great number of the simple Ideas, conveyed in by the Senses, as they are found in exteriour things, or by Reflections on its own Operations, takes notice also, that a certain number of these simple Ideas go constantly together; which being presumed to belong to one thing, and Words being suited to common apprehensions, and made use of for quick dispatch, are called so united in one subject, by one name; which by inadvertency we are apt afterward to talk of and consider as one simple Idea, which indeed is a complication of many Ideas together; Because, as I have said, not imagining how these simple Ideas can subsist by themselves, we accustom our selves, to suppose some Substratum, wherein they do subsist, and from which they do result, which therefore we call Substance (Essay, II, 23:1).

The distinction between the "real" and the "seeming" has its meaning for Lockean empiricism in the accuracy of conformity insofar as various complex ideas, thought to subsist in a substratum (=object), represent external archetypes really existing independent of the knowing mind. Concerning the nature of truth and falsity Locke writes: "Our complex Ideas of Substances, being made all of them in reference to Things existing without us, and intended to be Representations of Substances, as they really are, are no farther real, than as they are such combinations of simple Ideas, as are really united, and co-exist in Things without us. On the contrary, those are fantastical, which are made up of such Collections of simple Ideas, as were really never united, never were found together in any Substance..." (Essay, II, 30: 5). The epistemological question arises, accordingly, in context with the notion of conformity. The criterion for the "real" must furnish a means for determining the accuracy of conformity. "The Question then is," writes Locke, "which of these [complex ideas] are real, and which barely imaginary Combinations: what Collections agree to the reality of Things, and what not?" (Essay, II, 30:3).

If there are no intrinsic and logical interconnections between simple ideas, what criteria are there for accepting any specific combination of simple ideas as really representative of the supposed external object that affects the mind? In short, how is the real to be known? The answer to this question is of greatest importance for the understanding of Locke's position as the father, so to speak, of the aesthetics of life.

Knowledge must be certain, instructive (i.e. synthetic) and real.[19] This is a very strict definition of knowledge. Anything less is probability, opinion, or faith. Locke finds that there are different types of knowledge. For instance, there is knowledge about the identity or non-identity of ideas, e.g. the idea of black is not that of white. This type of knowledge is obviously tautological and not very instructive. Mathematical knowledge is instructive but only formal, i.e. its truth has nothing to do with whether or not there are real objects that conform to its propositions.

Locke believed that knowledge of the self is real and also the demonstration of God's existence is real. But what about knowledge about the existence of any other thing? "The knowledge of the existence of any other thing we can have only by sensations" (Essay, IV, 11:1). Although it is true that the existence of other things is made manifest by sensation, Locke does not yet answer the question as to whether or not the sensations accurately represent the substance, to say nothing of complex ideas. Locke's answer is: "The Notice we have by our Senses of the existing of Things without us ... is an assurance that deserves the Name of Knowledge. If we persuade ourselves that our Faculties act and inform us right concerning the existence of those Objects that affect them, it cannot pass for an ill-grounded confidence: For I think nobody can, in earnest, be so sceptical as to be uncertain of the Existence of those Things which he sees and feels . . . As to myself, I think GOD has given me assurance enough of the Existence of Things without me" (Essay, IV, 11:3). This answer is anything but satisfactory. Indeed, it assumes that which is to be proved, i.e. it assumes that man's faculties inform man rightly of the existence of external objects, but this is what needs to be demonstrated. In short, Locke still has not answered the question as to why ideas, particularly complex ideas, are to be accepted as real and reliable representations of objective reality.

In order to understand Locke's solution a brief restatement of Locke's problem will help. Consciousness involves a unity of the manifold. The contents of consciousness involve (1) a manifold (simple ideas) and (2) a unity (complex ideas). Locke's problem is (1) to ascertain how accurately complex ideas represent the real and (2) to discover a criterion for determining this accuracy. For example, the mind's imagination can just as easily concoct an image of a centaur as that of a man. Both represent a unity of the manifold. How is the self to judge which complex idea is real or not. Locke's answer is: "The Understanding Faculties being given to Man, not barely for Speculation, but also for the Conduct of his Life, Man would be at a great loss if he had nothing to direct him but what has the Certainty of true Knowledge. . . .He that will not eat till he has Demonstration that it will nourish him; he that will not stir till he infallibly knows the Business he goes about will succeed, will have little else to do but to sit still and perish" (Essay, IV, 14:1).

This answer suggests a practical answer to a theoretical problem. Man has needs and they must be met if man is to maintain his wellbeing. Speculative knowledge about the deepest secrets of reality is not necessary for a successful practical life. This means facing up to the fact that man's knowledge (i.e. absolutely certain knowledge) is very narrow. "We shall not have much Reason to complain of the narrowness of our Minds, if we will but employ them about what may be of use; for of that they are very capable" (Essay, I, 1:5). "Our Business here is not to know all things, but those which concern our Conduct" (Essay, I, 1:6). "Conduct" and "of use" are key words for understanding Locke's solution. Practicality is a sufficient epistemological criterion for the way man should organize the manifold of experience. Man must seek his well-being. To do this he must seek good and avoid evil. This means organizing and interpreting experience (sensations) in such a way that it is amenable to human needs. This practical imperative justifies Locke (1) in his abandonment of absolutely certain knowledge as the only source to cognition of reality and (2) in positing practicality as an ultimate criterion for deciding which complex ideas are to be accepted as real and which as mere works of the imagination.[20]

The significance of the practicality criterion needs further amplification. That which is of use is good. That which is not of use is evil. Furthermore, good and evil refer to that which gives pleasure or pain. "Things then are Good or Evil only in reference to Pleasure or Pain" (Essay, II, 20:1). Man's being is governed by pleasure and pain. "Nature, I confess, has put into Man a desire for Happiness and an aversion to Misery: These indeed are innate practical Principles which . . . do continue constantly to operate and influence all our Actions without ceasing: These may be observed in all Persons and all Ages, steady and universal" (Essay, I, 3:3). Thus, it seems to follow that that which is of an emotional and irrational nature is a very important determining factor in the cognitive construction of man's experience.

From the above exposition of Locke I believe that the essential empirical principles involved in Locke's thinking can be grasped. (1) First, the empiricist views sensations and reflection upon the mind's activity as the origins or originals of all knowledge. Sensations are the ultimate brute given of consciousness. (2) Next, the method of discovering truth must be based upon close observation of the "facts" and their interconnections. Furthermore, these interconnections are generally not of a logical nature; rather they usually result from repeated occurances in spatial and temporal contiguity. (3) Therefore, complex ideas generally are a result of inductive generalization. (4) Such demonstrations lack, however, apodictic certainty of the kind demanded by the ideal of absolutely indubitable knowledge. (5) Because experience does not give an indubitable cognitive criterion for distinguishing between true and false complex ideas, the empiricist is forced to turn to the needs of the subject for such a criterion. If knowledge is practically efficacious, i.e. if it sustains man's needs, this is all that is required of it. The influence of practical need in the structuring of the manifold of experience can be called the Principle of Life. (6) The principle of life means that the individual's psychology, i.e. his striving after pleasure and avoidance of pain, is of great importance in determining his experience as a synthetic unity. "Objectivity" becomes thereby a function of subjectivity viz. practical life. But what is of even more importance, the psychology of an individual has its dynamism not rooted in mathematical reason. Pleasure is not just unclearly experienced intellectual joy as it was for Leibniz. Pleasure and pain are ultimate irrational (or a-rational) psychic units of experience, i.e. they are simple ideas (or impressions) that occur in conjunction with other simple and complex ideas. This turn from a formal and cognitive interpretation of things by rationalism to a sensible and emotional (and hence psychological) interpretation of things is one of Locke's more important contributions to the revolution in thought throughout the eighteenth century.

Associationism and the "Constants" of the Empiristic World

"The analysis of mental processes which the English school [of psychologists] carried out is a logical result of their philosophical attitude. These [18th century] writers employed the empirical method in philosophy."[21] British theorists did, indeed, as Warren asserts, examine the "mental processes" of man from the standpoint of their philosophical position. However, the relationship between the empiricistic theory of mental dynamics and an empiricistic metaphysics is more than one of methodology. Not only did philosophical paradigms furnish the theorists of life with analytical principles for a theory of mental activity (=psychology), but psychological theory completed the philosophical project. Experience evinces a uniformity and this uniformity is amenable to orderly analysis. In other words, experience shows itself to be an organized system and, therefore, manifests a oneness, a synthetic unity. However, the metaphysical analysis of the manifold of experience had resulted in an ontological atomism. As far as the human mind is concerned, there is no "objective" uniformity given that can unite the manifold into a whole. The epistemological solution to this Lockean problem was to seek a substitute in the connection of ideas. The unity of experience derives from the mind's capacity to "compound" ontological atoms into complex wholes. Locke himself had basically focused upon the epistemological aspects of such "compounded" unities. In other words, the mind can seemingly concoct an infinite variety of complex unities. Which ones are reflective of "reality" and which are not? As shown above, the principle of life was the epistemological criterion suggested by Locke.

Locke did not, however, focus much upon the compounding activity itself, particularly conceived as a psychological process. In other words, the genesis of complex ideas as products of the mind's activity was not adequately considered by Locke. But the "objective world" which confronts the individual is precisely the product of such mental activity. Furthermore, as Dessoir notes, "Locke had subordinated to psychology essentially the entire range of the experienceable. A step farther, and one came to the opinion, which was later current [in the 18th century], that psychology is the fundamental science."[22] It is precisely the task of psychology to explain how the sensations of experience are organized into the knowable world and the knowledge thereof.

At this point (ca. 1740 on), the psychological analysis as carried out by empiricism begins to leave Locke behind. Theorists such as John Gay, David Hartley, Mark Akenside, George Turnball, and especially David Hume began to investigate the "compounding" dynamics of the human mind. Such thinkers were impressed with the "empirical" fact that sensations, regularly repeated and contiguous, evince a "bond" that connects them, i.e. one empirical content "naturally" introduces the next. The fact of such a "bond" grounds the organization of knowledge and of experience. The technical term applied to the process of bonding was "association."[23] Hume designated the principle of association as "a kind of ATTRACTION, which in the mental world will be found to to have as extraordinary effects as in the natural, and to shew itself in as many and various forms" (Treatise, I, 1:4). Indeed, Hume could well have said that the "natural" world as an object of human experience is part of the "mental" world or, at least, its construct.

In the ensuing analysis, I shall briefly focus upon Hume's version of associationism. I shall not attempt to be comprehensive. I simply wish to show tht the aim of the theorists of life was to account for the organization of consciousness as a product of an associative operation. Hume's analysis is a particularly excellent example of the empiricistic doctrine of associationism.

Hume distinguishes three fundamental laws of association: namely resemblance, contiguity, and causality. I shall limit my examination of Hume's theory of association to the proglem of causality. The category of causality is, of course, one of the most important "constants" of objectivity. Without causality the unity of experience dissolves into random congeries. The manifold of experience, consequently, cannot transcend the subjectivity of the experiencing mind. Causality, on the other hand, structures, the manifold into temporally and spatially ordered units of dependencies (grounds and consequents). Causality thereby introduces "necessity" and hence "objectivity" into the kaleidescopic manifold of subjective experience. Indeed, "necessary connection" is the defining feature of causality according to Hume.

Hume's philosophical task was to ascertain the nature of causal necessity.[24] This task seems, however, to be impossible. Sensible experience certifies no such "impression" of necessary connection. The causal links escape empirical experience. Rational demonstration, Hume contends, cannot "prove" a priori the existence of causal connections in any and all given cases. In short, there is nothing in reason or in the impressions presented to the mind that can justify the inference of one object (or state of affairs) from another one. It is at this point that the principle of life becomes evident in the world-view (or world-constructing) of empiricism. Because Hume cannot find an explanation of causality in the contents present to the mind, he seeks it in the activity of the knowing mind itself. In other words, Hume undertakes a psychological analysis and seeks a psychological solution for a philosophical problem.

Hume notes that the mind is presented with "facts" or objects that are contiguous in time. The same experience continually repeat themselves. After a sufficient number of repetitions, a habit is produced in the mind which "determines" the mind to view two objects as "connected." In other words, Hume contends that:

> after a repetition of similar instance, the mind is carried by habit, upon the appearance of one event, to expect its usual attendant, and to believe that it will exist. This connexion, therefore, which we feel in the mind, this customary transition of the imagination from one object to its usual attendant, is the sentiment or impression from which we form the idea of power or necessary connexion...What alteration has happened to give rise to this new idea of connexion? Nothing but that [the individual] now feels these events to be connected in his imagination, and can readily foretell the existence of one from the appearance of the other (Enquiry, § 59).

Causality as an "objectivity constant" now reveals itself in empiricistic philosophy to be an internal feeling of the mind's own complusion to experience two things as "necessarily" connected. The "necessity" lies in the mind's impulse, not in the objects themselves. Hume writes:

> The idea of necessity arises from some impression. There is no impression conve'd by our senses, which can give rise to that idea. It must, therefore, be derived from some internal impression

of reflection. There is no internal impression, which has any relation to the present business, but that propensity, which custom produces, to pass from an object to the idea of its usual attendant. This therefore is the essence of necessity. Upon the whole, necessity is something, that exists in the mind, not in objects; nor is it possible for us ever to form the most distant idea of it, consider'd as a quality in bodies. Either we have no idea of necessity, or necessity is nothing but that determination of the thought to pass from causes to effects and from effects to causes, according to their experienc'd union (Treatise, I, 3:14).

The unity in things is for empiricism a function of the unity (or, rather, of the unifying activity) of the self. That which connects the unity of the self with external reality is "custom" or habituation. Habituation is, of course, a structure in the mind, not in things. Also, "custom" is essentially a category of life. "Custom, then", writes Hume, "is the great guide of human life. It is that principle alone which renders our experience useful to us, and makes us expect, for the future, a similar train of events with those which have appeared in the past. Without the influence of custom...we should never know how to adjust means to ends, or to employ our natural powers in the production of any effect. There would be an end at once to all action, as well as of the chief part of specualtion" (Enquiry, § 36). The key here is "useful to us" and "action." Custom as an associative principle is itself a function of human "life", i.e. of the individual and social activities of man in pursuit of what "is useful" to his needs. Consequently, the de facto "objectivity" that confronts man finds its constants (and hence reality) in the "life" needs of man. The empiricistic world does, indeed, reveal itself to be a world of "associations" produced by the principles of association. Hume was well aware that the "objective" world of empiricism was but a function of the associative power of the human mind. In 1740 Hume wrote:

'Twil be easy to conceive of what vast consequence these principles [of association] must be in the science of human nature, these are the only links that bind the parts of the universe together, or connect us with any person or object exterior to ourselves...[T]hey are really to us the cement of the universe, and all the operations of the mind must, in a great measure, depend upon them.[25]

The parts of the universe are "cemented" together by the principles of association, particularly by the principle of causality as produced by "custom." The associative production itself occurs within the context of "life", of man's pursuit of pleasure and avoidance of pain, of man's satiation of his needs.

Sympathy as the Gravity of "Life"

Man's cognitive life is both genetically and structurally a function of life, i.e. of man's pursuit of what is useful. An object, once obtained, produces pleasure or pain. Pleasure and pain constitute the utility or disutility of things and function as a mediator between man and his environment, between subject and object. The pursuit of pleasure and the avoidance of pain constitute the "life" springs of the mind's operations. Hume writes: "The chief spring or actuating principle of the human mind is pleasure or pain... The most immediate effects of pleasure and pain are the propense and averse motions of the mind..." (Treatise, III, 3:1). The manifold of human activities evinces a unity because of man's attempt to achieve pleasure and to avoid pain. This doctrine is one of the essential doctrines of British empiricism and of the philosophy of "life."

Despite his acceptance of the thesis that man pursues what is pleasurable and avoids what is painful, Hume did not wish simply to affirm a theory of purely egotistical utility, rather one of general utility. In other words, purely self-directed pleasure is a poor basis for grounding social cooperation and harmony. Self-interest alone could easily exercise an atomizing and centrifugal influence upon society. One specific self-interest can easily be opposed to another one or to the needs of society. Somehow a general utility - a universal "bond" - must be operative in the individual if society is to function as a cohesive whole and if human consciousness is to reflect a cohesion derived from such universal association. More specifically, pleasure and pain, conceived as motives for activity, must be "associated" with benevolence, love, generosity, etc. or, in short, with the utility of the many. Morality is precisely that science that deals with the universality (or the universal validity) of judgments concerning general utility. Morality, in effect, deals with the social "gravity" that "cements" the individual many into the social one.[26]

The "gravity" of the social world is, according to Hume, sympathy.[27] "No quality of human nature", writes Hume, "is more remarkable, both in itself and in its consequences, than that propensity we have to sympathize with others, and to receive by communication their inclinations and sentiments, however different, or even contrary to our own....To this principle we ought to ascribe the great uniformity we may observe in the humours and turn of thinking of those of the same nation..." (Treatise, II, 1:11). Man, according to Hume, has an innate propensity, respectively, to take pleasure (or pain) in the pleasure (or pain) of others. Social cohesion arises out of sympathy. Hume asserts: "The minds of all men are similar in their feelings and operations, nor can any one be actuated by the affection, of which all others are not, in some degree susceptible. As in strings equally wound up, the motion of one communicates itself to the rest; so all the affections readily pass from one person to another, and beget correspondent movements in every human creature" (Treatise, III, 3:1). Hume's imaginative description of sympathy, given in the last statement, clearly manifests the source of unity for the social world, namely the sympathetic universal in each "atom" of subjectivity. The objectively given impressions of experience are atomistically separate and diverse. No connection between any two distinguishable entities seems possible. As Hume notes: "So that, upon the whole, there appears not, throughout all nature, any one instance of connexion which is conceivable by us. All events seem entirely loose and separate. One event follows another; but we never can observe any tie between them. They seem conjoined but never connected."[28] The notion of any individual content does not include any reference to any other content. Things are not related as Grund and Folge. However, it now turns out that there appears to be some exceptions, e.g. causality. Causality is a necessity felt by the mind to proceed from one event to another. This necessity is a "connection." But it is an impulse of the mind, not of exterior things. It also turns out that man possesses a "need" to find pleasure in what is useful to others and this need appears to be an absolute in the structure of the human self. "Here [sympathy] is a principle, which accounts in great part, for the origin of morality...It is needless to push our researches so far as to ask, why we have humanity or a fellow feeling with others. It is sufficient, that this is experienced to be a principle in human nature...No man is absolutely indifferent to the happiness and misery of others. The first has a natural tendency to give pleasure; the second, pain" (Enquiry, § 178 and 178n).

Pain and pleasure, the structural heart of the principle of life, are not simply atomistically enclosed in upon themselves, rather evince a universal form which can be formulated as the thesis that "wherever we go, whatever we reflect on or converse about, everything still presents us with the view of human happiness or misery, and excites in our breast a sympathetic movement of pleasure or uneasiness" (Enquiry, § 180). Rationalism found unity in the mathematical identity of the pure self. This identity was articulated as the principles of contradiction and of sufficient reason. The ontological product of applying such principles to being was the construction of a connexial reality. The manifold of objectivity becomes real insofar as it is informed by a connexial bond. This unity is "perfection" and ultimately grounds the principle of form. Empiricists such as Hume could find no unity in things. Only the psychological structure of man evinces a connexial like unity. Both the cognitive and conative activities of the self entail a bonding feature. Cognitively the mind, habituated by custom, feels "determined" to experience two events as connected. Similarly, pleasure and pain as volitional impulses entail reference to the many conceived in generality as humanity. The conative oneness is sympathy. Sympathy as the center of the principle of life is, indeed, the creator of worlds. Sympathy structures the associative or bonding process and hence contributes to the construction of a universe of "life."

Concluding Remarks on the Principle of Life

Thus far I have limted my discussion of the objective structure of the universe of life to two representatives, namely Locke and Hume. Although British thinkers often disagreed with each other, there is enough unity between many of them such that one can speak of a "school" life. The philosophy of life entailed at least three basic features:

1) Locke, as shown above, located the criterion between the real and the seeming in practicality. Speculative reason cannot reach the ontological heart of things. Nevertheless, the practical usefulness of a cognitive thesis functions sufficiently as the criterion for the truth in things. This practical criterion can be seen in the thought of 18th century British thinkers. Even philosophers of the Scottish school of "Common Sense", despite their opposition to Locke and Hume, grounded in part their "evident principles" upon the criterion of life. Thomas Reid, the leading representative of this school, wrote: "One who applies to any branch of science...must have exercised his reason, and the other powers of his mind in various ways. He must have formed various opinions and principles, by which he conducts himself in the affairs of life. Of those principles, some are common to all men, being evident in themselves, and so necessary in the conduct of life that a man cannot live and act according to the rules of common prudence without them."[29] This is almost pure Locke.

2) Empiricists for the most part turned to psychology in their efforts to explain the obvious unity found in experience. The psychological doctrine of association was widely used in order to explain the "cement" that holds the atoms of experience together. Hume was not the first nor the most influential of associationists. David Hartley (1705-1757) developed a comprehensive theory of association in his Observations on Man, His Frame, His Duty, and His Expectations (1749). Hartley reduced association to the repeated contiguity of events. Hartley did, however, attempt to ground associationism on a physiological basis. Hartley's associationism was popularized greatly by Joseph Priestly (1733-1804) who in 1775 published an abridged edition of the Observations on Man and developed his own associationism in his Theory of the Human Mind (1775). Associationism became so prevalent that even the Scottish opponents to British empiricism utilized the principle of association in their discussions of the operations of the human mind.[30]

3) Consistent with their subordination of "speculative" theory to practical criteria, empiricists were very much interested in the social structure of "human" reality. Atomism clearly has limits relative to the social cohesiveness any society must have. In some sense the elements of the manifold had to transcend their atomistic separateness and become part of one "connexial" whole. The doctrine of sympathy fulfilled this need. The concept of sympathy can be found in many texts on moral or social theory in the 18th century. Perhaps the most comprehensive use of the doctrine can be found in Adam Smith. In his Theory of Moral Sentiments (1759) Smith laboriously describes the origins, development, and structure of human sociality (including moral judgments) by means of ubiquitous force of sympathy. Smith seeks to derive "generosity, humanity, kindness, compassion, mutual friendship and esteem, all the social and benevolent affections", from sympathy, the social "cement."[31]

Utility as the criterion of truth, the principle of association as the producer of the cohesion or unity of consciousness, and sympathy as the universal principle of mental operations - these three theses are integral constituents of the ontological, social, and psychological universe of the theorists of life. The reality that confronts man is a product of his life needs. These three theses furnished the analytical paradigms out of which the theorist of life derived questions concerning the aesthetic universe and the nature of beauty. It is to the aesthetic universe of life that we will turn now.

C. The Aesthetic Universe of the Aesthetics of Life

Methodology

British theories of aesthetics in the 18th century evince the influence of philosophical empiricism.[32] This is not, of course, to deny many differences, sometimes of great significance. In the ensuing analysis I shall focus somewhat upon the thought of Edmund Burke and supplement my interpretation of Burke with references to other theorists of life. In one important area, as shall be shown, Burke did deviate significantly from the general stream of an aesthetics of life.

In the "Preface" to the first edition of his work, Burke sets out the motives that led him to develop his own theory.[33] After having read many discussions of aesthetics Burke felt "that he was far from having an exact theory."[34] Burke sought, therefore, a "remedy" for this situation. This "remedy" involves (1) the rejection of any rationalist approach to aesthetics and (2) an adoption of an empiricistic methodology.

(1) Burke rejects the method of rationalism because he felt that it did not explain anything with its definitions and deductions. Rationalists sought, as a methodological ideal, to discover clear and distinct ideas and to formulate such ideas in comprehensive "definitions." The definitions then serve as premises for a series of deductive conclusions. Burke warns against the reliance upon definitions. "I have no great opinion of a definition, the celebrated remedy for the cure of this disorder [of the lack of scientific comprehension]. For, when we define, we seem in danger of circumscribing nature within the bounds of our own notions, which we often take up by hazard or embrace on trust, or form out of a limited and partial consideration of the object before us; instead of extending our ideas to take in all that nature comprehends, according to her manner of combining" (Phil. Enquiry, "Introduction", p. 12). Abstract concepts and definitions simply do not capture the particular characteristics of nature. Hence, to seek to explain the particular aspect of things by means of abstract notions, is to force nature into a restricted pattern, rather than to follow nature as it is in itself.

Burke's opposition to the use of "definitions" in the scientific process highlights the differences between the methodology of German rationalists and the methodology of British empiricists. In his German logic Christiann Wolff succinctly defines the essence of scientific thinking:

> Ich habe bereits in dem Vorberichte erinnert, daß ich durch die Wissenschaft eine Fertigkeit des Verstandes verstehe, alles, was man behauptet, aus unwidersprechlichen Gründen unumstößlich darzuthun. Da nun die Erklärungen [=definitions], die Grund-Sätze und klare Erfahrungen unumstößliche Gründe sind; die Demonstrationen aber die Schlüsse, welche unumstößlich sind, so weit hinauf führen, bis man in dem letzten Schlusse nichts als Erklärungen, klare Erfahrungen oder Grund-Sätze zu Förder-Sätzen hat; so ist die Wissenschaft nichts anders als eine Fertigkeit zu demonstriren.[35]

From the standpoint of German rationalism, the empiricistic method could do little more than to formulate acute "Beschreibungen" of things, i.e. it remains on the surface of things rather than penetrating to the ontological heart in things. Burke, on the other hand, following empiricistic thought, considers sensations, not ontological intelligibles, to be the "originals" of human knowledge. Consequently, Burke contends: "When we go but one step beyond the immediate sensible qualities of things, we go out of our depth" (Phil. Enquiry, IV, 1:129 -130). Hence, Burke demands close empirical observation of the object and its sensible characteristics rather than rational "demonstriren." The result is that reason as an a priori source of knowledge for aesthetic theory is considered to be inadequate, indeed, non-existent.

Not only is deductive reason incapable of explaining aesthetic experience, it is not even involved in the production of such experience, as the rationalist had believed. For instance, concerning the origin of beauty Burke writes that it "demands no assistance from our reasoning; even the will is unconcerned" (Phil. Enquiry, III, 1:91) and that "it is no creature of our reason" (Phil. Enquiry, III, 12:112). Because Burke rejects reason as a constituent element in the production of aesthetic awareness, he also rejects the contention of some of his contemporary theorists that "fitness" and "proportion" are causes of beauty. Both fitness and proportion are, according to Burke, rational concepts formed and grasped by man's faculty of reasoning. The cognition of fitness and proportion only, claims Burke, produces "the acquiescence of the understanding, but not love, nor any passion of that species" (Phil. Enquiry, III, 7:108). The passions and the imagination are left tranquil by the experience of order. Hence, "every idea of order...must...be considered as a creature of understanding rather than a primary cause acting upon the senses and imagination" (Phil. Enquiry. III, 2:92). In short, reason is not involved in man's emotional and sensible life and hence not in his experience of beauty. "I imagine", Burke writes, "that the influence of reason in producing our passions is nothing near so extensive as it is commonly believed" (Phil. Enquiry, I, 12:44).

(2) Aesthetic experience is not derived from the productive activity of reason. It involved the use of the imagination and the senses. Consequently, Burke concludes the investigator must pay strict attention to the immediate sensible aspects of nature. In this contention Burke is, of course, following in the footsteps of Locke and Hume. With the demand for close empirical observation in mind, Burke spells out the general method he will follow in the "Preface" to the second edition of his work.

> The characters of nature are legible it is true; but they are not plain enough to enable those who run, to read them. We must make use of a cautious, I had almost said, a timorous method or proceeding. We must not attempt to fly, when we can scarcely pretend to creep. In considering any complex matter, we ought to examine every distinct ingredient in the composition, one by one; and reduce everything to the utmost simplicity; since the condition of our nature binds us to a strict law and very narrow limits. We ought afterwards to re-examine the principles by the effect of the composition, as well as the composition by that of the principles. We ought to compare our subject with things of a similar nature, even with things of a contrary nature... The greater number of those comparisons we make, the more general and the more certain our knowledge is likely to prove, as built upon a more extensive and perfect induction (Phil. Enquiry, "Preface", p. 4).

This quotation exhibits clearly the methodology of empiricism. First Burke intends to break up all the complex units into simple ones and then to examine carefully the principle of combinations of such units. Finally, Burke will check his results by careful comparison so as to guarantee that he has reached his generalizations by means of an adequate induction. Burke, in summary, was following the empiricistic imperative to seek out the irreducible "atoms" of consciousness, out of which the complex edifice of experience is compounded. Just as Hume, in his analysis of the notion of "energy" contended that the investigator "must look for [the notion] in the [sensible] impressions from which it is originally deriv'd" (Treatise, I. 3:14), Burke similarly was seeking the "original" or "origin" of the ideas of beauty and sublimity in sensible contents of experience. Burke's term "origin" is synonymous with the Lockean and Humean designation of "original." Beauty for theorists of life is an idea, complex or simple, derived from certain irreducible "impressions" or originals. Applying this general empiricistic methodology to aesthetic experience, Burke sets out a three-step procedure for the development of his theory.

> Could this [problem of the lack of any exact aesthetic theory] admit of remedy, I imagined it could only be from a diligent examination of our passions in our own breasts; from a careful survey of the properties of things which we find by experience to influence those passions; and from a sober and attentive investigation of the laws of nature, by which those properties are capable of affecting the body, and thus of exciting our passions. If this could be done, it was imagined that the rules deducible from such an enquiry might be applied to the imitative arts, and to whatever else they concerned, without much difficulty (Phil. Enquiry, "Preface to the First Edition," p. 1).

(1) The first step that Burke proposes is to investigate the subjective side of aesthetic experience, (2) then to examine the objective side in order to determine the objective characteristic of things involved in aesthetic experience, and (3) finally to determine the efficient cause of the relationship between the objective and subjective side of aesthetic experience. In the process of the ensuing analysis the subjective, objective, and interrelational aspects of the aesthetic experience, as interpreted by theorists of life, will be examined.

Imagination, Taste, and the Aesthetic Universe

British aestheticians of the 18th century rivaled the Germans in quantity and perspicacity of aesthetic theories. However, a certain terminological difficulty arises in any attempt to compare the two groups of thinkers. It is clear that British theorists of life were interested in aesthetic phenomena or in explaining the nature of aesthetic experience. However, despite the plenitude of disquisitions on the matter, British thinkers had no general term for the "aesthetic." "Aesthetik" as a technical designation for the beautiful, etc. was, of course, an invention of Baumgarten. British thinkers made no use of this term. As a result, British aestheticians had to discuss the "aesthetic" in another terminological vocabulary.

Joseph Addison (1672-1719) more or less set the framework of British theory to 1712 when he sought to explain the aesthetic experience of beauty, sublimity, and novelty in terms of "The Pleasures of the Imagination" (as the title of his essays on the matter reveals).[36] This designation identifies both the producer of the aesthetic world (=the imagination) and the nature of the aesthetic (=pleasure). The "scientific" treatment of "the pleasures of the imagination" was subsumed by subsequent theorists under the rubrics of "taste." In 1759 Alexander Gerard asserted that "taste consists chiefly in the improvement of those principles, which are commonly called the powers of the imagination..."[37] Edmund Burke stated: "I mean by the word Taste, no more than that faculty or those faculties of the mind, which are affected with, or which form a judgment of, the works of the imagination and the elegant arts" (Phil. Enquiry, "Introduction", p. 1). Reid defined taste as "that power of the mind by which we are capable of discerning and relishing the beauty of Nature and whatever is excellent in the fine arts" (Intellectual Powers, I, 490). In 1777 Joseph Priestly (1783-1804) simply conceived taste as "the capacity of percieving the pleasures of the imagination."[38] Each of the four definitions just cited are but variants of the same basic position. The central idea is that of the imagination. Taste is improved (or developed) by the powers of the imagination. Taste is directed towards and hence forms judgments about products of the imagination (=works of art). Ultimately taste is the ability to experience the pleasures of the imagination, i.e. to have aesthetic experience. The term "taste" in British thought is roughly equivalent to the term "aesthetic" in German theory. Beauty was discussed by the theorists of life in the terms of the principles of taste. These principles in turn are derived from the principles governing the functioning of the imagination. "Taste", maintains Gerard, "...though itself a species of sensation, is, in respect of its principles, justly reduced to the imagination" (Essay, p. 160).[39]

In order to grasp the nature of the "aesthetic" for the theorists of life, we must first examine the function of the imagination in the construction of the "objective" outline of the aesthetic universe and, secondly, the function of "pleasure" as the principle of unity for the aesthetic world of life.

Imagination

Addison located the pleasures of the imagination, or more specifically, the imagination, in a gap between immediately present sensations and the understanding. Or as Addison succinctly put it: "The pleasures of the imagination, taken in their full extent, are not so gross as those of sense, nor so refined as those of the understanding" (Spectator, #411, p. 123). I shall attempt to illuminate the "powers" of the imagination and its pleasures in terms of this "gap." In order to reduce my exposition to manageable terms, I will focus mostly upon Hume's theory of the imagination. I am not contending that all theorists fully shared Hume's position.[40] Few of them were philosophers of any stature. Nevertheless, Hume's analysis of the imagination entails at least five features that seem, implicitly or explicitly, to be shared by most other theorists and to constitute the essence of the imagination for an aesthetics of life.

1) Imagination and vividity: According to Hume the mind possesses three basic powers, namely the capacity for immediate sensations, memory, and imagination. Such powers are, of course, not separate faculties, rather they are determined by the specific content upon which the mind is focused. Actually the mind is faced by three kinds of contents. The contents of consciousness, relative to types, fall into two basic classes for Hume, i.e. they are simple or complex. Simple contents (be they impressions or ideas) are, of course, the atomistic originals of consciousness. Complex contents are composits of simple contents. Such is the formal nature of the contents of the imagination. But this formal nature also pertains to the memory and to the immediate senses. The differences between the contents of the senses, memory, and imagination cannot, consequently, lie in the formal classifica-tion of their respective contents. The source of difference arises out of

the manner in which the contents present themselves to awareness. In other words, sensate contents can appear very vividly and forcefully (=impressions). This forceful vividity is that which makes such sense contents be the originals of consciousness. Sensate contents can also appear as faint(er) images of the sensate originals (=ideas). Such "faint" ideas constitute the domain of memory and imagination. Memory and imagination are to be distinguished by two features. Hume contends that "it be a peculiar property of the memory to preserve the original order and position of its ideas, while the imagination transposes and changes them, as it pleases" and that "the main difference betwixt [memory] and the imagination lies in its superior force and vivacity" or, conversely, "the ideas of the imagination [are] fainter and more obscure" than those of memory (Treatise, I, 3:5). Memory repeats its "faint" contents in the same order as they were originally received as vivid impressions. The imagination, on the other hand, can re-order such contents and create "new" compounds that have no "vivid" models. More importantly, however, the prime distinguishing feature is the vivid viz. faint manner in which the contents of the imagination are present to the mind. On the scale of vividity, the imagination has its contents at the faint end. This feature constitutes one of the boundaries of the "gap" between the senses and the understanding that the imagination fills. In this respect the imagination resembles the senses. Whatever can be done with such contents constitute the parameters of the imagination.

2) Imagination as a combiatoric power: The imagination can transpose and change its contents "as it pleases." In this sense the imagination is creative and free from the dominance of vivid originals. This combiatoric power of the imagination is the other side of the "gap" between the senses and the understanding. In this respect, the imagination resembles the understanding, i.e. it can subsume a manifold under a principle of unity. Concerning the free combiatoric power of the imagination Hume writes: "Nothing is more free than the imagination of man; and though it cannot exceed that original stock of ideas furnished by the internal and external senses, it has unlimited power of mixing, compounding, separating, and dividing these ideas, in all the varieties of fiction and vision" (Enquiry, §39). Whereas memory simply and quite mechanically reproduces the manifold and unity of the mind's "originals", the imagination can freely compound its contents and create an infinite number of "fictive" worlds. As Addison contended: "[F]or by this faculty [of imagination] a man in a dungeon is capable of entertaining himself with scenes and landscapes more beautiful than any that can be found in the whole encompass of nature" (Spectator, #411, p. 122).

3) Imagination as "fancy": The imagination's power of free compounding grounds its function as the source of artistic creation. In other words, the imagination can compound its contents into "imaginary" worlds, into fictive universes, which, in turn, mediate aesthetic experience to the mind. In 1762 Henry Home (Lord Kames) designated the imagination as a "singular power of fabricating images without any foundation in reality."[41] Such a power of fabricating in its artistic use was often called "fancy." Gerard explains fancy: "Fancy, by its associating power, confers upon the ideas of the imagination new ties, that they may not lie perfectly loose, ranges them in an endless variety of forms. Many of these being representations of nothing that exists in nature, whatever is fictive or chimerical is acknowledged to be the offspring of this faculty, and is termed imaginary" (Essay, p. 167).

The imagination conceived as fancy stands in direct opposition to "real" knowledge, or to "rational" reflection and, hence, is the opponent of philosophy. As Hume warned: "For it we assent to every trivial suggestion of the fancy; ... they lead us into errors, absurdities, and obscurities...Nothing is more dangerous to reason than the flights of the imagination, and nothing has been the occasion of more mistakes among philosophers" (Treatise, I, 4:7).

4) Imagination as the universal "cement": The imagination has the power to associate or connect contents together into "objects" and to bond these objects together into an orderly (though perhaps only fictive) world. It is precisely this associating power that grounds the unity of any objective world. In other words, as shown above, custom habituates the mind to connect impressions (viz. ideas) together. This "cement" between things lies not in the things, but in the mind's determination to infer one event from another. It is the mind's determination that constitutes and hence generates the "constants" of any objective world. It now turns out that this world creating power, this cementing force, is the imagination. As Hume contends: "Again, when I consider the influence of this constant conjunction [produced by custom], I perceive, that such a relation can never be an object of reasoning, and can never operate upon the mind, but by means of custom, which determines the imagination to make a transition from the idea of one object to that of its usual attendant, and from the impressions of one to a more lively idea of the other" (Treatise, I, 3:14). The imagination is, then, the cement of any world, fictitious or real. In conjunction with repeated empirical experience and functioning according to the constant principles of association (and also under the influence of sympathy), the imagination produces the system of constants that are experienced as the objective world. Freed from the regulative norm of repeated experience, the imagination can create endless fictional worlds.

5) The work of art as objectified imagination: Aesthetic experience entails, of course, an awareness of some contents viz. the work of art itself. Such an awareness must comprehend more than a chaotic or random congery of sensations. A work of art is an aesthetic object and, like any other object, it must evince an order, a coherence, a system of constants, even if such an object only possesses a fictional reality. In more general terms, any objective universe must consist of a unity of a manifold. For the aestheticians of life as well as for those of form, the manifold of the aesthetic universe consists of sensations (empirical contents). However, a sensate content was for the theorists of form ontologically a derivative, i.e. it is nothing but unclearly perceived intelligibility (form). Consequently, the unity pertaining between sensate contents are not derivative, rather ultimate. The empirical manifold consists of atoms of sensation. The unity that supplies the "constants" of any objective world is derived from the connecting, cementing, or associating act of the human mind (=imagination). This holds true for any aesthetic or fictional universe. Now it is precisely the imagination that supplied the "unity" of the aesthetic world viz. of any work of art. However, the proper domain of the imagination is that of "faint" sensations. With exception of faint images called forth in the mind by the literary word, it is obvious that works of art (e.g. paintings, sculpture, architecture, drama, etc.) are present quite vividly to the mind. Consequently, aesthetic objects can evince not only faint images, but also forcefully vivid ones. This fact does not, however,

pose an insuperable problem. The imagination can conceive an aesthetic world in the privacy of the artist's mind. The artist can then form a medium (e.g. clay) in accordance with the "faint" fabrications of the imagination. The formed medium becomes, then, a vivid object, a forcefully present fabrication of the imagination. In this sense, it can be said that a work of art is an objectification of the imagination.

Pleasure as the Aesthetic

Aesthetic consciousness entails, of course, an awareness of an object, i.e. of sensate atoms "bonded" together as stable complex ideas. The term "object" must be understood in a wide sense as it encompasses the complex unity of a work of music. The material of aesthetic objects consists of sensate atoms. These atoms are compounded together to create the aesthetic object or, more accurately, the object that produces the aesthetic experience. The fabrication of such an object is accomplished by the imagination. However, not all fabrications of the imagination are productive of aesthetic experience. Consciousness of the "sensate" qualities of an object is not per se aesthetic. The fabricated world of imagination is, to be sure, a sine qua non of an aesthetic experience, but it is not constituitively the aesthetic itself. What then constitutes the aesthetic? "There is scarcely any Object which our Minds are employ'd about, which is not thus constituted the necessary occasion of some Pleasure or Pain..."[42] So wrote Francis Hutcheson in 1725. Lord Kames echoed Hutcheson in 1762 when he wrote: "We are not so constituted as to perceive objects with indifference; they with very few exceptions appear agreeable or disagreeable; and at the same time raise in us pleasant or painful emotions" (Elements, p. 480). Both Hutcheson and Kames were thinking within the broad paradigms of Locke. The world of "objective" contents (=sensations) is in itself of secondary importance for man. Or, more accurately, sensations and their complex ideas receive importance from the bearing they have upon human happiness (=the obtainment of pleasure and the avoidance of pain). Hutcheson writes: "We generally acknowledge, that the Importance of any Truth is nothing else than its Moment, or Efficacy to make Men happy, or to give them the greatest and most lasting Pleasure..." (The Original of our Ideas, p. iii). This thesis certainly holds true for the fabrications of the imagination. Indeed, the imagination is particularly productive of pleasure(s). "Now the imagination," writes Burke, "is the most extensive province of pleasure and pain..." (Phil. Enquiry, "Introduction," p. 17). The vast majority of the theorists of life limited the pleasures of the imagination to those of the eye and (often derivatively) of the ear. Henry Home contends: "The fine arts are contrived to give pleasure to the eye and the ear, disregarding the inferior senses. A taste for these arts...is susceptible of much refinement; and is, by proper care, greatly improved. In this respect, a taste in the fine arts ...[is] rooted in human nature, and governed by principles common to all men" (Elements, p. 13).

The human mind can be aware of two basic kinds of contents: namely sensation and emotions of pleasure or pain. Sensations are constituted such that they, directly, or indirectly, produce pleasure or pain. Now this causal relationship between the object and emotions is the basis for aesthetic experience. Hume notes that "beauty of all kinds gives us a peculiar delight and satisfaction, as deformity produces pain" (Treatise, II, 1:8). In the context of the Treatise Hume uses the term "beauty" as effectively synonymous for the aesthetic or the experience of taste. In other words, Hume does not here differentiate beauty from sublimity or novelty (which are other categories of taste). What Hume says about beauty pertains to all the areas of taste and hence constitutes the aesthetic per se. Concerning the nature of, in effect, the aesthetic Hume writes that:

> beauty is such an order and construction of parts, as either by the primary constitution of our nature, by custom, or by caprice, is fitted to give a pleasure and satisfaction to the soul. This is the distinguishing character of beauty, and forms all the difference betwixt it and deformity, whose natural tendency is to produce uneasiness. Pleasure and pain, therefore, are not only necessary attendants of beauty and deformity, but constitute their very essence...[We] may conclude, that beauty is nothing but a form, which produces pleasure, as deformity is a structure of parts, which conveys pain...(Treatise, II, 1:8)

Pleasure as the principle of life is not just a concommitant effect of an aesthetic object, rather it is, instead, the very essence of the aesthetic itself. Pleasure is that which makes an experience to be an aesthetic experience. Pleasure is, of course, precisely the principle of life. Before articulating this fact, I first want briefly to point out the vast difference in the aesthetic for theorists of form and those of life.

The "real" for Vollkommenheitsmänner is intelligible oneness. Oneness as the principle of unity of a manifold is simply perfectio. Reality is a system of intelligibilia. However, the human mind, because it is finite, cannot grasp most intelligibilia in their rational purity. Instead, the mind often can only become "undeutlich" aware of the intelligible unity in things. The result is the derivative experience of sensate contents. Sensate contents are de facto ultimates in the human mind. In other words, the mind cannot penetrate the sensate "appearance" of things. The mind can and does, however, create fictitious worlds out of sensate contents and these worlds appear as aesthetic objects. The awareness of aesthetic objects does produce pleasure (Vergnügen) and this pleasure is an ingredient of the aesthetic. There is, then, a resemblance between the aesthetics of form and that of life. But only a resemblance! Ontologically, any object (or complex of objects) consists of metaphysical perfection. The pleasure arising from awareness of such "undeutlich" perceived perfection is constitutively an "undeutlich" content of awareness. Leibniz writes, instance:

> ...[E]t, qui plus est, les plaisers même des sens reduisent à des plaisers intellectuels confusement connus. La Musique nous charme, quoyque, sa beauté ne consiste que dans les convenances des nombres, et dans le compte dont nous ne nous appercevons pas, et que l'ame ne laisse pas de faire, des battements ou vibrations des corps sonnans, qui recontrent par certains intervalles.[43]

Moreover, the aesthetic pleasure itself is not simply a modification of the perceiving self. It is constituted by the perceived perfection of the object. Johann August Eberhard asserted in 1783 that "Vergnügen" is the "Endzweck" of beauty und "dieses [entsteht] aus dem Gefühl der Vollkommenheit" or, in short: "Das [aesthetische] Vergnügen [besteht] in dem

Anschauen der Vollkommenheit."[44] Perfectio which is "undeutlich" perceived
is a constituent ingredient of the aesthetic pleasure of form.

Pleasure in the philosophy of life is not an ontological derivative,
rather an ultimate and isolated atom. Objects cause feelings of pleasure and
pain. But such feelings are modifications of the subject, not an ontological
quality of the object. Referring to the aesthetic experience of a garden as
beautiful. Henry Home contends:

> When I turn my attention from the garden to what passes in my mind,
> I am conscious of a pleasant emotion, of which the garden is the
> cause: the pleasure here is felt, as a quality, not of the garden,
> but of the emotion produced by it....In a word...pleasant and
> painful are qualities of the emotions we feel;...they are felt as
> existing within us (Elements, p. 59).

The units of pleasure or pain are on principle not reducible to "undeutlich"
perceived intelligibilia. They are non-rational units of emotion. The
pleasurable as the essence of the aesthetics of life is a non-rational
feeling. This brings us back to the principle of life.

The primary feelings that a subject has in the aesthetic experience are
those of pleasure and pain. Pleasure and pain are the two basic and ultimate
elements involved in any aesthetic experience of beauty or of deformity.
They are, in effect, the essence of the aesthetic experience in its
subjective aspect. Pleasure and pain are positive, separate, and irreducible
psychological units. Consequently Burke, for instance, rejects any attempts
to view the two feelings as interdependent. "For my part, I am rather
inclined to imagine, that pain and pleasure, in their most simple and natural
manner of affecting, are each of a positive nature, and by no means
necessarily dependent on each other for their existence" (Phil, Enquiry, I.
2, p. 32). It should be understood that these terms have the widest possible
meaning for Burke. They do not only refer to immediate pleasurable or
painful feelings, although this is their most frequent meaning. They also
can refer to any experience, however complex, that either attracts or
repulses an individual. For instance, the psychological need to be praised
when satisfied is felt as a pleasurable experience.

Pleasure and pain are not isolated and secondary events in the life of
an individual. Instead, they are constituent factors in the conscious life
of the human self. As was shown in my analysis of Locke, the self of
empiricism is that which organizes the manifold into a unity. Above it was
shown that in Locke's thought the well-being of the self (i.e. the obtainment
of pleasure and the avoidance of pain) determines much of the organization of
cognitive experience. In a similar vein Burke postulates the well-being of
the self as the organizational principle of the emotional life and hence of
the aesthetic experience. The well-being of the self constututes the
principle of life. Life as a psychological notion contains at least four
theses. (1) The non-rationality of the affective life of man is the basic
premise. Reason or the understanding has no immediate and constituitive
effect upon the psychological mechanism of the individual self. (2) The
psychological life of the self is, therefore, emotional, not rational. (3)
The passions the self experiences are derived from the desire for pleasure
and the aversion to pain. (4) The self does not live in isolation. The

self is a social being. The social life of man, particularly under the influence of sympathy, is the ultimate organizing principle of the self's affective life and hence of the principle of life. I shall consider this fourth point in a subsequent section. Above it was noted that sympathy was perhaps the most important pleasure governing human life and hence cognition. At this stage I only wish to take note of this facit of pleasure. It suffices to close this section with a word from Lord Kames: "The principles of the fine arts, appear, in this view, to open a direct avenue to the heart of man" (Elements, p. 26). The principles of aesthetic theory are, indeed, a function of the heart of man for it is man's "heart" (=emotions, needs, pleasures), not his "head" (=reason), that determines his life and hence the aesthetic creations spawned by this life.

Life as the General Principle of Form

The work of art consists of objective and subjective aspects, i.e. it is a mixture of the fabrications and the pleasures of the imagination.The imagination can compound an endless variety of fictive worlds. Not all such worlds are, of course, capable of eliciting an aesthetic or pleasurable emotion in the perceiver. Above Hume was quoted contending that beauty is caused by certain structures in objects that cause pleasure. Similarly Reid contends:

> Our judgement of beauty is not indeed a dry and unaffecting judgment, like that of a mathematical or metaphysical truth. By the constitution of our nature, it is accompanied with an agreeable feeling or emotion, for which we have no other name but the sense of beauty. This sense of beauty, like the perceptions of our other senses, implies not only a feeling, but an opinion of some quality in the object which occasions that feeling...Beauty or deformityof an object results from its nature or structure...(On the Intellectual Powers, I, 492).

Reid, like other theorists of life, equated "beauty with pleasure" (I, 490). But Reid, like Hume and others, also held that a given object (called a work of art) must possess certain qualities that produce the aesthetic experience viz. feelings of pleasure. Such feelings are, of course, the essence of aesthetic experience. However, by extension, the term "beauty" can be applied to the object that causes aesthetic feelings.

The causal realtionship between object and pleasure enables the theorist of life to formulate a general principle of artistic form. This principle was enunciated by Mark Akenside in 1744 in his poem The Pleasures of the Imagination. Akenside writes:

> .... by the mixed effect
> Of Things corporeal on his passive mind
> [Man] judgeth what is fair. Corporeal things
> The mind of man impel with various powers,
> And various features to his eye disclose.
> The powers which move his sense with instant joy,
> The features which attract his heart to love,
> He marks, combines, reposits. Other powers
> And features of the selfsame thing (unless

>The beauteous form, the creature of his mind,
>Request their close alliance) he o'erlooks,
>Forgotten; or, with self-beguiling zeal,
>Whene'er his passions mingle in the work,
>Half alters, half disowns...............[45]

The imagination of man "marks, combines, [and] reposits" that which has given him joy. In other words, the imagination "alters" the elements of man's experience in order to emphasize and to recall "those features which attract his heart." The imagination fabricates a complex whole, that is not simply a reproduction of the mind's originals (now fainter images), in order to magnify the pleasures caused. The goal of magnification is functionally the principle of aesthetic form. The principle of life (=non-rational pleasure) reveals itself to be the "heart" or unity of a work of art. The manifold and organization of a work of art are all aimed to the production of pleasure.

Associationism and the Construction of the Aesthetic Universe

The form-principle of the aesthetics of life determines that the "objective" manifold of an aesthetic universe (viz. object) is so constituted (=compounded) that it elicits emotions of pleasure in its perceiver. Much of British aesthetic theory is concerned with just what in an object produces "pleasure" in the subject. As Hume wrote in 1758: "Though it be certain, that beauty and deformity, more than sweet and bitter, are not qualities in objects, but belong entirely to the sentiment, internal or external; it must be allowed, that there are certain qualities in objects, which are fitted by nature to produce these particular feelings."[46] Edmund Burke, for instance, proposes to make "a careful survey of the properties of things which we find by experience to influence those passions [of pleasure and pain]" (Phil. Enquiry, "Preface," p. 1). Burke contends, for instance, that beauty (i.e. the "taste" of pleasure) is uniformly produced as an immediate effect by certain qualities of an object. These effects are in no way mediated by reason, reflection, or psychological associations. Instead, the pleasure of beauty depends upon "properties [of objects] that operate by nature, and are less liable to be altered by caprice or confused by a diversity of tastes, than any other" (Phil. Enquiry, III, 18:117). Burke supplements his examination of the properties of objects with a proto-physiological theory, putatively explaining the subject's emotional reactions to the object's properties. Out of these physiological reactions pleasures and/or pains arise. Consequently, Burke contends that it is possible "by looking into physical causes...to give a sort of philosophical solidity" to a theory of taste (Phil. Enquiry, "Preface," p. 6). Such causes are, of course, integrally related to man's uniform "life" needs and hence principle of life.

Burke'a attempt to explain the pleasure of beauty solely as an immediate effect of physical causes is almost unique in 18th century British theory. Most theorists did, indeed, make use of physical explanations. But such explanations were not the only ones or, indeed, not even the most important type. By far the majority oi the theorists of life, particularly after the mid-century mark, utilized association psychology in their respective attempts to determine the "formal" properties of an aesthetic object. It is not my intention to outline the history of associational psychology in British critical theory, nor even to examine any of the arguments between different critical associationists.[47] I shall simply focus upon a significant mechanism in the associative process and indicate in general the manner by which this mechanism contributed to the construction of the aesthetic universe.

In my discussion of associationism in a previous section, I paid particular attention to Hume's doctrine of causation. The principle of causation, insofar as it refers to the relation between objects (or events), entails the repetition of objects temporally contiguous to each other. After a sufficient number of repetitions of such contiguity, the objects (or events) become "bonded," i.e. associated. David Hartley (1705-1757), rather than Hume, evolved a comprehensive theory based upon this principle of association and applied it to all areas of mental activity including aesthetic experience. Hartley formulated his principle of association in 1749 in the following manner: "Any Sensations A, B, C, &c. by being associated with one another a sufficient Number of Times, get such Power over the corresponding Ideas a, b, c, &c. that any one of the Sensations A, when impressed alone, shall be able to excite in the Mind b, c, &c. the Ideas of the rest."[48] Hartley goes on to show how various sensations and their associations come together (in the brain) to produce new and more intricate associations, ones different from the simple originals. "[I]f any two sensations, or more, belong to the same Region [of the brain] since they cannot exist together in their distinct Forms, A will raise something indeterminate between them [i.e. a new complex experience]" (Observations, I, 12:73). In this manner, the "simple" elements of the sensate manifold coalesce into "clusters" which govern man's affective life relative to morality and beauty. Hartley writes: "It appears also from Observations, that many of our intellectual Ideas, such as those that belong to the Heads of Beauty, Honour, moral Qualties, &c, are, in Fact, thus composed of Parts, which by degrees, coalesce into complex idea" (Observations, I, 12:74-75).

Hartley applied his principle of association to the pleasures of the imagination in a long proposition entitled "Of Pleasures arising from the Beauty of the natural World" (Observations, I, 94:418-442). Hartley's general thesis is that various pleasures are elicited or occur contiguously with "real" and vivid experience. Naturally an association arises between the specific pleasure and the concommitant objects (=situation). The "fainter" images that the imagination creates out of the original, in turn, recall similar pleasures. In short, the pleasure producing "power" of the qualities of objects is a function of their associations with real pleasures. Akenside expressed this principle of aesthetic associationism in his own poetic way when wrote:

> For when the different images of things,
> By chance combined, have struck the attentive soul
> With deeper impulse, or, connected long,
> Have drawn her frequent eye; how'er distinct
> The external scenes, yet oft the ideas gain
> From that conjunction an eternal tie,
> And sympathy unbroken. Let the mind
> Recall one partner of the various league;
> Immediate, lo! the firm confederates rise,
> And each his former stations straight resumes:
> One movement governs the consenting throng,
> And all at once with rosy pleasure shine,

Or all are saddened with the glooms of care.
....
Such is the secret union, when we feel
A song, a flower, a name, at once restore
Those long connected scenes where first they moved
The attention; backward thro' her mazy walks
Guiding the wanton fancy [=imagination] to her scope,
To temples, courts, or fields, with all the band
Of painted forms, of passions, and designs,
Attendant; whence, if pleasing in itself,
The prospect from the sweet accession gains
Redoubled influence o'er the listening mind
(The Pleasures, pp. 55-56).

In 1793 Frank Sayers, who grounded in part his aesthetic ideas upon Hartley, went so far as to contend in effect that it is precisely the association of pleasure with fabrications of the imagination that constitutes the aesthetic viz. beauty. Sayers writes:

[T]he view of a beautiful object occasions in us much more exquisite feelings of pleasure than the most delicious food, the most brillant colour, or the most grateful perfume: we must therefore seek...[a] cause of this peculiar sensation of delight: this cause will be found to depend upon an association of ideas: with the forms which we esteem beautiful, it will appear that certain pleasing ideas or emotions are associated in our mind, which, upon the presentation of such forms, regularly arise, and produce those sensations which we attribute to the beauty of the object. This power then, which an object possesses, of exciting pleasing ideas or emotions associated with it, is what determines us to ascribe to it beauty....

These arguments seem sufficient to prove that beauty is not inherent in forms, features or complexions, but depends entirely upon the ideas associated with them.[49]

Psychological associationism became a very fertile principle in the critical theorizing of such aestheticians as Archibald Alison, James Beattie, Henry Home, Alexander Gerard, Joseph Priestly, and Adam Smith, to name just a few.[50] Dr. John Baille more or less summed up the two principles used by British associationists: "Objects in general delight from two Sources: either because [they are] naturally fitted to please, from a certain Harmony and Disposition of their Parts, or because [they are] long associated with Objects really agreeable; and thus, tho' in themselves there be nothing at first delightful, they at last become so."[51] Baille's first principle is obviously related to Burke's thesis concerning the physical causes of pleasure and the second principle is, of course, the principle of association. The principle of association was used to explain the most diverse aesthetic phenomena, sometimes even conflicting data. For instance, this principle was used to explain and justify neo-classic uniformitarianism, i.e. the consensus gentium of taste and then to explain the divergences in aesthetic values, i.e. the relativity of taste. The uniformitarian position rested upon the assumption that, since human nature is basically the same, certain general associations arise from certain universal habits and customs. The relativist thesis rested upon the assumption that the social environment of individuals (or of individual peoples) is so different and that the specific differences between individuals is so great that associations formed will necessarily reflect different and differing subjective experiences. Indeed, both explanations can be found in the thought of the same theorist. Furthermore, both positions reflect the principle of life. In other words, the aesthetic world, both in regards its manifold and its "bonds" of unity, is a function of associations grounded in the individual's life needs, in his pursuit of pleasure and avoidance of pain. Such a function is variously viewed as idiosyncratic or universal. The same principle of life, nevertheless, remains as the generative principle of the aesthetic world.

In my discussion of association psychology I noted that "sympathy" was perhaps the heart of the bonding process of life. Parallels can be found in association aesthetics. I shall not now take up this feature of associationism, rather treat it in context of my discussion of the universe of beauty. At this point I only wish to note the existence of such a feature. It is now time to examine the world of beauty for an aesthetics of life.

D. Life as the Principle of Beauty

Method of Analysis

Aesthetic experience in its essence is constituted by feelings or emotions of pleasure. Pleasure is subjective in that it is in the mind, i.e. it is a modification of the self, and not located in the object. The object, nevertheless, is not without meaning in the analysis of the aesthetics, i.e. the object possesses qualities (or powers) or occurs in an associative context with such qualities as do produce the feelings of pleasure in the individual. The differences pertaining between different classes of objects and the differences pertaining between classes of pleasurable feelings can be correlated, usually as cause and effect. There is located in such "kinds" of differences the basis for a differentiation of aesthetic experience into its subordinate categories (e.g. beauty or sublimity). For instance, Sayers contends: "Among the variety of natural and artificial appearances, which occasionally attract our notice, it is not difficult to discover many classes of objects, from the contemplation of which peculiar sensations of pleasure are generally experienced....." (Disquisitions, p. 9). The various "peculiar sensations" are different types of aesthetic experience. Priestly evinced a similar position when he wrote "that by noting the properties which are common to those objects which affect our imagination in an agreeable manner, we may be enabled to give an enumeration of all the species of the pleasures of imagination that we are capable of..." (Course of Lectures, p. 133). Different types of pleasure, according to genus and species, are consequently, functions of the different types of objects. From this point of view, beauty, sublimity, etc. are subcategories of the genus of aesthetic experience viz. of taste. Home, for instance, contended that "agreeableness is the genus, of which beauty and grandeur [sublimity] are species" (Elements, p. 110). British theorists distinguished various "classes" of "peculiar sensations," i.e. of aesthetic experience. The categories of beauty and sublimity were in effect universally acknowledged. Most authors followed Addison in also considering the "taste" of novelty as aesthetic (cf. "On the Pleasures of the Imagination," Spectator, #412, VI, 126-131). Beattie adds elegance to the list and then asserts: "Sublimity, Beauty, and Elegance, are not the only things in art and nature, which gratify Taste. There is also a taste in imitations, in harmony, and in ridicule. He who takes delight in truth, in virtue, in simplicity, may be said to have a taste for it."[52] And Gerard adds the taste of harmony and of imitation to this list of aesthetic categories (cf. Essay on Taste, pp. 49-65). The list of categories varies from theorist to theorist. The addition of tastes for virtue and even for mathematical theorems certainly stretches the aesthetic meaning of the term "taste." However, perhaps the three most important categories are beauty, sublimity, and novelty.

The methods of analysis pursued by theorists of life was basically twofold, as is evident from above and from the quotation from Burke above. The structure of the object is correlated with the structure of aesthetic experience, i.e. of pleasure. Both the objective and subjective sides of the aesthetic experience were investigated and related to each other, usually causally, i.e. the object elicits in the subject certain "peculiar sensations" of one type or of another. In general terms, it can be said that the question before the theorists of life was: What constitutes the morphology of beauty (or of sublimity, etc.)? We shall now consider how this question was answered.

The Morphology of Beauteous Pleasure: Subjective Aspects

At this point I shall first focus upon the subjective aspect of beauty, i.e. upon the emotion or pleasure of beauty. All categories of aesthetics share the common feature of pleasure or agreeableness. The essence of beauty is, of course, as Hume maintained, pleasure. Consequently, the species-meaning of beauty sometimes becomes obscured as a genus term that is indiscriminately applied to all forms of aesthetic pleasure. Gerard notes: "There is perhaps no term used in a looser sense than beauty, which is applied to almost every thing that pleases us" (Essay on Taste, p. 45). The pleasure of beauty in a strict sense can, however, be distinguished from the pleasure of the other categories. For instance, sublimity entails a type of pleasure. However, this pleasure is first mediated in some manner through displeasure (e.g. fear or terror). The pleasure of sublimity is distinguishable from that of beauty precisely through this element of negativity viz. displeasure. Beauty, on the other hand, entails no basic mediation, i.e. its pleasure is pure or positive. Burke, for example, contends that "whatever produces pleasure, positive and original pleasure, is fit to have beauty engrafted upon it" (Phil. Enquiry, IV, 3:131). Pleasure that is "positive and original" stems from feelings that are neither too intense (and thereby irritating) nor too dull (and also irritating), i.e. from moderate and calming feelings. And it is precisely the notion of moderation which was meant by "agreeable." Reid referred to beauty as "a certain agreeable emotion or feeling in the mind" (Intellectual Powers, I, 498). Stewart even contended that the attribution of beauty to colors, forms, or motion "arises solely from their undistinguishable cooperation in producing the same agreeable effect..."[53] Beauty, in short, is a pleasure that satisfies the human soul. Addison asserts: "But there is nothing that makes its way more directly to the soul than beauty, which immediately diffuses a secret satisfaction and complacency through the imagination...The very first discovery of it strikes the mind with an inward joy, and spreads a cheerfulness and delight through all its faculties" - ("Pleasures of the Imagination," Spectator, #412, VI, 128-129).

Joy, cheerfulness, delight, complacency, satisfactions, etc. are, so to speak, the elements of the morphology of beauteous pleasure. Pleasure, as shown above, is a function of the principle of life. Indeed, it, along with the avoidance of pain, constitutes the essence of the term "life." Insofar as a "peculiar sensation" of pleasure evinces cheerfulness, delight, etc., it will be experienced as beautiful, as beauty. Beauty is, then, that pleasure which, so to speak, composes the human self. Home, for one, notes that "beauty...lends its name to express every thing that is eminently agreeable...[A]ll the various emotions of beauty maintain one common character, that of sweetness and gaiety" (Elements, p. 103). Sayers, for his part, contends that "the emotions produced by a view of one of these classes [of peculiar sensations], the beautiful, although very impressive, have something in them of a gentle and soothing kind..." (Disquisitions, p. 9). Beauty, contends Priestly, entails a certain "leisure or opportunity for [the mind's] perceiving those more delicate beauties, which constitute the chief merit of works of taste and imagination" (Course of Lectures, p. 139). Similarly, Reid notes: "The emotion produced by beautiful objects is gay and pleasant. It sweetens and humanizes the temper, is friendly to every benevolent affectation, and tends to allay sullen and angry passions. It enlivens the mind, and disposes it to other agreeable emotions, such as those of love, hope, and joy" (Intellectual Powers, IV, 498). Burke contends that beauty "is a name I shall apply to all such qualities in things as induce in us a sense of affection and tenderness, or some other passion the most nearly resembling these" (Phil. Enquiry, I, 18:51). According to Gerard, the verdure of fields is beautiful because it suggests "the pleasant idea of fertility" (Essay on Taste, p. 43). Beattie summed it up when he contended that "the effect of beauty is, to compose...the soul..." (Dissertations, p. 116).

Above Locke was quoted writing: "Nature, I confess, has put into Man a desire for Happiness and an aversion to Misery: These indeed are innate practical Principles which...do continue constantly to operate and influence all our Actions without ceasing: These may be observed in all Persons and all Ages, steady and universal" (Essay, I, 3:3). This thesis, enunciated by Locke, is the principle of life. The only thing innate and hence structural in the human self is the need for life. We have seen that Locke used this principle as a epistemological criterion for distinguishing between the real and the seeming, i.e. to determine which complex ideas are reflective of reality. Knowledge and, indeed, the compounded world known, are functions of life-need. Pleasure and pain constitute the dynamic principle of life. Knowing is but one type of "action" that is governed by the desire for happiness (and the aversion to misery). This twin principle of life also determines the "action" of the imagination and hence of its pleasures. More accurately, pleasure (and pain) is the determining principle of the imagination's world creating, compounding, and cementing activity. Such a "fabricated" world in its objectivity constitutes the aesthetic world. This "fictive" world is structured so as to elicit pleasure in its perceiver. Pleasure, however, is not simply homogenous. There are different types of pleasure. Beauty is one such type. The epithets for beauty are various. Joy, delight, gentle, smoothing, delicate, gay, pleasant, sweet, enlivening, tender, complacent, and composing are some of the designations morphologically descriptive of that species of pleasure called beauty. However different such attributions are, they all agree in the idea that beauty is a positive, moderate, calming, and satisfying feeling of life. This multifaceted feeling is, indeed, the principle of life as the basis for beauty within an aesthetics of life.

The Morphology of Beauty: Objective Aspects

The methodology of British theorists, as noted previously, entails "a careful survey of the property of things" that elicit aesthetic pleasure (cf. Burke, Phil. Enquiry. "Preface," p. 1). We have seen that, morphologically, beauteous pleasure entails a composing positivity or, as Burke claims, "qualities in bodies...cause love, or some passion similar to it" (Phil. Enquiry, III,1:91). Such a "composing" effect sets, of course, limits to the nature of the qualities an object can have, if it is to be considered as "beautiful," In other words, a beautiful object must, morphologically or formally, possess certain "delicate" features. Theorists of life evince considerable deviance in their respective analyses of such features. Some theorists, such as Burke, sought to establish a mechanical and causal link between object and subject. Others, such as Priestly or Beattie, claimed an associative relationship. Still others, such as Gerard, focused upon active response of the human self to the influence of the object as the source for aesthetic pleasure. All sought in some way to correlate certain objective properties with the "delicate" structure of beauteous pleasure.

Burke, for instance, grounds his mechanical thesis in a physiological theory. Burke contends that "our minds and bodies are so closely and intimately connected, that one is incapable of pain or pleasure without the other" (Phil. Enquiry, IV, 4:133). The mind feels pleasure when the body is "pleasantly" stimulated by an object. The emotion of beauty is a tender, composing, or delicate feeling. The physical effects upon the body which are felt as pleasurable are, reasons Burke, relaxing in nature since "a relaxation somewhat below the natural tone seems to me to be the cause of all positive pleasures" (Phil. Enquiry. IV, 19:150). The physical properties of objects must not, consequently, be too stimulating in nature. For example, the physical property of "smoothness" was conceived by Burke as a universal feature of beauty. Burke asserts that the "gentle stroking with a smooth hand allays violent pains and cramps, and relaxes the suffering part from unnatural tension..." (Phil. Enquiry. IV, 20:151). The feeling effected by relaxation is, of course, that of beauty. This is because "the sense of feeling is highly gratified with smooth bodies" (Phil. Enquiry, IV, 20:151). Other properties such as sweetness, smallness, and certain colors also have similar pleasurable effects and are, accordingly, beautiful. Burke himself constructs a partial morphology of the objective properties of beauty:

[B]eautiful [objects are] comparatively small: beauty should be smooth and polished; ...beauty should shun the right line; ...beauty should not be obscure; ... beauty should be light and delicate; ...[beauty is founded] on pleasure...(Phil. Enquiry, III, 27:124).

The features of beauty (i.e. those qualities of an object that elicit in the subject the composing pleasures of beauty) just listed by Burke are by no means exhaustive, either of Burke's own theory or of the theories of other aestheticians of life. Simplicity, unity in variety, variation, proportion, etc. are other features that various theorists of life fastened upon. The main point that interested such theorists was to seek a correlation between certain properties of objects, either in isolation or compositionally, that produce the "peculiar sensations" subsumable under the heading of "composing" pleasure. Beauty itself is <u>properly</u> a feature of the subject's feelings. It is a delicate, satisfying, and composing pleasure. Derivatively, however, beauty can be ascribed to those features of objects that produce beauty proper. This relationship between subject and object underlies Reid's definition of beauty.

> All the objects we call beautiful agree in two things, which seem to concur in our sense of beauty. <u>First</u>, When they are perceived, or even imagined, they produce a certain agreeable emotion or feeling in the mind; and, <u>secondly</u>, This agreeable emotion is accompanied with an opinion or belief of their having some perfection or excellence belonging to them (<u>On the Intellectual Powers</u>, II, 498).

The specific "excellencies" of an object that constitute the objective morphology of beauty are readily seen as a function of the principle of life, namely of positive pleasure. Just as Locke's cognitive world is a function of life-needs, so too is the aesthetic world of the aesthetics of life.

Sympathy: The Heart of the Aesthetics of Life

Beauty consists of positive pleasures. Pleasure is a prime category of life. Indeed, it (along with aversion to pain) constitutes the principle of life. The principle of life directs man's cognitive and volitional activities. Aesthetic creativity becomes, accordingly, an intensification of life, albeit by means of a fabricated or fictitious world.

Pleasure, as noted in the previous section on "Sympathy as the Gravity of 'Life'," is not without a certain ambiguity. Pleasure or, perhaps more accurately, pleasure-seeking can be quite egotistical and hence socially disruptive. Moralists such as Hume and Smith are well aware of the atomizing effect of pleasure. Consequently, both thinkers (and others) sought to discover a "bonding," rather than a divisive power in the principle of life. Without some sort of "life" gravity, social intercourse, which is the normal context of life, would become very problematic if not impossible. Hume designated such a social gravity as "sympathy." In a quaint comparison, Hume compared sympathy with equally wound up strings, "the motion of one communicates itself to the rest; so all the affections readily pass from one person to another, and beget correspondent movements in every human creature" (<u>Treatise</u>, III, 3, 1). "No man," Hume writes elsewhere, "is absolutely indifferent to the happiness and misery of others. The first has a natural tendency to give pleasure; the second, pain" (<u>Enquiry</u>, p. 178n). Henry Home echoed Hume when he wrote: "[B]ut as man is endowed with a principle of benevolence as well as of selfishness, he is prompted by his nature to desire the good of every sensible being that gives him pleasure; and the happiness of that being is the gratification of his desire" (<u>Elements</u>, p. 97). The principle of benevolence is simply the taking pleasure in the well-being of others. Paradoxically, the concern for others can be pleasurable when gratified, even if it is directed at the misery of others, i.e. so long as it motivates an attempt to alleviate such misery. Again Home writes: "But the principle of benevolence...makes [man] desire to afford relief; and by relieving the person from distress, his passion is gratified. The painful passion thus directed, is termed sympathy; which, though painful, is yet its nature attractive" (Elements, p. 98).

Beauty as the aesthetically experienced is pleasure. Pleasure is the principle of life. Perhaps the most important class of pleasures is that which derives from sympathy, from concern for others. Sympathy makes social bonds possible. It is, indeed, the principle of sociality. Aestheticians of life repeatedly assert sociality as a common feature of the "peculiar sensations" called beauty. As Reid notes: "[Beauty] sweetens and humanises the temper, is friendly to every benevolent affection, and tends to allay sullen and angry passions. It enlivens the mind, and disposes it to other agreeable emotions, such as those of love, hope and joy" (On the Intellectual Powers, II. 498). Beauty clearly has a socially ameliorative effect. Benevolent affections bring about social bonding. Similarly, Burke maintains "that the strongest sensations relative to the habitudes of particular society are sensations of pleasure. Good company, lively conversations, and the endearments of friendship, fill the mind with pleasure" (Phil. Enquiry, I, 11:43). And social pleasure is, of course, experienced as beauty. Burke accordingly constructs a more comprehensive definition of beauty. The origin of much sociality is sexual in nature and has to do with the propagation of the species. Beauty, however, is obviously more than sexual attraction. Man unlike the animals is designed by God to remain with one mate. Therefore, there are attractive "social qualities" that draw people together into a more permanent relation. "I call beauty a social quality," writes Burke, "for where women and men, and not only they, but when other animals give us a sense of joy and pleasure in beholding them (and there are many that do so), they inspire us with sentiments of tenderness and affection towards their person [=sympathy]; we like to have them near us, and we enter willingly into a kind of relation with them, unless we should have strong reasons to the contrary" (Phil. Enquiry, I. 10:42-43). Pleasure in beholding the socially bonding properties of things (people) is beauty. In more general terms: "By beauty, I mean that quality, or those qualities in bodies by which they cause love, or some passion similar to it" (Phil. Enquiry, III, 1: 91). The emphasis in the above definition rests upon the notion of love. Love is the social bond par excellence. Insofar as beauty, so to speak, exercises man's ability to sympathize, it not only produces the highest pleasure through a fictive world, but also makes man more able to live life in his real viz. social world. Home asserts:

> [D]elicacy of taste tends no less to invigorate the social affections, than to moderate those that are selfish. To be convinced of that tendency, we need only reflect, that delicacy of taste necessarily heightens our feelings of pain and pleasure [=the principle of life]; and of course our sympathy, which is the capital branch of every social passion. Sympathy invites a communication of joys and sorrows, hopes and fears: such exercise, soothing and satisfactory in itself, is necessarily productive of mutual good will and affection. (Elements, p. 15).

Sympathy is, in essence, the heart of beauty because it enables the individual to take the greatest pleasure in the life of others. Without sympathy a work of art would be impossible. Hume, for instance, contends:

> Most kinds of beauty are deriv'd from this origin [of sympathy]; and tho' our first object be some senseless inanimate piece of matter, 'tis seldom we rest there, and carry not our view to its influence on sensible and rational creatures. A man, who shews us any house or building, takes particular care among other things to point out the conveniences of the apartments, the advantages of their situation, and the little room lost in the stairs, antichambers and passages; and indeed 'tis evident, the chief part of the beauty consists in these particulars. The observation of convenience gives pleaaure, since convenience is a beauty. But after what manner does it give pleasure? 'Tis certain our own interest is not in the least concern'd; and as this is a beauty of interest, not of form, so to speak, it must delight us merely by communication, and by our sympathizing with the proprietor of the lodging. We enter into his interest by the force of imagination, and feel the same satisfaction, that the objects naturally occasion in him (Treatise, I, 2:5)
> ...Wherever an object has a tendency to produce pleasure in the possessor, or in other words, is the proper cause of pleasure, it is sure to please the spectator, by a delicate sympathy with the possessor (Treatise, III, 3, 1).

Sympathy enables a work of art to affect the spectator pleasurably and often it itself is the direct cause of beauty. Sympathy is the heart of the principle of life, is indeed, the highest principle of beauty.

For some theorists of life, beauty not only produces a social life of man with man, but also between man and God, through the mediation of nature or life itself. For instance, Addison writes:

> In the last place, [God] has made everything that is beautiful in all other objects pleasant, or rather has made so many objects appear beautiful, that he might render the whole creation more gay and delightful. He has given almost every thing about us the power of raising an agreeable idea in the imagination; so that it is impossible for us to behold his works with coldness or indifference, and to survey so many beauties without a secret satisfaction and complacency [in creation]...In short...we walk about like the enchanted hero in a romance, who sees beautiful castles, woods, meadows; and, at the same time, hears the warbling of birds, and the purling of streams...It is not improbable that something like this may be the state of the soul after its first separation [in death] in respect of the images it will receive from matter...("The Pleasures of the Imagination," Spectator, #413, VI, 134-135).

Beauty is, as Tuveson has shown, a means of grace for many 18th century aestheticians of life.[54] Just as beauty was a reflection of divinity in the aesthetics of form of Mengs, it can function as a mediator of the divine to man in the aesthetics of life.

Footnotes - Chapter III

[1] For a general review of the influence of Burke's Enquiry on Germany see Frieda Baune, Edmund Burke in Deutschland (Heidelberg, 1917), "Heidelberger Abhandlungen," Heft 50, pp. 4-15. In general Burke was well recieved in Germany. Lessing (as early as 1758), Herder, and Mendelssohn at one time or another planned to translate Burke. But it was not until 1773 that a full translation appeared by Christian Garve. Both Kant and Schiller acknowledged the influence of Burke upon them. Despite their often high praise of Burke and despite their admiration for Burke's astute empirical observations, Germans tended to feel that Burke did not develop an adequate theory in order to explain his observations.

[2] Geschichte der Aesthetik als philosophischer Wissenschaft (Wien, 1858), p. 222.

[3] The following is a select list of some secondary sources on Locke: R. I. Aaron, John Locke (London, 1947); Frederick Copleston, A History of Philosophy: Vol. V. Modern Philosophy: The British Philosophers, Part I, Hobbes to Paley (Garden City, 1964), pp. 76-152; J. Gibson, Locke's Theory of Knowledge and Its Historical Relations (Cambridge, 1917); Alfred Klemmt, John Locke: Theoretische Philosophie (Meisenheim, 1952); Martin Kallich, "The Association of Ideas and Critical Theory: Hobbes, Locke and Addison, "A Journal of English History, Vol. XII (1945), 290-315; and Ernest Lee Tuveson, The Imagination as A Means of Grace: Locke and the Aesthetics of Romanticism (Berkeley and Los Angeles, 1960), pp. 5-41.

[4] The Treatment of Personality by Locke, Berkeley, and Hume (Columbia, 1911), p. 17.

[5] Cf. Victor Delbos, "Le 'Cogito' de Descartes et la philosophie de Locke," L'Annee philosophique, XXIV (1914), 1-14.

[6] For two weeks concerning the position of Locke in the development of psychology see George Sidney Brett, Bretts History of Psychology, ed. R. S. Peters, (London/New York, 1953), pp. 402-408, and Howard C. Warren, A History of the Association Psychology (New York, 1921), pp. 36-40.

[7] Max Dessoir writes concerning the influence of Locke upon the further development thought in Europe: "Locke has subordianted to psychology essentially the entire range of the experienceable. A step farther, and one came to the opinion, which was later current, that psychology is the fundamental science." Cf. Outlines of the History of Psychology, trans. Donald Fischer (New York, 1912), pp. 11-112. Cf. also Denton J. Snider, Modern European Philosophy: The History of Modern Philosophy, Psychologically Treated (St. Louis, 1904), p. 419.

[8] An Essay Concerning Human Understanding, 4th edition (London, 1700), reprinted by the Clarendon Press, ed. Peter H. Nidditch (Oxford, 1975), Book II, Chapter 1: Paragraph 2. Hereafter, all references to this edition will be made in the text and abbreviated like the following: Essay, II, 1:2. The first early version of Essay appeared in 1690. Expanded editions, two and three, appeared respectively in the years 1694 and 1695.

[9] Cf. A Treatise of Human Nature: Being an Attempt to introduce the experimental Method of reasoning into Moral Subjects (London, 1739), Book I, Part I, Section 1. Hereafter this work will be referred to in the text in the following manner: Treatise, I, 1:1. Books I and II printed in 1739 and Book III in 1740.

[10] Cf. Etienne Gilson and Thomas Langan, Modern Philosophy: Descartes to Kant (New York, 1963), p. 103.

[11] Über die Evidenz in den metaphysichen Wissenschaften (1763) in Schriften zur Philosophie, Aesthetik und Apologetik, ed. Moritz Brasch (Leipzig, 1880), I, 82.

[12] Ibid., p. 79.

[13] Cf. John Locke, p. 99.

[14] Cf. Locke's Theory of Knowledge, p. 65. Aaron says essentially same thing. Cf. John Locke, pp. 1-28.

[15] Cf. Treatise, I, 4:3.

[16] An Enquiry Concerning Human Understanding (1748), reprinted in Enquiries Concerning Human Understanding and Concerning the Principles of Morals, ed. L. A. Selby-Bigge, 3rd ed. (Oxford, 1975), paragraph 13. The posthumous edition of 1777 was used for the reprint. Hereafter this source will be referred to in the text as Enquiry plus paragraph number.

[17] Concerning Locke's theory of substance see John L. Kraus, John Locke: Empiricist, Atomist, Conceptualist, and Agnostic (New York, 1968), pp. 117-132.

[18] The World and the Individual. First Series: The Four Historical Conceptions of Being (New York, 1959 [reprint of 1899 edition]), p. 97.

[19] For an excellent discussion of the problem of knowledge for Locke see Gibson, Theory of Knowledge, pp. 1-28.

[20] For an extended discussion of the relationship between practical and representational theories of knowledge in Locke's thought see Addison Webster Moore, The Functional versus the Representational Theories of Knowledge in Locke's Essay (Chicago, 1902).

[21] Warren, A History of the Association Psychology, p. 154.

[22] Dessoir, Outlines of the History of Psychology, pp. 111-112.

[23] For some sources on association psychology with particular reference to the British see Brett, History of Psychology, pp. 402-450; Dessoir, Outlines of the History of Psychology, pp. 107-125; Gardner Murphy, An Historical Introduction to Modern Psychology (New York, 1930), pp. 8-45; W. B. Pillsbury, The History of Psychology (New York, 1929)', pp. 67-105 and 123-136; and Warren, A History of the Association Psychology, pp. 23-80.

[24] Concerning Hume's theory of causality and belief see Constance Maud, Hume's Theory of Knowledge. A Critical Examination (London, 1937), pp. 266-304.

[25] An Abstract of a Book lately Published; Entitled a Treatise of Human Nature, &c. wherein the Chief Argument of that Book is further Illustrated and Explained (London, 1740), p. 32.

[26] Concerning British theories of ethics in the 18th century see Frederick Copleston, S. J., A History of Philosophy: Volume V. Modern Philosophy: The British Philosophers. Part 1: Hobbes to Paley (Garden City, 1964), pp. 182-212, and John Hermann Randall, Jr., The Career of Philosophy: Volume I. From the Middle Ages to the Enlightenment (New York/London, 1962), pp. 709-801.

[27] For some remarks on the function of "sympathy" in Hume's thinking see Rudolf Metz, David Hume. Leben und Philosophie (Stuttgart, 1929), pp. 249ff. and 270-273.

[28] See Hume's Enquiry Concerning the Principles of Morals (1748) in Enquiries (cf. footnote #16), paragraph 58. Hereafter this work will be referred to in the text as Principles of Morals plus the paragraph number.

[29] Essays on the Intellectual Powers of Man (1785) in Philosophical Works, with intro. by Harry M. Bracken (Hildesheim, 1967 [reprint of the 1895 edition]), I, 230. Hereafter referred to in the text as Intellectual Powers, I, plus page number.

[30] For example, see Dugald Stewart, Elements of the Philosophy of the Human Mind (1792) in The Works of Dugald Stewart (Cambridge, 1829), I, 203-296.

[31] Cf. The Theory of Moral Sentiments in The Works of Adam Smith (London, 1812), I, 59. Hereafter referred to in the text as Theory of Moral Sentiments plus page number. Concerning the function of sympathy in the ethics of Hume and Smith see Arthur O. Lovejoy, Reflections on Human Nature (Baltimore, 1968), pp. 247-264.

[32] For a general overview of 18th century aesthetics in Britain see: Raymond Bayer, Histoire de l'esthetique (Paris, 1961), pp. 180-228; Walter John Hipple, Jr., The Beautiful, the Sublime, and the Picturesque in Eighteenth-Century British Aesthetic Theory (Carbondale, 1957); Peter Kivy, The Seventh Sense. A Study of Francis Hutcheson's Aesthetics and Its Influence in Eighteenth-Century Britain (New York, 1976); Samuel H. Monk, The Sublime: A Study of Critical Theories in XVIII Century England (Ann Arbor, 1960); Max Schlasler, Kritische Geschichte der Aesthetik. Grundlegung for die Aesthetik als Philosophie des Schönen und der Kunst. Erste Abtheilung. Von Plato bis zum 19. Jahrhundert (Berlin, 1872), pp. 283-337; and K. Heinrich von Stein, Die Enstehung der neueren Ästhetik (Hildesheim, 1964 [reprint of the 1886 edition]), pp. 185-220. Also of some interest is James S. Malek, The Arts Compared. An Aspect of Eighteenth-Century British Aesthetics (Detriot, 1974).

33 For some important sources on Burke see: J. T. Boulton, "Editor's Introduction" to Burke's A Philosophical Enquiry into the Origin of our Ideas on the Sublime and Beautiful (London/New York, 1958), pp. i-cxxviii Katherine Everrett Gilbert and Helmut Kuhn, History of Esthetics (London, 1956), pp. 253-256; T. R. Henn, Longinus and English Criticism (Cambridge, 1934), pp. 117-123; Hipple, The Beautiful, the Sublime, and the Picturesque, pp. 83-98; Monk, The Sublime, pp. 84-100; Schlasler, Kritische Geschichte der Aesthetik, pp. 304-308; Tuveson, The Imagination as A Means of Grace, pp. 166-174; Dixon Wechter,"Burke's Theory of Words, Images and Emotions," PMLA, XL (1940), 167-181; and Robert Zimmermann, Geschichte der Aesthetik als philosophischer Wissenschaft, pp. 259-266.

34 Cf. A Philosophical Enquiry into the Origin of our Ideas of the Sublime and Beautiful (1756), ed. J. T. Boulton (London/New York, 1958), p. I. Hereafter all references to this edition will be made in the text according to book, section, and page number. The work itself will be abbreviated as Phil. Enquiry.

35 Cf. Vernünftige Gedanken von den Kräften des menschlichen Verstandes und ihrem richtigen Gebrauche in Erkenntnis der Wahrheit (1713) in Gesammelte Werke, ed. Hans Werner Arndt (Hildesheim, 1965), 1. Abtheilung. Band 1, 200.

36 Cf. "The Pleasures of the Imagination," The Spectator in The Spectator: With a Historical and Biographical Preface by A. Chalmers (New York, 1881), VI, 121-178, ##411-421. Hereafter referred to in text as Spectator plus issue and page number.

37 An Essay on Taste (London 1759), p. 1. Hereafter referred to in text as Essay on Taste plus page number.

38 A Course of Lectures on Oratory and Criticism (London 1777), p. 74. Hereafter referred to in the text as A Course of Lectures plus page number.

39 For an overview of British theories of taste see Hannelore Klein, There is no Disputing Taste. Untersuchung zum englischen Geschmacksbegriff im 18ten Jahrhundert (Münster, 1967).

40 Concerning Hume's theory of imagination see Metz, David Hume, pp. 203-211.

41 See Elements of Criticism, With Analyses and Translations of Ancient and Foreign Illustrations (1762), New Edition (New York, 1847), p. 480. Hereafter referred to in the text as Elements plus page number. For an overview of Kames' thought see Arthur McGuiness, Henry Home, Lord Kames (New York, 1970).

42 An Inquiry into the Original of our Ideas of Beauty and Virtue (London, 1752), p. v. Hereafter referred to in the text as The Original of our Ideas plus page number.

43 Cf. Principles de la Nature et de la Grace, fondés en raison (1714) in Die philosophischen Schriften von Gottfried Wilhelm Leibniz, ed. C. J. Gerhardt (Hildesheim, 1961 [reprint of 1885 edition]), VI, 605.

[44] *Theorie der schdnen Wissenschaften*. *Zum Gebrauche seiner Vorlesungen* (Halle, 1783), pp. 9 and 11.

[45] *The Pleasures of the Imagination* (1744) in *The Poetical Works of Mark Akenside* (London, 1894), pp. 102-103. Hereafter referred to the text as *The Pleasures* plus page number.

[46] *Of the Standard of Taste* (1757) in *Essays Moral, Political, and Literary*, ed. T. H. Green and T. H. Grose (London/New York/Bombay, 1898), I. 273. Hereafter referred to in the text as *Standard of Taste* plus page number.

[47] For a comprehensive history of the influence of associationism on British criticism see Martin Kallich, *The Association of Ideas and Critical Theory in Eighteenth-Century England. A History of a Psychological Method in English Criticism* (The Hague/Paris, 1970).

[48] *Observations on Man, His Fame, His Duty, and His Expectations. In Two Parts.* (London, 1749), Part I, Proposition 10, p. 65. Hereafter referred to in the text as *Observations* plus Part, Proposition, and page number. The above citation would read I, 10:65.

[49] *Disquisitions, Metaphysical and Literary* (London, 1793), pp. 16-17, 23. Hereafter referred to in the text as *Disquisitions* plus page number.

[50] Cf. Alison, *Essays on the Nature and Principles of Taste* (Edinburgh, 1790); Beattie, "Of Imagination," in *Dissertations Moral and Critical* (London, 1783), pp. 72-206; Gerard, *An Essay on Taste* (1759); Lord Kames, *Elements of Criticism* (1762); Priestly, *A Course of Lectures on Oratory and Criticism* (1773); and Smith, "Of the Influence of Custom and Fashion upon our notions of Beauty and Deformity," in *The Theory of Moral Sentiments* (1759), *The Works*, I, 335-346.

[51] *An Essay on the Sublime* (London, 1747), p. 34.

[52] *Dissertations Moral and Critical* (London, 1783), p. 165. Hereafter referred to in the text as *Dissertations* plus page number.

[53] *Philosophical Essays* (1810) in *The Works of Dugald Stewart* (Cambridge, 1829), IV, 199. Hereafter referred to in the text as *Phil. Essays* plus page number.

[54] *The Imagination as A Means of Grace*, pp. 132-163.

Chapter IV

Aesthetics of Living Form

A. Introduction

In the preceding two chapters I have, respectively, dealt with the aesthetics of form and of life. In both instances, my presentation was organized around the theoretical model developed in Chapter I. In other words, I first established the nature of the metaphysical universe of each school. Secondly, I showed how questions concerning the aesthetic universe were generated and answered in terms of the respective metaphysical universes. Finally, I focused upon the nature of the "beautiful" in light of the aesthetic universe concerned. In my analysis of Schiller's aesthetics of living form I shall, in broad outline, follow the tripart-division used in the previous chapters.

However, certain difficulties present themselves. Schiller explicitly noted that his concept of living form was based upon Kant's critical philosophy. Accordingly, I will examine Kant's critical thought in order to exposit the "metaphysical" universe grounding an aesthetics of living form. Schiller saw in Kant's philosophy a means for bringing the empirical back to principles or, conversely, the speculative back to experience. In other words, Kantian theory enabled Schiller to unite the aesthetics of form and of life into an integrated aesthetics of living form. Accordingly, I shall seek, however summarily, to explain the reconciliatory function of Kant's philosophical principles relative to rationalism and empiricism. Moreover, in order to facilitate an understanding of Kant's solution, I will first exposit the nature of the philosophical crisis of Kant's pre-critical thought. From around 1750 to 1781 rationalistic and empiricistic paradigms vied with each other for dominance in Germany and neither paradigm set won. This period, called by Max Wundt, "das dritte Menschenalter der Aufklärung," was a period of philosophical crisis.[1] I do not intend to give a history, even in outline, either of this period or of Kant's evolving pre-critical thought.[2] I wish only to focus upon a few philosophical difficulties of the period and upon their meaning for Kant's pre-critical situation. In terms of this situation I shall explain Kant's metaphysical universe and its meaning for Schiller's aesthetic universe. Also, in order to cast some more light upon Schiller's aesthetics, I will briefly examine Kant's aesthetic theory.

B. The Pre-Critical Crisis

Kant and Rationalism

The starting point of rationalistic philosophy was Descartes' cogito, ergo sum. The certainlty of the pure self was the source for philosophical theory. Moses Mendelssohn summed it up:

> Ich denke, worein...kein Zweifel zu setzen ist und woraus sich mit Gewissheit schliessen lässt: Also bin ich. Auf diesem Grundsatze muss sich das ganze philosophische Lehrgebäude aufführen lassen, ohne sich irgend auf ein anderes Zeugniss der äussern Sinne zu stützen. Denn was die Sinne von den äussern Dingen wahrnehmen ist verdächtig.........[3]

The rationalist sought ways, within the pure oneness of the cogito-sum consciousness, to deduce the objective outline of being or the thingness of things. Reality in itself does not disclose itself unmediated to human reason, to human subjectivity. Instead, human subjectivity finds in its pure selfhood, i.e. in the structure of its rational awareness, the outline of ontological objectivity. The dynamic principles of rational awareness, as shown in Chapter II, are the principium contradictionis the principium rationis sufficientis.

What is or can be, must be vorstellbar, i. e. evince a Grund-Folge-Struktur. The veritas metaphysica of being is accordingly the ordo plurium in uno, i. e. form. All of reality as a Ding-an-sich is analogous to a geometrical demonstration. Mendelssohn expressed the situation thusly:

> In dem Verstande Gottes ist alles Wissenschaft, hängen alle möglichen Wahrheiten so zusammen, wie die Sätze einer geometrischen Demonstration.....Ein unendlicher Verstand aber kann alle möglichen Bestimmungen wirklicher Dinge auf das allerdeutlichste erklären, und daher ihr Dasein, wenn ich vom Unendlichen menschlich reden darf, a priori beweisen. Daher hängen in ihm, vermöge des Satzes vom zureichenden Grunde, die Möglichkeiten und Wirklichkeiten auf das allergenaueste zusammen, und alle Wahrheiten machen ein einziges Ganz, eine einzige Wissenschaft, eine unendliche Demonstration aus, die der Allerhöchste mit einem Blicke übersieht ....[S]o harmonieren auch alle seine Einsichten und machen ein systematisches Ganze aus, in welchem sich eins aus allem und aus einemvernünftig erklären lässt (Über die Evidenz, I, 82).

Objective reality or the Ding-an-sich constitutes a connexial whole and is knowable as such. However, it is only totally knowable to a divine or infinite mind. In his Hamburgische Dramaturgie Gotthold Ephraim Lessing contends: "In der Natur ist alles mit allem verbunden; alles durchkreuzt sich, alles wechselt mit allem, alles verändert sich eines in das andere. Aber nach dieser unendlichen Mannigfaltigkeit ist sie nur ein Schauspiel für einen unendlichen Geist."[4] The Harmonia mundi is "really" there, but, alas, hidden to a great degree from human reason. Lessing's statement is not empty rhetoric. On the contrary, it is indicative of the crisis situation of Kant's pre-critical period. In itself reality is totally connexial. However, to man's de facto reason reality often appears atomistic, or non-rational. Mendelssohn comments:

> In unserm Verstand ist zwischen Möglichkeit und Wircklichkeit allezeit eine entsetzliche Kluft, indem wir niemals alle möglichen Bestimmungen eines Dinges verständlich erklären können, und daher das Dasein zufälliger [d. h. endlicher] Dinge nicht anders als aus der Erfahrung haben können (Ueber die Evidenz, I, 82).

In short, experience often evinces a de facto giveness, atomicisity, or unintelligibility. But, based upon his rationalistic faith, Mendelssohn had contended about reality in itself:

> Es ist schlechterdings unmöglich, dass eine Bestimmung wahr und unbegreiflich sein sollte....
> Gesetzt, es könnte etwas ohne allen Grund vorhanden sein, so wäre

das Dasein desselben eine Wahrheit, die mit keiner anderen Wahrheit verknüpft ist, eine isolirte Insel im Reich der Wahrheiten, zu welcher auf keinerlei Weise zu gelangen ist (Ueber die Evidenz, I, 79, 82).

In practice, however, the determinations of experience often appear isolated and unbegreiflich. If it should turn out that reality truly evinces contents which not only appear unbegreiflich, but are such, then it would follow that the pure reason cannot grasp being by means of its essentialistic concepts. The evolution of German philosophy between 1750 and 1781 is precisely the metamorphosis of this "if" situation into a real one.

An example of the evolving crisis can already be found in Georg Friedrich Meier's Betrachtungen über die Schrancken der menschlichen Erkenntnis (1755).[5] This short work, influenced by Meier's reading of John Locke, was published in the same year as the first volume of his Metaphysik. This work relativizes the Metaphysik. Rationalists (such as Meier in his Metaphysik) conceived the Dasein of individual reality as the most concrete "Bestimmungen" that flow from the essence of a thing. Friedrich Christian Baumeister (1709-1785), a Wolffian, summarized the rationalistic position: "Individuum est...ens omnimode determinatum, seu in quo determinata sunt omnia, quae eidem insunt."[6] Existence and individuality reveal themselves to be but modes of essentiality, determinations of essential being. The individual existence is, in short, the individual "Folge" of a general "Grund."

In his work Meier distinguishes between individual cognition and general cognition. Concerning general cognition Meier writes:

Nehmlich die abstracte oder allgemeine Erkenntniß besteht in dem Inbegriffe aller abstracten Begriffe und aller allgemeinen Urtheile und, Sätze und Schlüsse; oder in der Erkenntniß der Uebereinstimmung und Aehnlichkeit der einzelnen Dinge. Aus der Vernunft-Lehre ist bekant, daß alle abstracten Begriffe...in der Vorstellung der Aehnlichkeiten und Uebereinstimmungen der Dinge [bestehen] (Betrachtungen über die Schrancken, pp. 11-12).

In short, general knowledge focuses upon the connexiality, or oneness inherent in the many. General knowledge is, consequently, directed towards essentiality. Individual cognition is, however, aimed at a different content.

Wer also von einem eintzeln Dinge eine eintzelne Erkenntniß haben soll, der muß ausser seinen Aehnlichkeiten mit andern Dingen dasjenige von demselben erkennen, was ihm eigen ist, und wodurch es von allen übrigen eintzeln Dingen unterschieden ist (Betrachtungen über die Schrancken, p. 48).

Individual cognition is simple "dasjenige, was [dem Dinge] allein und eigenthümlich zukommt, und wodurch es von anderen Dingen verschieden ist" (Betrachtungen über die Schrancken, p. 20).

Without being fully aware of the fact, Meier has in effect exploded the rationalistic notion of individuality. For the rationalistic Meier the individual is but the most determinate "Bestimmung" of essence. It is specified generality. But now it appears that individuality excludes all that is general, that is, essential. Individual cognition focuses upon that which is "eigenthümlich." Simply stated, the concrete predicates of a thing stand outside of essential commonality and would appear not to be deducible from a ratio sufficiens. Meier clearly did not want to conclude so much. However, in effect, the individual cannot be approached through concepts, and is, accordingly unbegreiflich, or "eine isolirte Insel im Reiche der Wahrheit." General knowledge for Meier is completely inadequate. Meier writes:

> Man nehme die gantze allgemeine Erkenntniβ in ihrem gantzen Umfange so wie sie möglich ist, und in dem Verstande Gottes würcklich angetroffen wird: so muβ man zugestehen, daβ dasjenige, was wir davon wissen, der Theil derselben der uns bekant ist, in Absicht auf denjenigen, der uns unbekant ist, unendlich klein sey, und daβ der erste gegen den letztern in kein Verhältniβ gesetzt werden könne, welches uns Menschen verständlich und begreiflich seyn solte (Betrachtungen über die Schrancken, p. 37).

Meier has in effect introduced a heterogeneity into the "oneness" of the rationalistic universe. Individuality does not appear to be open to conceptual comprehension. Human knowledge based upon cognition of essentiality appears to be "unendlich klein."

If "pure" reason, de facto or on principle, cannot grasp the individuality of objective being, what, then, is the source for human cognition? Mendelssohn's answer was: "aus der Erfahrung." In other words, the mind is furnished with sensate contents, with empirical atoms. Meier writes: Die menschliche eintzelne Erkenntniβ [ist] deswegen so sehr eingeschrenckt: weil wir uns von keiner Sache, die ein eintzelnes Ding ist, einen rechten Begrif machen können, welchen wir nicht empfunden und erfahren haben...Alle unsere Erkenntniβ besteht in unsern Empfindungen und denen Begriffen, die wir aus ihnen herleiten.... Folglich können wir nichts als ein eintzelnes Ding dencken, was wir entweder nicht erfahren haben, oder was keiner eintzelnen unserer Empfindungen ähnlich ist (Betrachtungen über die Schrancken, p. 58).

Despite epistemological difficulties, thinkers such as Christian August Crusius (1715-1755) came to place ever more emphasis upon the empirical as the starting point of philosophy. In other words, reason should not so much apply pure or a priori concepts to reality as it should analyze sense experience. Crusius contends:

> Denn wir müssen unsere Erkenntnis von den Sinnen anfangen, da wir also auf Begriffe kommen, die unauflöslich sind und die nicht mehr als die gemeine Deutlichkeit haben können. [Einige Denker] schmähen ziehmlich unbedachtsam auf die Sinne. Sie wollen lauter Begriffe haben, die der Verstand aufgelöst hat. Wenn sie an die obersten Grenzen aller menschlichen Erkenntnis gekommen sind, so wollen sie die einfachen Begriffe ebenfalls durch eine fernere Auslösung definieren und deutlich machen. Notwendig müssen sie sich aber als dann in einem Wirbel herumdrehen und können nicht weiter kommen. Sie flechten und wirren eins in das andere und definieren erst dieses durch jenes und hernach jenes durch dieses. Weil sie die

rechte Methode, einfache Begriffe deutlich zu machen, aus der Acht lassen: so verfallen sie dabei auf bloβ relativische und negativische Begriffe, wobei sie aber das absolute und positive aus der Acht lassen und nicht als pure Cirkel und leere Worte übrig behalten.[7]

Failure to derive metaphysical concepts from sense experience cannot but lead to philosophical error. In 1747, Johann Gottlob Justi, in a prize winning essay, criticized quite subtly Leibniz's monadology. Monads are Leibniz's ontological equivalents to his mathematical-like world. Leibniz, claimed Justi, tried to reduce the rich manifold of empirical experience to the concept of "das Einfache" - a concept derived from purely mathematical concepts. Justi objects:

Allein wie kan man in der Metaphysic auf den Satz kommen; wo zusammengesetzte Dinge sind, da müssen auch einfache seyn. In der ganzen Natur siehet man nichts von einfachen Dingen...Da wir nun in der ganzen Natur von einfachen Dingen nichts wahrnehmen; ...so darf ein Metaphysicus bey der Untersuchungen der Cörper schlechtdings nicht auf einfache Dinge verfallen, wenn ihn nicht die Ordnung seiner vorhergehenden Schlüsse, und die natürliche Folge aus denselben unumgänglich darauf führen. Thut er es dennoch; so ist es offenbar, daβ er fremde und nicht hierher gehörige Begriffe einmischet...
...Allein so bald man einen geometrischen Begriff mit einem metaphysichen verbindet: so entstehet daraus allemahl ein falscher Schluβ ....Man kan gar nicht leugnen, daβ der Begriff des zusammengesetzten hier metaphysich ist. Da man nun den geometrischen Begriff des einfachen mit demselben verbinden will; so muβ der Schluβ nothwendig falsch seyn.[8]

In short, metaphysical concepts, not derived from sense experience and, as pure concepts, have no application to reality itself. "Pure" reason shows itself to be out of place.

Rationalists assumed that being in itself is rational, i. e. structured like a geometrical demonstration. However, de facto experience seems to confront the mind with non-rational congeries of sensations. Philosophical evolution tended to change the "seems" into an "is." I have cited above various thinkers in order to illustrate this developing quandry. Such difficulties become specifically pre-critical Kantian insofar as Kant crosses the line separating the "seems" from the "is." For the purposes of my analysis of Kant's pre-critical philosophy, I shall treat two transformations of the philosophical situation that were enacted by Kant.

First of all, Kant changed fundamentally the manner in which sensate experience was theoretically examined. For the rationalist man possesses only one single Vorstellungskraft. Rationalists, particularly under the influence of Leibniz's monadology, held that the mind represents, albeit "finitely," reality from the point of view of the body. Sensation arises as "undeutlich" experienced being (=essentiality). The rationalists hoped to grasp the individual, the concrete by means of a conceptual analysis and formation. The individual, conceived as "das Besondere," is derived (derivable) from "das Allgemeine." The difference resides in "Klarheit" and/or "Deutlichkeit." Kant transformed the continuum between the general and the individual into a discontinuous opposition - one between the concept (Begriff) and intuition (Anschauung). This change in philosophical thinking is very evident in Kant's inaugural dissertation of 1770. Here man is represented not as possessing one single vis repraesentativa, rather as having two separate cognitive faculties. Kant writes:

> Sensualitas est receptivitas subiecti, per quam possible est, ut status ipsius repraesenativus obiecti alicuius praesentia certo modo afficiatur. Intelligentia (rationalitas) est facultas subiecti, per quam, quae in sensus ipsius per qualitatem suam incurrere non possunt, repraesentare valet. Obiectum sensualitatis est sensibile; quod autem nihil continet, nisi per intelligentiam cognoscendum, est intelligibile...Cognito, quatenus subiecta est legibus sensualitatis, est sensitiva, intelligentiae, est intellectualis s. rationalis.[9]

Meier has admitted that man's intelligentia cannot in effect penetrate to the concrete individual as a determination of essence. Crusius had insisted that sensations should be the starting point for philosophical analysis. Justi had even claimed that concepts derived solely from intelligentia are not metaphysically applicable to the sense world. Kant now asserts that the mind has to be presented with the objects through sensations. The individual presented to the mind is given in Anschauung. In other words, the mind does not posit out of its one Vorstellungskraft its sensate contents, rather it possesses a passive or receptive faculty - one that must be "affiziert." Furthermore, the sensate contents are coordinated in time and space (=forms of sensation) by the faculty of sensibility, not by reason. Space and time are, accordingly, alogical forms of order, forms not derived from intelligentia as a faculty of concepts. The result is that, for Kant, the individual as sensate appearance is not the determination of essence, rather a content sui generis, i. e. on principle different from conceptual "reality." A fundamental difference pertains between sensation and conceptualization.

Secondly, Kant not only removed the empirical individual from the grasp of reason, but Dasein itself. Mendelssohn, Leibniz, Wolff, et. al. had conceived of existentia as but the most determinate mode of essentia. The possible differs from the actual in that the possible does not possess all its potential predicates. However, should a possible object possess all possible predicates (=complimentum), it is thereby made actual, real. In short, it exists. In his Der einzig mögliche Beweisgrund zu einer Demonstration des Daseins Gottes (1763) Kant disintegrates the essentialistic concept of existence as a complimentum possibilitatis. Kant writes: "Die Wolffische Erklärung des Daseins, daß es eine Ergänzung der Möglichkeit sei, ist offenbar sehr unbestimmt. Wenn man nicht schon vorher weiß, was über die Möglichkeit in einem Dinge kann gedacht werden, so wird man es durch diese Erklärung nicht lernen."[10] In order to illustrate his point that Dasein cannot be conceived as a predicate Kant writes: "Nehmet ein Subjekt, welches ihr wollt, z.E den Julius Cäsar. Fasset alle seine erdenkliche Prädikate, selbst die der Zeit und des Orts nicht ausgenommen, in ihm zusammen, so werdet ihr bald begreifen, daß er mit allen diesen Bestimmungen existieren oder auch nicht existieren kann" (II, 72). Consequently, Kant concludes: "Das Dasein ist gar kein Prädikat oder Determination von irgendeinem Dinge"

(II, 72). Kant was a long way from explaining what Dasein is. But he knew what it is not, namely it is not a logical determination of essentia. Kant used such a distinction in order to refute the ontological proof for God's existence. Rationalists, such as Baumgarten, had sought to conclude from God's possibility (essentiality) to His reality (existence). If essence and existence are on principle distinct, i.e. its existence is not a mode of essence, then such a proof is illicit.

Since rationalist man could only transcend his subjectivity by means of his rationality (his principia cognitionis), the positing of existence beyond the realm of essentiality was simultaneously to place ontological reality beyond the cognitive powers of pure reason. Contrary to Mendelssohn's hopes, Dasein is an isolated island to which there is no access, i.e. by pure reason, by concepts. The cognitive crisis of 18th century Germany resides in the inability of the root metaphor of mathematicism to deal adequately with the problem of existence. Intellectual intuition seems to be brought to a halt before existence and empirical appearance.

Kant and Empiricism

German rationalism developed problems revolving around the meaning of the empirical. Kant's evolving thought certainly manifests such a tendency. Kant's concern for the empirical could not but open him to influence from Britain. As Kant noted in his Prolegomena, Hume "was eben dasjenige, was mir vor vielen Jahren zuerst den dogmatischen Schlummer unterbrach und meinen Untersuchungen im Felde der speculativen Philosophie eine ganz andre Richtung gab."[11] The direction that Hume inspired was not so much one of embracing Humean empiricism, rather one of refuting it. Let us now examine Hume's meaning for Kant.[12]

British empiricism entails two key concepts, namely that of heteronomy and unintelligibility. For the empiricist (particularly for the Humean philosopher), there is no such thing as a homogeneous and intellectual consciousness that determines a priori the formal and necessary structure of reality. Instead, there is an irreducible plurality of atomistic perceptions that exhibit no common and homogeneous structure. Reality and knowledge thereof are heteronomous. In other words, the ultimate units of reality are not related to each other as ratio to rationatum, Grund to Folge. Instead, they are isolated and ultimate atoms. A clear and distinct conception of any specific object or aspect of reality in no way contains a reference to any other object. Referring to the meaning of Hume's critique of causality, Kant writes: "[Hume] bewies unwidersprechlich: daß es der Vernunft gänzlich unmöglich sei, a priori und aus Begriffen eine solche [kausale] Verbindung zu denken...; es ist aber gar nicht abzusehen, wie darum weil Etwas ist, etwas anderes nothwendiger Weise auch sein müsse, und wie sich also der Begriff von einer solchen Verknüpfung a priori einführen lasse" (Proloegonema, IV, 257) Since there is no intelligible essence or form involved in the very conception of any existing thing that implies the existence of any other thing, then the nature of things and their inter-connections lie beyond the a priori structures (i.e. intelligible constructions) of "pure" reason. Thus the finely spun intellectual web of rationalism is torn asunder into an infinite number of fragments. In short, metaphysics seems to be an impossibility. Kant summarizes Hume's meaning for philosophy:

Hieraus schloß [Hume]: die Vernunft habe gar kein Vermögen, solche [ontologischen] Verknüpfungen auch selbst nur im Allgemeinen zu denken, weil ihre Begriffe alsdann bloße Erdichtungen sein würden; und alle ihre vorgeblich a priori bestehende Erkenntnisse wären nichts als falsch gestempelte gemeine Erfahrungen, welches eben soviel sagt, als: es gebe überall keine Metaphysik und könne auch keine geben (Prolegomena, IV, 158).

The relationship between things is not intrinsic and logically determined. Instead, the relationship is extrinsic. How, then are the relations between things to be ascertained. Hume's answer was, of course, through a posteriori experience. As Hume wrote: "'Tis therefore by Experience only that we can infer the existence of one object from that another."[13]

Hume seems to have destroyed completely the rationalistic ideal of a priori, necessary, and hence metaphysical knowledge. That which can be said about reality is only possible through experience, i.e. only the observation of a conjunction between two objects at a specific "now" and at a specific place can yield knowledge. Hume seems to have triumphed. Kant's rejection of rationalism would have, if he had followed Hume's direction of philosophy, led him into a philosophical scepticism relative to metaphysics. But, paradoxically, Hume's very empiricism contains the seeds (or inner contradictions, to use Hegel's terminology) of its own destruction and transcendence.

Kant's dissatisfaction with Hume's empiricistic grounding of knowledge becomes quite striking in Hume's attempt to explain causality. Causality was the key "objectivity constant" in Hume's analysis of the world. Knowledge about the relationship between things was for Hume a function of causality. In other words, experience furnishes knowledge about the future by means of causal links inherent in or (structuring) present and/or past "nows." Hume clearly saw that causal or objective relations between objects differs from the merely sequential relation between objects, no matter how many times repeated, and that it is "neccessity" that constitutes such a difference, Hume writes: "An object may be contiguous and prior to another, without being consider'd as its cause. There is a NECESSARY CONNEXION to be taken into consideration.." (Treatise, I, 3:2).

But what is the origin of the notion of "necessity?" What is its structure? When Hume examined causality by means of his "experimental method," he could find no "objective" relation of necessity pertaining between objects. Events, spatially contiguous and temporally sequential, repeat themselves frequently. But repetition alone can never be "seen" to constitute necessity. Since Hume could find no "connexion" objectively in and between the objects upon which his mind focused, he sought such unity in the mind itself, i.e. in the manner in which the mind relates itself to its contents and its contents to itself. According toHume, constantly repeated events "cause" the mind to become habituated to view such events ordered in a specific way. Concerning necessity Hume contends:

Necessity... is nothing but an internal impression of the mind or a determination to carry out thoughts from one object to another...- Upon the whole, necessity is something that exists in the mind, not in objects.... 'Tis a common observation, that the mind has a great propensity to spread itself on external objects, and to conjoin with them any internal impressions, which they occasion, and which always make their appearance at the same time that these objects discover themselves to the senses (Treatise, I, 3:14).

Causality or necessity is simply the "determination" of the mind to view two events as combined, connected, or bonded. In short, a causal "connexion, tie, or energy lies merely in ourselves, and is nothing but that determination of the mind, which is acquir'd by custom, and causes us to make a transition from an object to its usual attendant, and from impression of one to the lively idea of the other" (Treatise, I, 4:7).

But Hume's analysis of causality is quite faulty and entails an inner contradiction. Hume contends that constant repetition "causes" the mind to become habituated in a specific manner. In simple terms, Hume uses the concept of causality in the very manner that he is seeking to prove to be illicit. How can constant repetition (event set one) bring about, produce, or cause a habituated mind (event set two), if the necessity of causality reveals itself to be nothing but a determination of the mind. Hume is asserting that a causal relation "really" pertains between events and the mind, although his theory contends that no such "objective" relations can be. Hume's very description of the objective genesis of the "impression" of necessity can, on the basis of his theory, be no more than a subjective determination of the mind to so think. The objective use of causality grounds Hume's thesis that such an objective use is illicit![14]

However, without the existence of causal links between the contents of experience, experience will decompose into random congeries of sense perceptions. Without the "determination" of the mind to connect events causally, there are no objectivity constants whereby "seems" and "is" can be distinguished. But such a mental "determination" cannot be explained as habituation because habituation cannot be explained without an illicit use of causality. Hume, in effect, leaves the mind with certain structural tendencies without being able to explain them. An atomistic, empiricistic, and nominalistic explanation of causality reveals itself to be impossible. Kant could never have been satisfied with Hume's empiricistic explanation of the unity of experience. Since the senses cannot furnish the necessary connexion between things, it would appear that Kant's only choice would be to examine the faculty of reason in order to discover the necessary unity for experience. This would mean that metaphysics is not dead. In other words, it must be the understanding that thinks the connexion of things a priori. Such thinking is, moreover, metaphysical. Concerning the direction of his thought as inspired by Hume, Kant wrote:

Ich suchte mich [der] Zahl [der a priori Verknüpfungen] zu versichern, und da dieses mir nach Wunsch, nämlich aus einem einzigen Prinzip, gelungen war, so ging ich an die Deduction dieser Begriffe, von denen ich nunmehr versichert war, daß sie nicht, wie Hume besorgt hatte, von der Erfahrung abgeleitet, sondern aus dem reinem Verstande entsprungen seien...Da es mir nun mit der Auflösung des Humischen Problems nicht blos in einem besondern Falle, sondern in Absicht auf das ganze Vermögen der reinen Vernunft gelungen war: so konnte ich sichere, obgleich immer nur langsame Schritte thun, um endlich den ganzen Umfang der reinen Vernunft in seinen Grenzen sowohl, als seinen Inhalt vollständig und nach

allgemeinen Principien zu bestimmen, welches denn dasjenige war,
was Metaphysik bedarf, um ihr System nach einem sicheren Plan
aufzuführen (Prolegomena, IV, 260-261).

Kant's Critical Problem

I am now in a position to formulate Kant's philosophical dilemma the
solution to which will reveal the nature of the "objectivity constants" in
Kant's mature thinking (and in Schiller's aesthetics). Scientific knowledge,
be it physical, psychological, or metaphysical, was for Kant a judgement
about objects. The metaphysician, for instance, aims his judgments at the
most fundamental feature of an object, of objectivity, namely at the distinction between "is" and "seems" that is valid for any and all things. Based
upon this distinction the metaphysician articulates the "objectivity
constants" of being or the "thingness" of things. The mind knows its
objects, understands reality by means of concepts. But a concept can only
constitute real knowledge when it has an object to which it refers.
Knowledge for Kant is knowledge about an object, about an objective world.

Kant agreed with Hume that experience alone (=sense perceptions)
furnishes the mind with objects to be known. What is, is given to the mind
by means of the faculty of sensibility. The mind must, in short, be
"affiziert" by an object if it is to have something to know. Kant also
agreed with Hume that experience cannot mediate to the mind universal and
necessary knowledge. Temporally conjoined events cannot be translated into
genuine universal knowledge - and it was such knowledge that Kant sought.
Furthermore, Hume's empiricistic explanation of the prime objectivity
constant, namely of causality, failed. Indeed, it revealed itself to be
self-contradictory. Only the faculty of reason functioning "purely" (i.e.
independent of all sensate content) can construct universal and necessary
concepts. But such "pure" concepts of "pure" reason are simply a product of
the human mind. The faculty of reason does not intuit any objects nor does it
produce any. Reason produces the form of universal knowledge, but not the
content, not the objects so known. Rationalists had held that the principia
cognitionis to be ontologically and objectively valid because they were
grounded in the cogito, ergo sum of Descartes. The principles of reason for
Kant have, the contrary, no immediate reference to any objectivity.

If universal and necessary knowledge is to be had, Kant had to determine
the relation between rational concepts in the mind (or produced by the mind)
with objects outside the mind. In short, how can subjective constructs
possess objective reference? Kant formulated his critical problem quite
clearly in a letter (February 21, 1712) to his friend and former student,
Marcus Herz. Kant wrote:

> Die reine Verstandesbegriffe müssen also nicht von den Empfindungen
> der Sinne abstrahiert sein, noch die Empfänglichkeit der Vorstel-
> lungen durch Sinne ausdrücken, sondern in der Natur der Seele zwar
> ihre Quellen haben, aber doch weder insoferne sie vom Objekt
> gewirkt werden, noch das Objekt selbst hervorbringen. Ich hatte
> mich in der Dissertation damit begnügt, die Natur der Intellektual-
> vorstellungen bloß negativ auszudrücken: daß sie nämlich nicht
> Modifikationen der Seele durch den Gegenstand wären. Wie aber denn
> sonst eine Vorstellung, die sich auf einen Gegenstand bezieht, ohne

vom ihm auf einige Weise affiziert zu sein, möglich, überging ich
mit Stillschweigen. Ich hatte gesagt: die sinnliche Vorstellungen
stellen die Dinge vor, wie sie erscheinen, die intellecktuale, wie
sie sind. Wodurch aber werden uns denn diese Dinge gegeben, wenn
sie es nicht durch die Art werden, womit sie uns affizieren; und
wenn solche intellektuale Vorstellungen auf unsrer innern Tätigkeit
beruhen, woher kommt die Übereinstimmung, die sie mit Gegenständen
haben sollen, die doch dadurch nicht etwa hervorgebracht werden,
und die axiomata der reinen Vernunft über diese Gegenstände, woher
stimmen sie mit diesen überein, ohne daß diese Übereinstimmung von
der Erfahrung hat dürfen   Hulfe entlehnen?[15]

C. "Critical" Objectivity

Kant's "Copernican" Revolution

Kant offered a solution to his critical problem in his so-called
Copernican revolution in metaphysics.[16] Just as Copernicus had changed the
viewpoint for judging the relationship between the viewer and the heavens, so
too did Kant alter the viewpoint for determining the relationship between the
knower and the known. Kant expressed his revolution: "Bisher nahm man an,
alle unsere Erkenntnis müsse sich nach den Gegenständen richten; ...Man
versuche es daher einmal, ob wir nicht in den Aufgaben der Metaphysik damit
besser fortkommen, daß wir annehmen, die Gegenstände müssen sich nach unserem
Erkenntnis richten..."[17]

Kant had contended that reason cannot penetrate (by means of concepts)
to the existence of things-in-themselves. For example, the objectivity
constants of substance and causality, which are concepts of the understand
ing, have no ontological reference. As Kant wrote: "[D]enn von der
Möglichkeit einer solchen Verknüpfung des Daseins habe ich keinen Begriff"
(Prolegomena, IV, 311). Reason cannot ascertain how such conceptual
possibilities have any ontological possibility, i. e. possibility for things-
in-themselves. Consequently, a priori knowledge of a thing-in-itself is an
impossibility. Despite this fact, it is, nevertheless, clear that the world
of experience is not chaotic, rather orderly. The "Erfahrungsurtheile" of
reason do not refer to subjectivity, rather to the objective order in
appearing things. Kant contends: "[S]o müssen wir [ein Erfahrungsurtheil]
auch für objectiv halten, d. i. daß es nicht blos eine Beziehung der Wahrnehmung auf ein Subject, sondern eine Beschaffenheit des Gegenstandes ausdrücken
..." (Prolegommena, IV, 298). How can such judgments refer to an object?
The answer will reveal the "objectivity constant" for Kant.

For there to be an objective unity of perception(s), i.e. experience,
(1) there must first be an intuitive apprehension of the various parts of the
manifold that will constitute the matter of unity. These apprehensions take
place in time. For example, the apprehension of a book is not simultaneous.
First the front, then the sides, etc., appear to consciousness. The fact of
the successive apprehension leads to the second aspect of an object. (2) The
apprehended manifold must be reproduced in the imagination if a complete
determination of an object is to be possible. For instance, a direct and
head-on apprehension of the front of a book will not result in the experience
of an object unless there are also represented to the mind the back and the
sides. (3) Correlative to the idea of the reproduction and apprehension of

the manifold is the recognition that the various parts of the manifold are
related together as parts of an on-going whole. In other words, the manifold
must be linked together and recognized as such if there is to be an object.
However, this is not all there is to the construction of the objectivity of
an object of experience.   (4) The perception of the multiplicity occurs in
time. There is, therefore, relative to the perceiver, a subjective order of
apprehension. If the mind "viewed" perceptions simply according to its own
subjective and contingently determind order of reception, there would be no
object, just congeries of random sensations. For instance, a book as a
perceptual front, two sides, and a back. The order of arrangement between
the front, sides, and back is not simply determined by the subject's arbitrary order of perception. On the contrary, the back is necessarily not
attached to the front, but necessarily to the sides. Destroy the necessary
order of relationship between the parts of a book and the book as an object,
as an objectivity, disappears. Therefore, the fourth element of objectivity
is the necessary synthesis of perceptions.

At this point, the importance of Kant's Copernican revolution becomes
evident.   Reason itself takes up the sensate contents given to it in
intuition and orders them before they reach consciousness as the contents of
experience. In this sense, one can say that the objects of experience must
accord themselves to the necessities of the intellect. This guarantees the
possibility of a priori knowledge. Kant claims:

Wenn die Anschauung sich nach der Beschaffenheit der Gegenstände
richten müßte, so sehe ich nicht ein, wie man a priori von ihr
etwas wissen könne; richtet sich aber der Gegenstand (als Objekt
der Sinne) nach der Beschaffenheit unseres Anschauungsvermögens, so
kann ich mir diese Möglichkeit ganz wohl vorstellen (KdrV, B, p.
xvii).

In short, Kant claims, "daß wir nämlich von den Dingen nur das a priori
erkennen, was wir selbst in sie legen" (KdrV, B, p. xviii).

Experience evinces objectivity constants because subjectivity qua its
nature forms the manifold of experience according to universal structures or
categories.   Hume had sought for the causal objectivity constant in the
mind's "determination" to connect two events together. Hume, unsuccessfully,
tried to explain such a "determination" as a habit of the mind. Kant agreed
that the mind determines the contents of experience to be ordered into a
lawful whole. However, Kant insisted that the mind (reason) is not a passive
object to be habituated, rather a categorical or structural function.   In
other words, the mind evinces "determinations" because it is, prior to
experience, so structured. Furthermore, it is possible to determine the
nature of such a structure and hence to determine a priori to experience
certain universal and necessary constants - constants that transform
atomistic perceptions into manifestations of an objective unity, of
objectivity. The ordering function of subjectivity must be further examined.

The objectivity constant of unity is a function of the intellect's
categorical structure.   The intellect supplies the connections for the
manifold and thereby combines the manifold into a synthetic unity. "Allein
die Verbindung (coniunctio) eines Mannifgaltigen überhaupt kann niemals durch
Sinne in uns kommen und kann also auch nicht in der reinen Form der

sinnlichen Anschauung zugleich mit enthalten sein; denn sie ist ein Aktus der Spontaneität der Vorstellungskraft, und, da man diese, zum Unterschiede von der Sinnlichkeit, Verstand nennen muss, so ist all Verbindung . . . eine Verstandeshandlung, die wir mit der allgemeinen Bennenung Synthesis belegen werden. . ."(KdrV, B. pp. 129-130). Thus the ultimate act of synthesis is an intellectual act.

The consciousness of the synthetic unity of the manifold necessarily entails a unity or sameness in the consciousness that experiences the unity. If each single awareness of each single aspect of experience were not related (present) to a unity of consciousness, there could not be an experience of a synthetic unity of the manifold. The identity of the representations of differing times necessarily implies a unity of consciousness that transcends- (and includes) all the separate differing states of consciousness. Kant called this ultimate consciousness "die transcendentale Einheit des Selbstbe- wusstseins" (KdrV, B, p. 132), i.e. the transcendental self. This self is the logical subject for the experiencing of all objects. "Die synthetische Einheit des Bewuβtseins, ist also eine objektive Bedingung aller Erkenntniβ, nicht deren ich bloβ selbst bedarf, um ein Object zu erkennen, sondern unter der jede Anschauung stehen muβ, um für mich Object zu werden, weil auf andere Art, und ohne diese Synthesis, das Mannigfaltige sich nicht in einem Bewuβt- sein vereinigen würde" (KdrV, B. p. 138). This unity is beyond all temporal, spatial, and conceptual determinations of the phenomenal world. It is rather their prerequisite. Insofar as the ultimate self is beyond the phenomenal world Kant assigns it to the noumenal world.

Although the transcendental unity of apperception is not found in direct self-intuition, it is possible to obtain some knowledge about this ultimate self by examining it as a functional prerequisite for the synthetic unity of the manifold. (1) The manifold only becomes unified by being synthesized. To synthesize is to gather a multiplicity and to combine this multiplicity by means of a concept. The combination takes place in a spontaneous act of the understanding. "Begriffe," writes Kant, "gründen sich also auf der Spontaneität des Denkens, wie sinnliche Anschauungen auf der Rezeptivität der Eindrücke"(KdrV, B, p. 93). It is only in the act of combining that the transcendental self is. To be a self is to be active. (2) Insofar as the ultimate self brings together plurality into a unity it forms. The activity that the self participates in is an activity of forming (Gestalten). The self generates the unity of cognition. (3) The function of the self is actively to form a cognitive whole, i.e. to conceptualize the manifold. Consequently, the ultimate self is essentially an intelligence. "...und ich existere als Intelligenz, die sich lediglich ihres Verbindungsvermögens bewuβt ist..." (KdrV B, p. 158). The essence of the Kantian self is to be a Verbindungsvermögen. (4) Insofar as the self is beyond the phenomenal world, it is self-determining. Self-determination is a correlative notion to the idea of actively forming. Insofar as the self forms (determines), it is not being formed (determined). Conversely, that which is not being determined and is not passive, is therefore determining. The principle of self-determination was called by Kant the principle of autonomy.

"Verbindung" as the Objectivity Criterion of Critical Philosophy

Following the model established in Chapter I, I have attempted to explain the aesthetic universes of form and of life in terms of their respective metaphysical universes. A universe qua its nature entails a mainfold (the many) structured by a unity (the one). The manifold becomes a universe precisely by the unity that it manifests. Rationalism and empiricism evince different universes, metaphysically and aesthetically, because they entail conflicting principles of unity.

Rationalism, for instance, conceives of unity as ontologically objective, i.e. unity inheres in things-in-themselves. Such unity is grounded in an analytical oneness. To be is to be one. Insofar as oneness unifies a manifold it does so as a Grund-Folge-Struktur, as a web of essentiality. This structure appears as order. The maximinization of order is perfection. Perfection is, in other words, the "form" of oneness in a manifold.

Empiricism, on the other hand, views unity as subjective, i. e. there is no unity inherent in things-in-themselves. Things are present to human consciousness as atomistic contents, as sense perceptions. Unity is introduced into the manifold by the mind (=subjectivity). The mind synthetically combines or holds the many together. This unity resides in the "determination" of the mind to view sense perceptions together. Such a synthesizing act, insofar as it transcends mere spatial and temporal conjoining, is habit (=inclination). The synthetic activity itself is a function of a deeper principle of unity, namely that of life. In other words, the determination of the mind to connect things is structured by the dual principle of pursuing pleasure and avoiding pain, that is of life. The principle of life, as the principle of unity, entails constructing a world that maximizes life.

Kant's critical concept of unity reconciles the opposition between the unities of form and of life. Unity - necessary, universal, and a priori - is the general form of objectivity as it appears to human consciousness in Kant's critical thought. This concept entails four features. (1) Critical unity is not a mere viewing things together as in empiricism. Critical unity entails universality and necessity. Consequently, it embodies in itself a genuine oneness as in rationalism. (2) This oneness, however, does not inhere in things-in-themselves, i. e. it has no objective locus in being. (3) Oneness must be imposed upon the phenomenal many by an act of subjectivity. Conversely, the many must be synthesized by the universality of oneness. This is accomplished by subjectivity. (4) Unity is the objectivity constant par excellence because it is a "Verbindung" pertaining between perceptions as prescribed by the subjective universality of reason. Objective unity is a function of subjective unity, i.e. of a synthetic activity by subjectivity. Kant himself claimed:

> daß wir uns nichts, als im Objekt verbunden, vorstellen können, ohne es vorher selbst verbunden zu haben, und unter allen Vorstellungen die Verbindung die einzige ist, die nicht durch Objekt gegeben, sondern nur vom Subjekte selbst verrichtet werden kann, weil sie ein Actus seiner Selbsttätigkeit ist (KdrV, B, P. 130).

Verbindung as the principle of unity implies both a state and an act. Verbindung is a state insofar as it constitutes the objective outline of nature, i.e. it is the universal structure relative to which the many are connected. It is an act insofar as it refers to the subject's forming activity. Objective unity is essentially a combining act - a combining according to universal and necessary rules. The principles of combination are forms of oneness insofar as oneness structures a synthesizing activity. Such principles generate and constitute the "real" of appearances, i. e. the invariable in opposition to the variable. Subjective combining according to universality and the resultant combination are two reciprocal aspects of objectivity in Kant's critical thought.[18]

Kant' reconciliation of empiricism and rationalism leads to a peculiar proposition. Universal, necessary, and a priori cognition does not reveal anything about objective things-in-themselves, rather it reveals what the deeper universal self, unconsciously, has formed. More accurately, the principles of forming (or the form of rational activity) are brought to consciousness in a priori cognition. The self sees itself in the order of nature since the nature of the self is essential for the constitution of nature. Universal knowledge is really a manifestation of the self's formative powers to the self. Concerning this proclivity of Kantian thought H. A. Korff writes: "Denn dann besteht Kants Lehre gar nicht eigentlich darin, daβ unsere Vernunft die Dinge an sich nicht erkennen kann, sondern sie gar nicht zu erkennen sucht, weil sie überhaupt nicht 'erkennen', sondern formen will...[U]nser Geist will ja nichts wissen, sondern formen bzw. wissen, was er geformt hat."[19] Korff has in effect come upon a new principle of life inherent in Kant's notion of Verbindung. The cognitive process itself appears to be subordinated to a process of self-revelation. What comes into consciousness is the forming power of the self. This power constitutes a new principle of life. Life is no longer the dynamics of pleasure or pain, rather the activity of universal forming power. This problem will be taken up in my discussion both of Kant's and Schiller's aesthetic theories.

D. The Aesthetic Universe of Critical Philosophy

The Problem of a "Critical" Aesthetics

In the previous chapters I have shown how theorists of form and of life applied their respective "objectivity constants" to aesthetic phenomena in order to derive the "nature" of the aesthetic universe. The initial effect of Kant's Kritik der reinen Vernunft was not propitious for a Kantian or critical aesthetics. In his first Kritik Kant expressed the opinion that a reduction of aesthetic judgments (i.e. judgments of taste) to principles of reason is impossible. Kant writes:

Die Deutschen sind die einzigen, welche sich jetzt des Worts Aesthetik bedienen, um dadurch das zu bezeichnen, was andre Kritik des Geschmacks heiβen. Es liegt hier eine verfehlte Hoffnung zum Grunde, die der vortreffliche Analysist Baumgarten faβte, die kritische Beurteilung des Schönen unter Vernunftprinzipien zu bringen, und die Regeln derselben zur Wissenschaft zu erheben. Allein die Bemühung ist vergeblich. Denn gedachte Regeln, oder Kriterien, sind ihren vornehmsten Quellen nach bloβ empirisch, und können also niemals zu bestimmten Gesetzen a priori dienen, wonach sich unser Geschmacksurteil richten müβte...(KdrV, B. p. 35)

Taste would appear to be a function of the empiricistic model. Examples of beautiful objects could, of course, be collected, compared, and empirical generalizations derived. But such "inductive" judgments are all a posteriori or, conversely, they are never a priori legislative for an aesthetic universe. In the strict Kantian sense there can be no "science" of aesthetics - at least in the KdrV. Indeed, in Kantian terms one can hardly speak about an aesthetic universe, since the necessary objectivity constants (the form of a universe) are lacking.

Kant and his followers did not long remain content with a mere empiricistic interpretation of aesthetic phenomena. For instance, Karl Heinrich Heydenreich evolved a "critical" aesthetics before Kant published his own Kritik der Urteilskraft (1790). In 1790 Heydenreich published his System der Aesthetik in which he constructed in a most unsatisfactorily manner a critical aesthetics.[20] Heydenreich explicitly attempted to answer Kant's objections to a science of aesthetics as raised in the KdrV (Cf. System. pp. 81ff.). According to Heydenreich: "Eine wahre Philosophie des Schönen...muß die gemeinschaftliche Abkunft dieser [aesthetischen] Empfindungen von höheren Prinzipien zeigen, .. muß endlich nach sichern Grundsätzen den wahren für alle gültigen Werth, dieser verschiedenen Klassen [von aesthetischen Gegenständen] bestimmen" (System, p. 87). In order to achieve this goal Heydenreich subsumes beauty (or aesthetic phenomena) under the general heading of Empfindung. More specifically, beauty is "lediglich das Gefühl des Angenehmen oder Unangenehmen selbst..." (System, p. 91). Heydenreich next asserts that there are two basic groupings of pleasant sensations. One group, is equivalent to the English model, i.e. it consists of immediately pleasing sensations, caused physiologically or by association. Similar to his English predecessors, Heydenreich does not specify the differences between merely pleasant sensations (e.g. sweetness) and the specific pleasantness of aesthetic sensations.

There is another group of aesthetic objects that are pleasing because they agreeably affect man's "Verstand." Expressed differently: "Warum reizt uns Ordnung, Uebereinstimmung, Verhältnißmäßigkeit so sehr an Gegenständen des Gesichts ...Warum Zweckmäßigkeit und Ordnung in Gedanken...? Weil in allen diesen Fällen die Gesetze der Vorstelkraft, des Verstandes, der spekulativen oder praktischen Vernunft beobachtet werden. Darum hat man von ieher Schönheit für den Verstand...angenommen" (System, p. 103). Heydenreich's second thesis turns out to be a reworking of the rationalist's principle of form. The "Vernunftprinzip" that grounds this second group of aesthetic pleasantness is:

Kann man alle mannichfaltigen Schönheiten unter ein und dasselbe Vernunftprinzip ordnen? ...Unter allen mir bekannten Meynungen der Weltweisen über diesen Gegenstand ist nur eine, die für eine Antwort auf [diese] Frage gelten kann: nämlich dieinige, nach welcher man alle Schönheiten auf Einheit in der Mannichfaltigkeit zurückführen zu können glaubt. Einheit is ist die Seele, das innere Leben der Vernunft... (System, pp. 111-112).
...[Der Erklärung der Schönheit] zufolge nämlich, soll Schönheit, sinnliche Gewahrnehmung der Vollkommenheit, der Einheit im Mannigfaltigen seyn..." (System, p. 130).

Heydenreich goes on in his work to cite Yves André's translation into French of St. Augustin's thesis concerning unity as the heart of beauty (Cf. System, pp. 111ff.).

Despite Heydenreich's critique of Baumgarten's principle of form, he comes up with little better. This is not unique to Heydenreich. For instance, Lazarus Bendavid, a worthy successor to Moses Mendelssohn,[21] evolved a critical aesthetics.[22] Bendavid credibly interpreted the various art forms as ways in which space and/or time are aesthetically schematized. Bendavid's intent was to show, "wie unsere Sinnlichkeit die Dinge anschauen muss, ... um sie schön zu finden" (Beyträge, "Vorrede"). Despite Kant's obvious influence upon Bendavid and although Bendavid makes references to a "free play" of the imagination (as did Kant), he repeatedly takes recourse to the traditional rationalistic formula of unity in variety. For example: "...desto mehr Mannichfaltigkeit stimmt zu einer Einheit zusammen, und desto mehr Schönheit finden wir in der Form....desto grössere Mannichfaltigkeit entdecken wir in einer Einheit zusammengestellt, und desto schöner finden wir auch das Werk" (Beyträge, pp. 6, 16). Similarly Salomon Maimon, one of Kant's most important early followers, accepted a rationalistic sounding definition of beauty. "Schönheit ist die sinnliche Uebereinstimmung des Mannichfaltigen zu einem Zweck..."[23] Indeed, Maimon even considered Wolff's definition of beauty, properly understood, to be the exact same as Kant's (or more accurately, Kant's to be the same as Wolff's).[24] Similar to Heydenreich, neither Bendavid nor Maimon was able to construct a "critical" aesthetics that added anything new to the definition of beauty, i.e. anything that seriously transcended the principle of form.

Relative to his twofold division of aesthetic objects, Heydenreich writes: "Ich begreife nicht, was selbst Kant gegen diese genauere Klassifikation der Schönheiten, und die darauf gegründete Einschränckung und Richtung der Frage über die Möglichkeit der Vernunftprinzipien für den Geschmack einwenden könnte. Sie stimmt mit seiner Art zu philosophieren völlig überein" (Systems, pp. 109-110). I do not know if Kant ever took cognizance of Heydenreich. However, Heydenreich was wrong. His aesthetics only marginally resembled Kant's "critical" way of philosophizing. Heydenreich did not ground the a priori and hence necessary basis for a "science" of aesthetics. Indeed, Heydenreich evinces two incompatible theories. Aesthetic objects are divided into two groups for which, respectively, empiristic and rationalistic models are suggested. How such diverse "causes" can produce the same, namely aesthetic, effect is not explained. Heydenreich admits: "[S]o müssen wir sogleich erkennen, daß keineswegs die Schönheit von allen....... Klassen, die ich aufgestellt habe, Principien der Vernunft untergeordnet werden können" (System, pp. 105-106). Indeed, Heydenreich explicitly contends "daß [Schönheiten] nicht auf ein gemeinschaftliches Princip reduciert werden können" (System, p. 104). Heydenreich, in effect, has conceded that he cannot construct a science of aesthetics in a Kantian manner. A science with inconsistent principles is not, on a Kantian basis, a "science"!

Kant's immediate followers were not able to evolve an adequate critical science of aesthetics. Instead it was Kant himself who first achieved this goal in a significant manner. In the ensuing I shall not attempt, even in outline, to exposit Kant's aesthetic theory. This has been done frequently, and with much success.[25] It will be recalled that Schiller was of the opinion that only critical philosophy can reconcile the empirical with the speculative (=principles of reason). I intend briefly to focus upon certain aspects of Kant's "critical" aesthetics that illustrate Schiller's contention.

Kant's "Critical" or "Transcendental" Grounding of Aesthetics

In his Kritik der reinen Vernunft Kant was able to deduce the "objectivity" of nature. In other words, Kant proved that there are a priori, necessary, and universal concepts that constitute the "objectivity constants" of nature and, indeed, ground nature as a "universe" for which theoretical knowledge is possible. Kant achieved this deduction not by means of a metaphysical analysis, rather "transcendentally" (or critically) by determining the necessary condition, grounded in the structure of the knowing self, that makes experience of objectivity possible, that, indeed, makes "Erfahrung" in opposition to mere "Wahrnehmung" possible. In order to achieve his transcendental analysis Kant focused upon man's theoretical "Erkenntnisvermögen" that furnishes the "Principien a priori" viz. the categorical "Bedingungen" that constitute the "Dingheit" of objects as they appear, not as they are in themselves. This cognitive faculty was called "Verstand." The a priori principle of "Verstand" in general simply is "Gesetzmäßigkeit," i.e. objects of nature possess objectivity to the degree that they are part of a single system of laws. "Gesetzmäßigkeit" is, accordingly, the necessary, a priori, universal, and hence transcendental condition for the experience of nature as a universe. It is by means of a transcendental principle that the objectivity of the natural universe is grounded. Concerning a transcendental principle Kant writes: "Ein transcendentales Princip ist dasjenige, durch welches die allgemeine Bedingung a priori vorgestellt wird, unter der allein Dinge Objecte unserer Erkenntniß überhaupt werden können."[26] The universe of nature is not the only universe for which Kant established a transcendental principle. Man not only makes judgments about nature, but also about his activities as guided by his will. In other words, man makes moral judgments. Man is motivated to act within nature in order to realize specifically desired values. Judgments about such acts can also be organized into a science, i.e. be shown to be subsumable under a priori, necessary, and universal principles. Kant, following his critical method in the Kritik der praktischen Vernunft, undertook a transcendental analysis of man's "Begehrungsvermögen" - a second faculty of man's "Gemüth." Such a faculty directs human activity relative to desired good. As a faculty functioning morally, it derives its principle(s) from man's "Vernunft," i.e. from that part of the synthesizing self that seeks absolute unity viz. "das Unbedingte." "Vernunft" is, accordingly, aimed at the realm of the supersensible as this realm realizes itself in the sensible realm. The "Princip a priori" of "Vernunft," when applied to moral activity, constitutes a universal and necessary value to be realized. The realization of absolute value requires the principle of "Endzweck." All activity must be ordered and subordinated to the actualization of a final purpose. And this purpose is nothing less than "Freiheit" (or autonomy). In other words, "Freiheit" is the mode in which "Vernunft" functions as a principle regulating the objects aimed at by the "Begehrungsvermögen." These objects are simply "moral acts." Kant discriminated, articulated and transcendentally grounded the principles of practical reason as the a priori condition for moral experience (viz. activity). In this way a moral universe is constituted, about which it is possible to make practical judgments.

In summary, a judgment or judging entails at least two features for Kant. Kant writes: "Die Urtheilskraft überhaupt ist das Vermögen, das Besondere als enthalten unter dem Allgemeinen zu denken" (KdU, p. xxvi). A judgment entails always an assertion about "something," about a content, about a particular. Conversely and secondly, the particular content is subsumed under a general concept. Concerning the "object" of transcendental philosophy Kant contends:

> So weit Begrifie a priori ihre Anwendung haben, so weit reicht der Gebrauch unseres Erkenntnißvermögens nach Principien und mit ihm der Philosophie....
> Unser gesammtes Erkenntnißvermögen hat zwei Gebiete, das der Naturbegriffe und das des Freiheitsbegriffs; denn durch beide ist es a priori gesetzgebend. Die Philosophie theilt sich nun auch diesem gemäß in die theoretische und die praktische.... Die Gesetzgebung durch Naturbegriffe geschieht durch den Verstand und ist theoretisch. Die Gesetzgebung durch den Frieheitsbegriff geschieht von der Vernunft und ist bloß praktisch. Verstand und Vernunft haben also zwei verschiedene Gesetzgebungen auf einem und demselben Boden der Erfahrung, ohne daß eine der anderen Eintrag thun darf... (KdU, pp. xvi-xviii).

In the light of the above, the first point to establish for a critical philosophy of aesthetics is: What is the object of a judgment of taste? Or, what determines a judgment to be an aesthetic assertion? Or, more qnerally, what constitutes the aesthetic about which judgments are made?

Let us take any judgment of taste: "This building is beautiful." In Kant's philosophy, such a judgment cannot be a theoretical assertion. Philosophy has not established "beauty" as one of the objectivity constants of "Verstand." Consequently, a judgment of taste cannot be about an objective structure in the phenomenal universe. This means, of course, that Kant rejected the rationalistic attempt to determine beauty metaphysically as a predicate of reality, of objectivity. Also, quite obviously, a judgment of taste is not about the moral quality of practical acts or about the "goodness" of a moral value. In other words beauty is not a principle inherent in "Vernunft." Since beauty is neither a principle of "Verstand" nor of "Vernunft," it cannot be included the "Gestzgebunq" of either the natural or moral universe.

Both theoretical and moral judgments seek to relate a particular content to the respective objectivity constants of each universe. In other words, the material particular is subsumed under the universal form of a given universe, i. e. if judgments about that particular are to be objective. This type of relating is not entailed in a judgment of beauty. Within Kant's discussion of the human mind there is one area about which judgments can be made that has not yet been discussed. The material contents of experience, i. e. Empfindungen, can become the object of assertions. Sensations divide themselves, however, for Kant into two basic classes. Sensations can mediate to the subject information about the world. In other words, objects are given to the human mind in intuition by means of Empfindunqen. Thus an object is given to the human mind via sight qua its color. Sensations can also refer to internal experience, i. e. specifically to the experience of pleasure and/or pain that accompanies the representation of an object. Such internal sensations were called by Kant "Gefühl." Gefühl refers entirely to the status of the subject, albeit as the subject is affected by the object. Kant writes: "Dasjenige Subjective aber an einer Vorstellung, was gar kein Erkenntnißstuck werden kann, ist die mit ihr verbundene Lust oder Unlust; denn durch sie erkenne ich nichts an dem Gegenstande der Vorstellung, obgleich sie wohl die Wirkung irgend einer Erkenntniß sein kann" (KdU, p. xliii).

Once having been affected by an object, the percipient can make judgments about the accompanying feeling of pleasure or pain. Such a judgment cannot be, in Kant's terms, theoretical, i. e. it cannot represent a cognitive grasp of an object, because it does not refer to any predicate of an object. It is precisely the non-cognitive or subjective nature of such a judgment that makes it aesthetic. Kant contends:

> Mit der Wahrnehmung eines Gegenstandes kann unmittelbar der Begriff
> von einem Objecte überhaupt, von welchem jene die empirischen
> Prädicate enthält, zu einem Erkenntnißurtheile verbunden und
> dadurch ein Erfahrungsurtheil erzeugt werden....
> Mit einer Wahrnehmung kann aber auch unmittelbar ein Gefühl der
> Lust (oder Unlust) und ein Wohlgefallen verbunden werden, welches
> die Vorstellung des Objects begleitet und derselben statt Prädicats
> dient, und so ein ästhetisches Urtheil, welches kein Erkenntniß-
> urtheil ist, entspringen (KdU, p. 147).

It is now possible to specify the material content to which aesthetic judgments are directed. Judgments can be called aesthetic which refer to the feeling of the pleasure or pain that accompanies the representation of an object. Kant writes:

> Um zu unterscheiden, ob etwas schön sei oder nicht, beziehen wir
> die Vorstellung nicht durch den Verstand auf das Object zum
> Erkenntnisse, sondern durch die Einbildungskraft...auf das Subject
> und das Gefühl der Lust oder Unlust desselben. Das Geschmacksur-
> theil ist also kein Erkenntnißurtheil, mithin nicht logisch,
> sondern ästhetisch, worunter man dasjenige versteht, dessen Bestim-
> mungsgrund nicht anders als subjectiv sein kann. Alle Beziehung
> der Vorstellungen, selbst die der Empfindungen aber kann objectiv
> sein (und da bedeutet sie das Reale einer empirischen Vorstellung);
> nur nicht auf das Gefühl der Lust and Unlust, wodurch gar nichts im
> Objecte bezeichnet wird, sondern in der das Subject, wie es durch
> die Vorstellung afficirt wird, sich selbst fühlt (KdU, pp. 3-4).

Kant has adopted the British model. That to which the term aesthetic refers is (1) the feeling of pleasure or pain an (2) such feeling is subjective, i. e. it is not a predicate of an object, rather the state of the percipient subject. Subjectivity and feeling are, accordingly, the "object" of an aesthetic judgment. In other words, the principle of life constitutes that about which one judges aesthetically. Kant writes:

> Ein regelmäßiges, zweckmäßiges Gebäude mit seinem Erkenntnißver-
> mögen (es sei in deutlicher oder verworrener Vorstellungsart) zu
> befassen, ist ganz etwas anders, als sich dieser Vorstellung mit
> der Empfindung des Wohlgefallens bewußt zu sein. Hier wird die

Vorstellung gänzlich auf das Subject und zwar auf das Lebensgefühl desselben unter dem Namen des Gefühls der Lust oder Unlust bezogen..." (KdU, p. 4).

The feeling of life is, then, the "object" of aesthetic judgments. The aesthetic judgment: "This building is beautiful" means that the specific building, as it enters consciousness, affects the subject pleasantly, i. e. causes the subject to be conscious of a pleasant feeling. An assertion about this feeling is simply a "Geschmacksurtheil."

Kant would seem to be caught within the confines of empiricism. If judgments of beauty refer to the status of the subject, then aesthetic judgments are particular, empirical, and merely subjective. The judging percipient would simply be making a descriptive statement about his state of feeling, not be asserting anything subsumible under the "objectivity constants" of a universe. What is peculiar of one subject could by no means lay claim to a priori, necessary, and universal validity. In short, the individual's judgment would appear to stand outside of any transcendental justification. It is at this point that Kant deviates from empiricism and takes up, although only to a degree, certain features of an aesthetics of form. In other words, Kant claims that a "Princip a priori" can be found for aesthetic judgments, such that an individual's aesthetic judgment can lay claim to the judgment of other individuals. Kant formulated his task:

> Diese Aufgabe kann auch so vorgestellt werden: Wie ist ein Urtheil möglich, das bloß aus dem eigenen Gefühl der Lust an einem Gegenstande unabhängig von dessen Begriffe diese Lust, als der Vorstellung desselben Objects in jedem andern Subjecte anhängig, a priori, d. i. ohne fremde Beistimmung abwarten zu dürfen, beurtheilte? (KdU, p. 148).

The Formal Object of Aesthetic Judgments (=Aesthetic Objectivity)

A transcendental grounding of a science is for Kant a function of the a priori conditions of consciousness. Because "oneness" or a mode of oneness is a necessary structure of the knowing subject, the subject's cognitive faculty furnishes the "objectivity constants" for the given universe to be known. In other words, knowing in itself is conceived as a type of activity. The subject knows as it makes judgments. Judgments about an aesthetic universe are, however, not judgments about the natural or moral universe. A priori oneness, if it is to ground transcendentally an aesthetic universe, cannot be "inserted" into the manifold of nature or of practical acts, but must reside in the subject itself, i. e. in the judging subject. Judgment as the form of judging activity must itself contain a "Princip a priori" for its own activity. In other words, not the "object" judged (=Gefühl der Lust oder Unlust), rather the very form of the aesthetic judgment about Gefühl is what can possibly ground a scientific aesthetics. Gefühl remains the material content (in this sense the "object") of aesthetic judgments. As such, however, Gefühl per se does not generate an "aesthetic universe." Any universe for Kant must be a function of necessary, a priori and universal principles. And feeling in its empirical content is always contingent and particular. Only form can constitute a manifold as a universe.

The form (or objectivity constant) of an aesthetic universe cannot lie in Gefühl as the content (manifold) of aesthetic awareness, rather only in the reflective act whereby the percipient subject determines itself to its affective contents. The difference between the judgments "X is sweet (to me)" and "X is beautiful (to all)", i. e. the difference between a subjective and empirical judgment and a transcendental and necessary judgment of taste, resides in the manner (or form of the manner) or judging Gefühl.

Before I specify further Kant's solution to the problem of a "critical" aesthetics, I should like to recall a point made above. The objectivity constant of the natural universe was for Kant Verbindung. The notion of Verbindung entails two sub-concepts. First of all, Verbindung refers to the unity, oneness, or form that is inserted into a manifold in order to transform the manifold into an objective universe. Verbindung also entails a second and dynamic meaning, i. e. it refers to the synthesizing activity of the self as it participates in the generation of a universe to be known. The synthetic unity of a universe is a function of the analytical unity of the self. But this analytical unity is not the static oneness of rationalism, rather it is precisely the synthesizing activity of the self. The form of such self-activity is of course the a priori, necessary, and universal constants of any universe. The emphasis must be placed in Kant's critical philosophy not upon the static notion of unity, rather upon the activity, or spontaneity of thinking itself. That the Verbindung is legislative for objectivity is not derived from the object, "weil sie ein Actus seiner Selbsttätigkeit ist" (KdrV, B, p. 130). In other words, knowledge consists in the mediation to the self of its own "Selbsttätigkeit."[27] Implicit in this position is the thesis that the final goal knowledge is the knowing of this pure "Selbsttätigkeit."

This goal casts light upon the deeper meaning of the principle of life in Kant's philosophy. Life is not merely an empirical awareness, even of the pleasure of moral acts, rather it is a universal forming power that seeks self-awareness. It is this deeper notion of life that Kant integrates into his aesthetic theory as its transcendental grounding. Vollkommenheit was the universal and necessary manifestation of objective being in rationalism. Furthermore, Vollkommenheit constitutes the principle of form. Kant appropriates this principle of form and subjectivizes it, i. e. refers it to the perfection of the subject. The subject is in its depths oriented towards universal and necessary oneness. Aesthetic awareness entails in some way the Vollkommenheit of the Kantian self (=the principle of objective unity).

Kant integrates this "critical" notion into his philosophy in his doctrine of the "Urtheilskraft." Kant, as noted above, defined the Urtheilskraft as the faculty of thinking the particular as contained under the universal. Verstand and Vernunft furnish principles by means of which judgment can subsume the particular under the universal form of either the natural or practical universe. However, in itself the Urtheilskraft, Kant contends, also contains its own "Princip a priori" and therefore must be viewed as the third cognitive faculty.

There is, moreover, a deeper meaning to the Urtheilskraft. The Urtheilskraft is not only a faculty, but it also entails the very "life" principle of Selbsttätigkeit.[28] The Urtheilskraft functions under the direction of Verstand or Vernunft by simply subsuming the particular under the universal concept furnished by either faculty. This act is one of the conceptual determination. But the Urtheilskraft can also be faced with a particular for which it has been given no universal, for which it must seek universality. This type of activity was called "reflective" by Kant. Reflective judging reveals itself to be the demand for total unity (=the manifestation of the synthetic power of the self). For example, Verstand guarantees that "nature" must be structured by the objectivity constant of causality. But causality is simply a "form" of nature, it does not reveal specific causal laws (e.g. gravity). Consequently, the myriad of empirical laws in nature can possibly conflict with each other. In other words, Verstand does not guarantee that the material laws of causality must be self-consistent. If they are not, however, nature will not be a totally unified universe. It is precisely such all-encompassing unity that the principle of the Urtheilskraft demands. This demand constitutes the a priori principle the Urtheilskraft. Kant writes:

> Allein es sind so mannigfaltige Formen der Natur, gleichsam so viele Modificationen der allgemeinen transcendentalen Naturbegriffe, die durch jene Gesetze, welche der reine Verstand a priori giebt, weil dieselben nur auf die Möglichkeit einer Natur...überhaupt gehen, unbestimmt gelassen werden, daß dafür doch auch Gesetze sein müssen, die zwar als empirische nach unserer Verstandeseinsicht zufällig sein mögen, die aber doch, wenn sie Gesetze heißen sollen..., aus einem, wenn gleich uns unbekannten, Prinzip der Einheit des Mannigfaltigen als nothwendig angesehen werden müssen. Die reflectirende Urtheilskraft, die von dem Besondern in der Natur zum Allgemeinen aufzusteigen die Obliegenheit hat, bedarf also eines Princips, welches sie nicht von der Erfahrung entlehnen kann...Ein solches transcendentales Princip kann also die reflectirende Urtheilskraft sich nur selbst geben...(KdU, pp. xxvi-xxvii).

This demand for total unity is ultimately a demand that the universe should be structured according to the exigencies of the cognitive needs (=life) of the human self. Kant contends: "[D]ie besondern empirischen Gesetze...[müssen] betrachtet werden, als ob gleichfalls ein Verstand.. sie zum Behuf unserer Erkenntnißvermögen, um ein System der Erfahrung nach besonderen Naturgesetzen möglich zu machen, gegeben hätte (KdU, p. xxvii). Such a demand requires in effect that nature be constructed according to the purpose of realizing the exigencies of the human mind. Purposiveness is, accordingly, the a priori principle directing the Urtheilskraft. "[S]o muß die Urtheilskraft, die in Ansehung der Dinge unter möglichen (noch zu entdeckenden) empirischen Gesetzen bloß reflectirend ist, die Natur in Ansehung der letzteren nach einem Princip der Zweckmäßigkeit für unser Erkenntnißvermögen denken, welches dann in obigen Maximen der Urtheilskraft ausgedrükt wird" (KdU, p. xxxiv). Selbsttätigkeit - the ground and goal (Zweck) of knowledge - is so structured that it requires the manifold to exhibit a "form" that manifests the self's inner essence. Such a transcendental principle is not "objective" in the Kantian sense, i.e. it does not legislate for an objective universe of nature, rather it is simply determinant for the way that the Urtheilskraft must function for itself. "Die Urtheilskraft hat also auch ein Princip a priori für die Möglichkeit der Natur, aber nur in subjectiver Rücksicht in sich, wodurch sie nicht der Natur (als Autonomie), sondern ihr selbst (als Heautonomie) für die Reflexion über jene, ein Gesetz vorschreibt..." (KdU, p. xxxvii). Zweckmäßigkeit is the principle (or form) of how the mind must judgmentally look at any contents, not an objective principle of how the objects must necessarily appear. Consequently, the universe of the Urtheilskraft is ultimately its own acts. It is, however, legislative hence a transcendental ground for this universe.

Pleasure (or pain) arises in human consciousness when an object affects perfectingly (or unperfectingly) the self's subjectively grounded needs. In other words, when the self is enabled by an object to function in a manner that realizes the needs of its subjectivity, it will experience pleasure. For example, an object that fulfills the physiological structure of an individual, will set the physiological self into a state such that the self feels the sensation of pleasure. However, all judgments about such pleasures can only be contingent, empirical, and relative. The physiological structure of individuals differ (however slightly) and hence the reaction of different individuals to the same stimulus will vary. Furthermore, an agreement in judgment in such matters can only be accidental. In other words, agreement cannot be demanded as an a priori condition of awareness.

There is, however, one class of judgments about Gefühl which is necessarily connected with the a priori condition of consciousness. When the self that is structured for a given need becomes aware of an object that fulfills the need, the self will experience pleasure. Now the human self, because it necessarily possesses an Urtheilskraft, is a priorily bound to need to experience design or purposiveness. Should an object (or a complex of objects) be so formed that it appears to embody purposiveness, it must necessarily and universally affect pleasantly the percipient subject. In other words, such pleasure must be universally valid for every individual because it arises out of the relationship between the transcendental structure of subjectivity per se and the form of an object necessarily demanded by subjectivity. Kant writes:

> Die Erreichung jeder Absicht ist mit dem Gefühl der Lust verbunden; und ist die Bedingung der ersten eine Vorstellung a priori, wie hier ein Princip für die reflectirende Urtheilskraft überhaupt, so ist das Gefühl der Lust auch durch einen Grund a priori und für jedermann gültig bestimmt: und zwar bloß durch die Beziehung des Objects auf das Erkenntnißvermögen...
> ...Es gehört also etwas, das in der Beurtheilung der Natur auf die Zweckmäßigkeit derselben für unsern Verstand aufmerksam macht, ein Studium ungleichartige Gesetze derselben wo möglich unter höhere, obwohl immer noch empirische, zu bringen, dazu, um, wenn es gelingt, an dieser Einstimmung derselben für unser Erkenntnißvermögen, die wir als bloß zufällig ansehen, Lust zu empfinden (KdU, pp. xxxix-xl).

Gefühl that is produced in the manner just described is subject to necessary and universal judgments. In other words, aesthetic judgments about Gefühl do not determine whether a specific feeling is pleasant or not (that is an immediate function of empirical awareness), rather they assert that a given pleasure, bounded up with the awareness of the form of purposiveness of an object, ought to be felt as pleasant by every one, i. e. be judged beautiful by everyone.

Also ist es nicht die Lust, sondern die Allgemeingültigkeit dieser Lust, die mit der bloßen Beurtheilung eines Gegenstandes im Gemüthe als verbunden wahrgenommen wird, welche a priori als allgemeine Regel für die Urtheilskraft, für jedermann gültig, in einem Geschmacksurtheile vorgestellt wird. Es ist ein empirisches Urtheil: daß ich einen Gegenstand mit Lust wahrnehme und beurtheile, Es ist aber ein Urtheil a priori: daß ich ihn schön finde, d. i. jenes Wohlgefallen jedermann als nothwendig ansinnen darf.
....Wenn eingeräumt wird, daß in einem reinen Geschmacksurtheile das Wohlgefallen an dem Gegenstande mit der bloßen Beurtheilung seiner Form verbunden sei: so ist es nichts anders, als die subjective Zweckmäßigkeit derselben für die Urtheilskraft, welche wir mit der Vorstellung des Gegenstandes im Gemüthe verbunden empfinden...[S]o muß eine Vorstellung mit diesen Bedingungen der Urtheilskraft als für jedermann gültig a priori angenommen werden können (KdU, pp. 150-151).

Zweckmäßigkeit as the form of an object perceived is the "cause" of the aesthetic pleasure felt. Because of this connection between the perceived object and the experienced pleasure, Kant often extends the designation beauty to the object itself. Thus Kant can contend: "Schönheit ist Form der Zweskmäßigkeit eines Gegenstandes..." (KdU, p. 61). Such an ascription of beauty to the object is only an analogous extension of the concept of beauty. The aesthetic universe consists of judgments about the feelings of subjectivity under specific conditions. One such condition is the non-conceptual appearance of the form of purposiveness in an object. As such the object can be analogously designated as beautiful This, however, is not a "proper" use of the aesthetic category. The aesthetic universe refers to the evaluation of Gefühl made by the Urtheilskraft under the conditions of perceiving the non-conceptual form of purposiveness. In other words, the aesthetic universe refers to the conditions of the judging self when the very transcendental and hence universal Selbsttätigkeit of the self's faculties is harmoniously affected by the form of an object. A judgment of taste is directed at the perfection of the transcendental status of the self. This assertion necessarily entails universal validity. It is not too far off to say that the aesthetic judgment is concerned with the subjective feeling viz. empirical awareness of the self's supersensible power of forming, of the Kantian principle of life. In this way "form" and "life" coalesce, are united, and are reconciled in the aesthetic experience. This world creating power of life necessarily generates an aesthetic universe in which the "objectivity constants" of universal and necessary validity reign.

I shall bring my exposition of Kant's aesthetic to a close at this point. Any further discussion would add nothing more relative to the problem of Schiller's aesthetics. The above discussion of Kant should be adequate to grasp his meaning for Schiller.[29] At this point, I shall turn to Schiller.

E. Schiller's "Aesthetic" Universe

Schiller's Relationship to 18th Century Aesthetics

In his published letters to Gottfried Körner (1793), entitled Kallias oder über die Schönheit (1793), Schiller related himself in a summary manner to the aesthetic schools of the 18th century. Schiller writes:

Es ist interessant zu bemerken, daß meine Theorie eine vierte
mögliche Form ist, das Schöne zu erklären. Entweder man erklärt es
objecktiv oder subjektiv; und zwar entweder sinnlich subjektiv
(wie Burke u.a.), oder subjektiv rational (wie Kant), oder
rational objektiv (wie Baumgarten, Mendelssohn und die ganze Schar
der Vollkommenheitsmänner), oder endlich sinnlich objektiv: Ein
Terminus, wobei Du dir freilich jetzt noch nicht viel wirst denken
können, außer wenn Du die drei andern Formen miteinander
vergleichst.30

I shall work out briefly just such a comparison.

Schiller considered that each one of the previous theories encompassed
part of the truth. But each theory was, nevertheless, onesided, and it is
this one-sidedness that constitutes its error. "Jede dieser vorhergehenden
Theorien hat einen Teil der Erfahrung für sich und enthält offenbar einen
Teil der Wahrheit, und der Fehler scheint bloß zu sein, daß man diesen Teil
der Schönheit, der damit übereinstimmt, für die Schönheit selbst genommen
hat" (KB, p. 394-395).   The onesidedness of each theory allows for a
comparison.

Burke or the aesthetics of life places the aesthetic in the very
subjectivity of the percipient subject. Moreover, the aesthetic is in the
subject as a manifestation of the subject's affectibility, i. e. of the
ability to feel pleasure or pain. In this sense, the aestheticians of life,
compared with the Vollkommenheitsmänner who sought a rationally objective
determination of the beautiful, constitute progress. The Burkeans etc. have
a point in locating the aesthetic in man's "Sinnlichkeit," rather than in his
reason. "Der Burkianer hat gegen den Wolfianer vollkommen recht, daß er die
Unmittelbarkeit des Schönen, seine Unabhängigkeit von Begriffen behauptet..."
(KB, p. 395). However, the locating of the aesthetic in the mere sensate life
of the subject is too onesided in that it limits the aesthetic to the
particular "Sinnlichkeit" of an individual.   From this point of view,
aesthetic theory cannot generate any universality or necessity, as Kant
clearly saw. "[A]ber[der Burkianer] hat unrecht gegen den Kantianer, daß er
es in die bloße Affektibilität der Sinnlichkeit setzt" (KB, p. 395). Kant
also located the aesthetic in subjectivity. However, Kant showed that
subjectivity itself evinces a rational structure. This structure generates
universality in judgments of taste. The interpretation of subjectivity as a
forming universality constitutes an advance over the aesthetics of life.
However, Kant's aesthetics is onesided relative to the object that causes the
aesthetic experience. Kant, and correctly according to Schiller, sought to
free the aesthetic object from any conceptual determination. Therefore,
beauty cannot be Vollkommenheit. Vollkommenheit is a conceptual determination of rationality. But Kant went too far in freeing the aesthetic from
conceptuality. A mere play of form was for Kant the essence of a pure
aesthetic judgment. If the perceived object, e.g. the human form, should
easily entail conceptualization, it could not, according to Kant, be the
object of pure aesthetic experience. According to Schiller, Kant contends,
"daß also eine Arabeske und was ihr ähnlich ist, als Schönheit betrachtet,
reiner sei als die höchste Schönheit des Menschen.   Ich finde, daß sine
Bermerkung den großen Nutzen haben kann, das Logische von dem Ästhetischen
zu scheiden, aber eigentlich scheint sie mir doch den Begriff der Schönheit
völlig in zu verfehlen" (KB, p. 395).   Kant is, accordingly, onesided in

locating the aesthetic simply in the subject, however rational the subject be interpreted. In the last analysis, the Vollkommenheitsmänner are correct in situating the aesthetic in the object. They are onesided and hence wrong in their attempt to explain such a location in terms of reason. That which is "sinnlich" cannot be reduced, even as "Undeutlichkeit," to a "Vernunftprincip." In this sense, an adequate aesthetics must be "sinnlich" for Schiller. However, this fact does not exclude it from also being "objektiv." The aesthetic is in some sense inherent in the object or forms from the object and is, hence objective.

> Denn eben darin zeigt sich die Schönheit in ihrem höchsten Glanz, wenn sie die logische Natur ihres Objekts überwindet, und wie kann sie überwinden, wo kein Widerstand ist? Wie kann sie dem völlig formlosen Stoff ihre Form erteilen? Ich bin wenigstens überzeugt, daß die Schönheit nur die Form einer Form ist...(KB, p. 395).

Insofar as the aesthetic is the form of a form (of an object), it is objective. In the ensuing I shall seek to explain what Schiller meant. Suffice to say, it will be shown that "lebende Gestalt" is precisely this form of a form and hence an objective appearance. This thesis concerning objectivity connects Schiller with the Vollkommenheitsmänner. In his own way Schiller was able to combine, to reconcile the aesthetics of form, the aesthetics of life, and Kant's critical aesthetics into a higher synthesis of living form.

Schiller's "Transcendental" Intent

Before Schiller explains his theory of living form in his Über die ästhetische Erziehung des Menschen, he explicitly sets forth an investigatory procedure similar to Kant's (as described above).[31] Schiller explicitly rejects the contention that empirical experience should be the source from which to develop a theory of aesthetics. "Aber vielleicht ist die Erfahrung der Richterstuhl nicht, vor welchem sich eine Frage wie diese ausmachen läßt."[32] The reason why empirical instances of art works cannot ground an adequate aesthetic theory resides in the fact that the individual instance itself must be judged by some general criteria, if beauty is to be more than purely individual feeling. Individual cases are always contingent, and the contingent cannot yield universal, necessary, and a priori knowledge. It is only by means of universally valid truth that the ideal scope of aesthetics can be determined and the individual case be judged. Furthermore, the universally necessary can only be obtained by means of a transcendental analysis of the a priori conditions of aesthetic experience. Such an analysis is a conceptual process, not simply the reporting of individual experience. "Zwar wird uns dieser transcendentale Weg eine Zeitlang aus dem traulichen Kreis der Erscheinungen und aus der lebendigen Gegenwart der Dinge entfernen und auf dem nackten Gefild abgezogener Begriffe verweilen" (AEM, x, p. 600). And aesthetic experience, like all forms of experience, is only possible by a subject. Hence a transcendental analysis of aesthetics requires a conceptual analysis of the structure of the subject. The subjective foundation of aesthetic experience is, moreover, human nature. Consequently, the formal and ideal essence of all aesthetic experience can be determined by an abstract and conceptual investigation of human nature. "Zu dem reinen Begriff der Menschheit müssen wir uns also nunmehr erheben" (AEM, x., p. 600).

Moreover, human nature in its most abstract or transcendental structure entails for Schiller (as it does for Kant) an aspect that is "sinnlich" and an aspect that is "vernünftig." The theoretical analysis of beauty must show that beauty arises out of and is grounded in this transcendental essence.

Dieser reine Vernunftbegriff der Schönheit, wenn ein solcher sich aufzeigen ließe, müßte also - weil er aus keinem wirklichen Falle geschöpft werden kann, vielmehr unser Urteil über jeden wirklichen Fall erst berichtigt und leitet - auf dem Wege der Abstraktion gesucht und schon aus der Möglichkeit der sinnlich-vernünftigen Natur gefolgert werden können: mit einem Wort: die Schönheit müßte sich als eine notwendige Bedingung der Menschheit aufzeigen lassen (AEM, x, p. 600).

Schiller's intended approach to aesthetic theory entails the analysis of the abstract (=transcendental) notion of human nature for the purpose of ascertaining the absolute a priori conditions of astheitc experience and then, once these conditions are undertsood, to explain the nature of the aesthetic universe and how it is brought about.

In seeking to explain Schiller's aesthetics I will first pay attention to the AEM. This work concentrates upon the transcendental ground of aesthetic experience. Some reference, to be sure, is made to the aesthetic object. Indeed, the notion of living form is evolved. Nevertheless, the emphasis rests upon the dynamics of human nature in the aesthetic experience, rather than upon the object that is experienced. In order to grasp the features of the beautiful object I will turn to the KB. In this work Schiller delineates the objective structure of the beautiful object. However, this work lacks an adequate transcendental grounding. Such a foundation is found in the AEM. In my judgment, both works are basically commensurate with each other. Indeed, the one compliments and supplements the other. Together they reveal a relatively coherent aesthetic theory, an aesthetics of living form. At any rate, my interpretation of Schiller's aesthetics is the product of my attempt to integrate both works together.

Schiller's Transcendental Grounding of Aesthetics

Schiller's concept of human nature has much in common with Kant's. For Kant (and for Schiller) experience involves a manifold held together in a synthetic unity. In all experience there is a plurality of determinations that are woven together to form a synthetic whole. The synthetic unity is only possible as an object for the transcendental and analytical unity of consciousness Thus, from the point of view of the transcendental subject, there is present to it a multitude of concrete perceptions. Moreover, the subject can only be determined to individual representations as long as it maintains a permanent or on-going unity of consciousness In other words, a subject can be said to be determined in a plurality of cases only insofar as it is the same subject in each case of determination. In more abstract terms, plurality is only possible by means of unity. Plurality and unity are correlative notions. Schiller uses these correlative notions in the formulation of this most basic conceptualization of human nature. "Wenn die Abstraktion so hoch, als sie immer kann, hinaufsteigt, so gelangt sie zu zwei letzten Begriffen, bei denen sie stille stehen und ihre Grenzen bekennen muß. Sie unterscheidet in dem Menschen etwas, das bleibt, und etwas, das sich unaufhörlich verändert. Das Bleibende nennt sie seine Person, das Wechselnde seinen Zustand" (AEM, xi, p. 601).

Schiller's Person is the necessary subject of all conditions or determinations that the human mind experiences. In God, as an infinite being, the subject of experience and the material of experience are essentially the same. "In dem absoluten Subjekt allein beharren mit der Persönlichkeit auch alle ihre Bestimmungen, weil sie aus der Persönlichkeit fließen. Alles, was die Gottheit ist, ist sie deswegen, weil sie ist; sie ist folglich alles auf ewig, weil sie ewig ist" (AEM, xi, p. 601). But man as a finite being must receive the material of his experience from without. As a Kantian, Schiller believed that the subject and the object are necessary and correlative terms. There can be no subject without an object and the reverse. Thus, if man is not to remain a pure possibility (but to exist), man must be actualized, i. e. made a real subject of some objective material. As a finite being man must receive this material from without. Furthermore, since man as a subject is finite, he cannot grasp an infinite matter, rather he must grasp matter in separate, successive, and limited amounts. Successive determination is only possible within time, time is the absolute condition for succession.[13]

The Person itself does not partake in time or succession as it is the absolute condition for time. "Die Person, die sich in dem ewig beharrenden Ich und nur in diesem offenbart, kann nicht werden, nicht anfangen in der Zeit, weil vielmehr umgekehrt die Zeit in ihr anfangen, weil dem Wechsel ein Beharrliches zum Grunde liegen muß. Etwas muß sich verändern, wenn Veränderung sein soll: dieses Etwas kann also nicht selbst Veränderung sein" (AEM, xi, p. 602). As the unchanging Ich, the self is a noumenon: ". . . denn der Mensch ist nicht bloß Person überhaupt, sondern Person, die sich in einem bestimmten Zustand befindet. Aller Zustand aber, alles bestimmte Dasein entsteht in der Zeit, und so muß also der Mensch, als Phänomen, einen Anfang nehmen, obgleich die reine Intelligenz in ihm ewig ist" (AEM, xi, p. 602). Schiller has, obviously enough, constructed a Kantian interpretation of human nature. Man in his determined aspects is phenomenal while in his unchanging he is noumenal. Both aspects are necessary for man's existence. "Ohne die Zeit, das heißt, ohne es zu werden, würde [der Mensch] nie ein bestimmtes Wesen sein; seine Persönlichkeit würde zwar in der Anlage, aber nicht in der That existieren" (AEM, xi, p. 602).

As a subject the human Person is confronted with a plurality of empirical contents and hence it is determined in various ways by this ever changing matter. "Diesen in ihm wechselnden Stoff begleitet sein niemals wechselndes Ich - und in allem Wechsel beständig er selbst zu bleiben, alle Wahrnehmungen zur Erfahrung, d. h. zur Einheit der Erkenntnis, und jede der Erscheinungsarten in der Zeit zum Gesetz für alle Zeiten zu machen, ist die Vorschrift, die durch seine vernünftige Natur ihm gegeben ist" (AEM, xi, p. 602). Man as the absolute subject of the manifold needs "in allem Wechsel beständig er selbst zu bleiben." This imperative is essentially a demand to form a manifold into a manifestation of the Person. "[D]er Mensch formt die Materie, wenn er...Beharrlichkeit im Wechsel behauptet und die Mannigfaltigkeit der Welt der Einheit seines Ichs unterwürfig macht" (AEM, xi, p. 603).

Schiller has in effect transformed Kant's transcendental unity of apperception, conceived as a universal prerequisite for any experience, into an existential requirement for empirical life. The self as Person is, so to speak, torn asunder by the matter that limits it to a specific series of representations at specific times and specific places. If the self were nothing more than these determinations, it would, indeed, be like Hume's self. For Hume, human beings "are nothing but a bundle or collection of different perceptions, which succeed each other with an inconceivable rapidity, and are in a perpetual flux and movement" (Treatise, I, 4:6). But the self, because of its unity and its existential imperative, takes this manifold and unites it into a synthetic unity as a phenomenal object for its own transcendental and analytical unity. Thus the centrifugal tendency of the manifold is overcome by the centripetal force of the self's forming activity. The unification of the manifold to form a unified experience for the self as Person is only possible by means of the categories of reason. The self's vernünftige Natur is that by means of which the Person unites the manifold. Therefore, it is only by having a rational nature that the self can give form to the manifold and maintain its permanence. "Giving form" and "maintaining permanence" are necessary and correlative notions for Schiller. It is only by "giving form" that the self's permanence is maintained. In essence, the self's permanence is its ordering activity.[34]

Schiller has obviously adopted Kant's notion of the self as exposited above. The self exists as a permanent subject only, insofar as it is active by giving form to matter. The idea of the self as a lawgiver gives rise to the "Idee des absoluten, in sich selbst gegründeten Seins, d. i. die Freiheit" (AEM, xi, p. 601). Thus Schiller's self has as its basis, as its generative or dynamic power, Kant's critical principle of life. It is because it is governed by the principle of autonomy that the Person seeks to maintain its permanence by forming the chaotic manifold that is presented to it. Therefore, there flows from the nature of the Person a demand that constitutes one of the two fundamental laws of human nature. This law "dringt auf absolute Formalität: [der Mensch] soll alles in sich vertilgen, was bloß Welt ist, und Übereinstimmung in alle seine Veränderungen bringen: mit andern Worten: er soll alles Innere veräußern und alles Äußere formen" (AEM), xi, p. 603). It is only insofar as the self seeks formality that the self can remain permanent. That which must maintain its sameness or permanence must direct its activity towards that which is identical, i. e. form. Thus the internal existential imperative of the Person, when used as the a priori principle of the self's activity vis-a-vis the given manifold of experience, results in a striving for form. Schiller has very skillfully transformed the self's existential imperative into a psychological drive. The psychic integrity of the self results in a conscious drive for formality. Schiller calls this drive man's Formtrieb. This drive "geht aus von dem absoluten Dasein des Menschen oder von seiner vernünftigen Natur, und ist bestrebt, . . . bei allem Wechsel des Zustandes seine Person zu behaupten" (AEM, xii, p. 605).

This drive is at the basis for man's drive to be moral. To be moral is to act according to universal law. In short morality gives permanence, continuity, or form to man's practical activity. This drive is also behind man's longing to know truth. To know truth is to be conscious of the permanent and unchanging in experience. In more general terms, this drive is behind all human activity that is in any way related to order. It interests man in that which is permanent, universal, or formal in experience. Conversely, the formal is that which is the object of Formtrieb. Concerning the object of the Formtrieb Schiller writes: "Der Gegenstand des Formtriebes, in einem allgemeinen Begriff ausgedrückt, heißt Gestalt, sowohl in uneigentlicher als in eigentlicher Bedeutung; ein Begriff, der alle formalen Beschaffenheiten der Dinge und all Beziehungen derselben auf die Denkkräfte unter sich faßt" (AEM, xv, p. 614).

From the above exposition it is obvious that Schiller has, with his notions of Formtrieb and Gestalt, developed a position similar to that of the rationalists. According to rationalism that to which the self is attracted is form. Schiller's Gestalt has all the characteristics of the rationalist's form. It is orderly, universal, and connective. It excludes anything that is contingent, isolated, and non-connective. Therefore, it excludes sensation. For the rationalist, form constitutes the dynamic principle for all activity or appetition on the part of the self. Similarly, Schiller postulates his famous Fromtrieb. On the metaphysical level the rationalists maintained that reality is orderly or formal. Schiller too makes order into the Daseingrund for the Person. Thus far Schiller's conception of the self constitutes a transcendental justification of the rationalist's principle of form. Schiller's theory differs from the rationalists's in that form is not the whole of his theory. Sensation and emotional pleasure were for Schiller not unclearly perceived and unclearly enjoyed form (cf. Leibniz), not even analogous to form (cf. Baumgarten). Instead, they have a nature all their own that is independent of all formality. This second part of human nature must now be investigated.

As a Person the self is oriented to the formal, universal, and unchanging. Further, insofar as the self is oriented to that which is permanent in all possible experience, the self is interested in the infinite. But this orientation however unlimited, is mere potentiality unless it is actualized by some object. In a state of potentiality the self can be determined to an infinite number of possibilities. "Der Zustand des menschlichen Geistes vor aller Bestimmung, die ihm durch Eindrücke der Sinne gegeben wird, ist eine Bestimmtbarkeit ohne Grenze" (AEM, xix, p. 627). Without having any matter to actuate its potentiality, the self's infinite determinability must remain empty. "[S]o kann man diesen Zustand der Bestimmungslosigkeit eine leere Unendlichkeit nennen, welches mit einer unendlichen Leere keineswegs zu verwechseln ist" (AEM, xix, p. 627). Therefore, besides the self's Person, it also has Zustand, i. e. the state of being determined by matter. It is only insofar as the self is determined, that it is (exists). Therefore, the Zustand is an absolutely necessary correlative to the Person. Person and Zustand together constitute the a priori and hence universally necessary conditions for the existence of a human self and, therefore, they are the transcendental concepts involved in explanation of human experience.

The Zustand, i. e. the state of being determined, is only possible because something outside the self supplies the potential self with a matter that determines it. The subjective correlative on the self's part to the matter furnished is the capacity to be affected, i. e. to feel or to receive. "Die Materie der Thätigkeit also oder die Realität, welche die höchste Intelligenz aus sich selber schöpft, muß der Mensch erst empfangen ..." (AEM., xi, p. 602). The matter that the self feels or receives is called by Schiller Realität. This matter constitutes the empirical manifold of the Welt or Natur in which the self finds itself.

The matter experienced by the mind in an act of perception is different from the nature of the Gestalt of the Person's activity. Since the human self is not infinite, it must experience or intuit the matter of consciousness in limited and determinate amounts. The conditions for experiencing limited matter are time and space. Space is the a priori formal prerequisite for the possibility of simultaneous experience of a plurality of matter. Time is the a priori formal condition for the experience of succession of matter. Schiller has an essentially Kantian interterpretation of space and time. Kant believed that the essentially structured matter of experience must in some way be formed before it can become an object to human consciousness. Thus Kant believed that each intuition of the manifold involves the formal aspects of time and space which structure or relate the sensuous manifold together. By abstracting from any specific intuition with its specific content, Kant believed that it could be shown that space and time as the a priori formal aspects of all experience must be represented as an ininite given magnitude. Each limited space of each specific intuition, no matter how great or small, is in space itself and hence a part of space. Each limited space must be viewed as a determination of an undertermined, i. e. infinite space. The same is true of time. Since space and time are infinite magnitudes considered in abstraction from any specific determinate intuition, it is only by limiting the infinite that the specific finite determination that constitutes reality is possible. At the same time, however, the infinite potentiality is destroyed by the determination that reality gives to the self. "Realität ist also da, aber die Unendlichkeit ist verloren. Um eine Gestalt im Raum zu beschreiben, müssen wir den endlosen Raum begrenzen; um uns eine Veränderung in der Zeit vorzustellen, müssen wir das Zeitganze teilen. Wir gelangen also nur durch Schrancken zur Realität, nur durch Negation oder Ausschliessung zur Position oder wirklichen Setzung, durch Aufhebung unserer freien Bestimmbarkeit zu Bestimmung" (AEM, xix, p. 627). The essence of "Realität" is limitation of the universal. The self is actualized only when its potential infinity and universality are negated. The universal self is dissolved into the flux of determinate moments that follow each other in an endless process of becoming.

Da alles, was in der Zeit ist, nacheinander ist, so wird dadurch, daß etwas ist, alles andere ausgeschlossen. Indem man auf einem Instrument einen Ton greift, ist unter allen Tönen, die es möglicher Weise angeben kann, nur dieser einzige wirklich; indem der Mensch das Gegenwärtige empfindet, ist die ganze unendliche Möglichkeit seiner Bestimmungen auf diese einzige Art des Daseins beschränkt . . . der Mensch ist in diesem Zustande nichts als. . . ein erfüllter Moment der Zeit - oder vielmehr, er ist nicht, denn seine Persönlichkeit ist so lange aufgehoben, als ihn die Empfindung beherrscht und die Zeit mit sich fortreißt" (AEM, xii, p. 604).

That which fills up the limited units of time is Empfindung. "Dieser Zustand der bloß erfüllten Zeit heißt Empfindung" (AEM, xii, p. 604). Sensation is limited and successive. It is void of all universality. A specific sensation is felt in a specific time and at a specific place. Hence sensation is radically individual and in no way can it form a basis for universality. "Das Gefühl kann bloß sagen: Das ist wahr für dies Subjekt und in diesem Moment, und ein anderer Moment, ein anderes Subjekt kann kommen, das die Aussage der gegenwärtigen Empfindung zurücknimmt" (AEM, xii, p. 606).

The fact that man in order to be must be determined is the source of the second fundamental law of human nature. This law "dringt auf absolute Realität" (AEM, xi, p. 603). Only insofar as the self receives and seeks matter given to it from outside itself can the self exist. Thus, only insofar as the self undergoes change can it be. The self must have an innate orientation to sensation if it is to exist. This is the self's second existential imperative. Just as Schiller transformed the Person's existential imperative into a psychological drive, he also transforms the Zustand's existential need for sensation into a psychological drive. This drive Schiller called der sinnliche Trieb or the Stofftrieb.

The appetitive orientation that the sensuous self has to the sensuous manifold is one of momentary interest. Just as sensation cannot form the basis for universal truth for the intellect, it cannot form the basis für universal maxims for the will. "Die Neigung kann bloß sagen: Das ist für dein Individuum und für dein jetziges Bedürfnis gut; aber dein Individuum und dein jetziges Bedürfnis wird die Veränderung mit sich fortrießen, und was du jetzt feurig begehrst, dereinst zum Gegenstand deines Abscheues machen" (AEM, xii, p. 606). The sensuous manifold that constitutes the object of the sensuous impulse was called by Schiller Leben. "Der Gegenstand des sinnlichen Triebes, in einem allgemeinen Begriff ausgedrückt, heißt Leben in weitester Bedeutung: ein Begriff, der alles materiale Sein und alle unmittelbare Gegenwart in den Sinnen bedeutet" (AEM, xv, p. 614).

From the above exposition it is obvious that Schiller has, with his notions of Stofftrieb and Leben, developed a position similar to that of the empiricist. According to empiricism that to which the self is attracted is sensuous experience. Schiller's Leben has all the characteristics of sense pleasure. Indeed, Schiller, if anything, is more radical and consistent in his empiricism than Locke, Burke, or even Hume. Sensations are atomistic, isolated, and non-connective. Sensuous experience excludes anything that is orderly, universal, connective, or, in short, formal. For empiricism, sense pleasure (i. e. Leben) constitutes the dynamic principle of activity and appetition on the part of the self. Similarly, Schiller postulates the Stofftrieb. On a metaphysical level the empiricist tended to believe that the ultimate constituent elements of reality are atomistic and radically individual. Schiller makes the self's orientation towards the variety of the manifold (i. e. Zustand) into one of the fundamental principles of existence of the human self. Schiller's theory of Leben differs from empiricism in that this theory does not claim to reveal whole of human nature.

Thus far, Schiller has been able to give a transcendental basis in support of his contention that man feels as well as thinks. Human nature is, therefore, open to both Leben and to Gestalt. But Schiller has succeeded in doing this only at the apparent cost of destroying any internal harmony within man's psychological life. Each of man's basic faculties or laws of his nature have principles that operate totally independent of each other. "Der sinnlich Trieb schließt aus seinem Subjekt alle Selbstthätigkeit und Freiheit, der Formtrieb schließt aus dem seinigen alle Abhängigkeit, alles Leiden aus. Ausschließung der Freiheit ist aber physische, Ausschließung des Leidens ist moralische Notwendigkeit. Beide Triebe nötigen also das Gemüt, jener durch Naturgesetze, dieser durch Gesetze der Vernunft" (AEM, xiv, p. 613).

Not only are both drives by nature totally independent, they tend to be exclusive. The exclusive fulfillment of one drive must make the other drive feel constrained. "Jede auschliessende Herrschaft eines seiner beiden ist für [den Menschen] ein Zustand des Zwanges und der Gewalt. . ." (AEM, xvii, p. 623). Schiller himself gives an example of what he means. "Wenn wir jemand mit Leidenschaft umfassen, der unserer Verachtung würdig ist, so empfinden wir peinlich die Nötigung der Natur. Wenn wir gegen einen andern feindlich gesinnt send, der uns Achtung abnötigt, so empfinden wir peinlich die Nötigung der Vernunft (AEM, xiv, p. 613). Since man's highest destiny is to act morally, man's moral (rational) nature must suppress his sensuous nature in cases of conflict. "Sobald man einen ursprünglichen, mithin notwendigen Antagonism beider Triebe behauptet, so ist freilich kein anderes Mittel, die Einheit im Menschen zu erhalten, als daβ man den sinnlichen Trieb dem vernünftigen unbedingt unterordnet" (AEM, xiii, p. 607).

If man must always suppress his sensuous nature, it would seem, as Kant once suggested, that man would be better off without one.[35] But Schiller's concept of man does not allow for the getting rid of man's sensuous nature. Without sense determination man would not exist. "Sinnlichkeit" is part of man's transcendental nature and, hence, sensuous demands cannot be ignored. Thus Schiller is faced with the apparent dilemma of contradictory demands. He attempts to overcome this dilemma by maintaining that a middle way must be found through which both drives can work together in a complimentary manner rather than in an antagonistic manner.[36] Indeed, the very transcendental notion of human nature demands such a harmony. "Die Vernunft stellt aus transcendentalen Gründen die Forderung auf: es soll eine Gemeinschaft zwischen Formtrieb und Stofftreib. . . sein, weil nur die Einheit [der beiden Triebe]. . . den Begriff der Menschheit vollendet" (AEM, xv, p. 615). The unity of both drives constitutes "im eigentlichsten Sinne des Worts die Idee seiner Menschheit" (AEM, xiv, p. 612).

The Aesthetic as "Lebende Gestalt"

It is by means of the notion of harmony that Schiller's transcendental analysis of human nature leads him, as it did Kant, to the field of aesthetics. In Schiller's opinion, this middle state of harmony is the aesthetic state itself. "Sobald [die Vernunft] demnach den Ausspruch thut: es soll eine Menschheit existieren, so hat sie eben dadurch das Gesetz aufgestellt: es soll seine Schönheit sein" (AEM, xv, p. 615). Therefore, from this point on in his analysis, Schiller's theory of human nature is also a theory of aesthetics.

The question automatically arises as to just how Schiller can bring about this aesthetic middle state, especially when Schiller asserts that a third drive that is neither sensuous nor rational, rather in between, is impossible. "[E]in dritter Grundtrieb, der biede vermitteln könnte, ist schlechterdings ein undenkbarer Begriff" (AEM, xiii, pp. 606-607). The difference between sensuous determination and rational determining is infinite. There is no middle point between the principle of heteronomy and of autonomy. Therefore, there can be no middle state or drive that is toto genere different from both states. This raises an important question.

Wie heben wir nun diesen Widerspruch? Die Schönheit verknüpft die
zwei entgegengesetzten Zustände des Empfindens und des Denkens und
doch giebt es schlechterdings kein Mittleres zwischen beiden.
Jenes ist durch Erfahrung, dieses ist unmittelbar durch Vernunft
gewiß.
   Dies ist der eigentliche Punkt, auf den zuletzt die ganze
Frage über die Schönheit hinausläuft, und gelingt es uns, dieses
Problem befriedigend aufzulösen, so haben wir zugliech den Faden
gefunden, der uns durch das ganze Labyrinth der Aesthetik führt
(AEM, xviii, p. 625).

Schiller's solution is to suggest that a middle position is to be
obtained by combining, indeed, integrating the two drives in such a way that
both drives can be active, yet their antagonistic opposition is overcome.
"Jene zwei entgegengesetzten Zustände verbindet die Schönheit und hebt also
die Entgegensetzung auf.   Weil aber beide Zustände einander ewig
entgegengesetzt bleiben, so sind sie nicht anders zu verbinden, als, indem
sie aufgehoben werden.   Unser zweites Geschäft ist also, diese Verbindung
vollkommen zu machen, sie so rein und vollständig durchzuführen, daß beide
Zustände in einem dritten gänzlich verschwinden, und keine Spur der Teilung
in dem Ganzen zurückbleibt; sonst vereinzeln wir, aber vereinigen nicht"
(AEM, xviii, p. 625).[37]

Schiller's aesthetic state in which man is conscious of aesthetic
experience is a continuation of the reconciliatory tendencies of Kantian
philosophy.   Kant claims to show that sensate matter, when combined with form
(space and time), results in empirical experience and that the manifold of
empirical experience, when combined with the pure forms of the understanding,
results in experience of objects.   Similarly, Schiller seeks to show that
sensuous matter when it is combined with the form of man's rational nature
results in a new and distinct experience called beauty.   Although this middle
state is different from the sensuous and rational states, it is not a simple
and irreducible state, rather it is the result of the fusing together of the
two states.

Just as he postulated a Formtrieb as a result of the demands of man's
Person, and a Stofftrieb as a result of the demands of man's Zustand,
Schiller postulated a specific drive for the working together of the form and
sensuous drives.   "Derjenige Trieb also, in welchem beide verbunden wirken,
. . . ist der Spieltrieb . . . (AEM, xiv, p. 612).[38]   This drive when
fulfilled represents the fulfillment of human nature.

Just as the object of the Formtrieb is Gestalt and the object of
Stofftrieb is Leben, the object of the Spieltrieb is lebende Gestalt. "Der
Gegenstand des Spieltriebes in einem allgemeinen Schema vorgestellt wird also
lebende Gestalt heißen können; ein Begriff, der allen ästhetischen
Beschaffenheiten der Erscheinungen und, mit einem Worte, dem, was man in
weitester Bedeutung Schönheit nennt, zur Bezeichnung dient" (AEM, xv, p.
614). Beauty is neither mere form, nor mere life.   "Nun spricht aber die
Vernunft: das Schöne soll nicht bloßes Leben und nicht bloße Gestalt, sondern
lebende Gestalt, d. i. Schönheit sein" (AEM, xv. p. 617).   The exact nature
of living form will become clear in the exposition of the nature of the
reconciliation between Leben and Gestalt which will now be undertaken.

The first question to resolve is how it is possible for the apparently contradictory drives of form and of life to work together. "Wahr ist es, ihre Tendenzen widersprechen sich, aber was wohl zu bemerken ist, nicht in denselben Objekten, und was nicht auf einander trifft, kann nicht gegen einander stoßen. Der sinnliche Trieb fordert zwar Veränderung, aber er fordert nicht, daß sie auch auf die Person und ihr Gebiet sich erstrecke, daß ein Wechsel der Grundsätze sei. Der Formtrieb dringt auf Einheit und mit der Person sich auch der Zustand fixiere, daß Identität der Empfindung sei" (AEM, Xiii, p. 607). Since the two drives have two different objects, it is possible for the two to work together in reconciliation.

The second question to be answered concerns the general nature of the unity of the two drives. (1) The first characteristic is, of course, the complementary working together of the two drives. In the aesthetic experience man is both sensuously and formally active in such a way that neither activity interferes with the other. (2) Each drive must be limited to its own sphere. Neither drive is to be allowed to usurp the entire activity of man. "Beide Triebe haben also Einschränkung und, insofern sie als Energien gedacht werden, Abspannung nötig; jener, daß er sich nicht ins Gebiet der Gesetzgebung, dieser, daß er sich nicht ins Gebiet der Empfindung eindränge" (AEM, xiii, p. 610). Further, the limitations of the one activity are to be determined by the limitations of the other. "Mit einem Wort: den Stofftrieb muß die Persönlichkeit und den Formtrieb muß die Empfänglichkeit oder die Natur in seinen gehörigen Schranken halten" (AEM, xiii, p. 611). The two drives should be mutually limiting. (3) It is not enough that the two drives cooperate and mutually limit each other. They are still two separate drives with their own independent activities. The middle state is not yet reached. Not only must the two drives be united in the aesthetic experience, they must merge in a new and distinct drive in which all their antagonistic characteristics are discarded and only their complementary characteristics remain. In short, the Formtrieb and the Stofftrieb must disappear as separate drives by being smelted, so to speak, into the Spieltrieb. "Unser Geschäft ist also, diese Verbindung vollkommen zu machen, sie so rein und vollständig durchzuführen, daß beide Zustände in einem dritten gänzlich verschwinden, and keine Spur der Teilung in dem Ganzen zurückbleibt" (AEM, xviii, p. 625).

Just how Schiller brings about this Aufhebung, reveals the meaning of his aesthetics of living form. Before showing in some detail how Schiller reconciles the two drives, it will be worthwhile briefly to recall the nature of the two drives so that just what is to be reconciled will be clearly in mind. Specifically, two basic characteristics of each drive must be kept in mind: (1) the nature and object of each activity and (2) the interest (particularly appetitive) of each drive in its object.

The sensuous faculty: (1) Man's sensuous activity arises from the fact that human nature must be determined by a matter given to it from an outside source. The matter given to the sensuous faculty is, of course, sensation. This matter, before the pure forms of the understanding have been impressed upon it, is characterless, isolated, atomistic, and totally determinate. It constitutes the manifold of experience. This manifold consists of an infinite variety that is ever changing. The way in which the subject becomes conscious of the manifold is through feeling (fühlen). The very consciousness of the determinate atoms of the manifold, i. e. sensation, is feeling. (2) The interest that the Stofftrieb takes in sensation is, of course, a sensuous determination. This interest is one of grasping and consuming the sensuous object. For example, when a person is hungry, he wants to consume food, not just look at it. The gratification that is derived from sensuous indulgence is felt as pleasure (life).

The rational faculty: (1) Man's rational activity is derived from the Person's need for permanence. The permanence of a subject is achieved through the subject's giving form to a manifold. In other words, a subject remains (i. e. is permanent) only insofar as it is engaged in an ordering activity. The main way in which the rational faculty gives order to a manifold is to structure conceptually this manifold. As a result of its ordering activity, that which the Formtrieb seeks is the unifying, universal, eternal, or formal aspects of experience. The Formtrieb is indifferent to sensuous matter. Sensuous matter serves only as an occasion for the ordering activity. For example, a scientist interested in the laws of falling bodies is interested solely in universal laws. He may use a specific body to study his discovery of these laws, but he is not interested in the body qua that specific body, rather he is interested in the universal laws that govern it. (2) The way in which the rational faculty is interested in its object is not the same as the sensuous faculty is in its object. The Stofftrieb impels the individual subject to consume immediately its specific determinate object. The Formtrieb, on the other hand, is not interested in that which is immediate and determinate, but in that which is eternal and universal. This lack of immediate and determinate interest in an object on the part of the rational faculty puts, so to speak, distance between the subject and the object. Instead of seeking to consume the object, the rational faculty seeks to contemplate it or reflect upon it. Indeed, being reflectively aware of or contemplating the formal aspects of an object is the way in which the rational part human nature appetitively seeks its objects.

The pure sensuous faculty (1) feels its object and (2) seeks to consume it while the pure rational faculty (1) conceptually orders its object and (2) contemplates it. The respective pure activity of each of these faculties excludes the activity of the other and, therefore, the total dominance of one faculty necessarily results in the suppression of the other. In order to overcome this opposition between the two faculties, Schiller seeks to combine them by rejecting that aspect of each activity that is intrinsically opposed to the activity of the other faculty. The sensuous consumption of an object excludes any rational activity while the conceptualization of an object excludes any sensuous activity. Therefore, Schiller excludes these aspects of thinking and sensing and seeks to merge together the feeling of the object with the contemplation of it. How he does this will now be examined.

As a sensuous or rational subject, man is oriented to the objective in two ways. (1) Man seeks the object in an appetitive manner and, (2) man has a conscious (cognitive) relation to its object. As a physical or sensuous subject man desires to consume a specific, immediate, and determinate sensuous object. Also, as a sensuous subject, man is conscious of (i.e. feels) the specific determinate object. Sensuous man qua sensuousness is neither conscious of, nor interested in, anything beyond the immediate and determinate. Further, insofar as man is oriented to the determinate he may be said to be determined. As a sensuous being man is controlled by the laws of phenomena, i. e. man is heteronomously determined. Or in Schiller's own words: "So lange der Mensch in seinem ersten physischen Zustande, die Sinnenwelt bloß leidend in sich aufnimmt, bloß empfindet, ist er auch noch völlig eins mit derselben, und eben weil er selbst bloß Welt ist, so ist für ihn noch keine Welt" (AEM, xxv, p. 651). Being determined is the price of pure sensuous feeling.

Man becomes freed from being determined by means of his rational faculty, i. e. by contemplation or reflection. "Erst, wenn er in seinem ästhetischen Stande [die Welt] außer sich stellt oder betrachtet, sondert sich seine Persönlichkeit von ihr ab, und es erscheint ihm eine Welt, weil er aufgehört hat, mit derselben eins auszumachen" (AEM, xxv, p. 651). The very nature of the reflective activity frees man from nature's power. Reflection is a consciousness of the common, orderly, universal or formal. This type of consciousness is brought about by the rational faculty's actively taking up the manifold and actively forming it into a unity (Gestalt, Form) which the mind then contemplates. Thus man's appetitive interest is not to consume, but to observe form as an image of man's own Person. Contemplation removes the human mind from the appetitive determination by the sensuous faculty. "Die Notwendigkeit der Natur, die [den Menschen] vor der Leidenschaft der bloßen Empfindung mit ungeteiler Gewalt beherrschte, läßt bei der Reflexion von ihm ab, in den Sinnen erfolgt ein augenblicklicher Friede, . . . indem des Bewußtseins zerstreute Strahlen sich sammeln, und ein Nachbild des Unendlichen, die Form, reflectiert sich auf dem vergänglichen Grunde" (AEM, xxv, p. 652). Why does this distance give peace to the mind? To contemplate is to observe an object. But an object only appears to the human consciousness after the mind has formed the manifold according to universal objectivity constants which, in turn, are but modes of its own transcendental unity. This forming process requires activity on the part of the subject. In short, an object is only possible for a subject after that subject has become active and has objectified its forming powers in the object as its Gestalt. Thus Schiller concludes: "Was [dem Menschen] Objekt ist, hat keine Gewalt über ihn, denn um Objekt zu sein, muß es die seinige erfahren. So weit er der Materie Form giebt, und so lang er sie giebt, ist er ihren Wirkungen unverletzlich" (AEM, xxv, p. 652). In other words, for there to be an object, there must be relations. Now the matter is not the source of the relations, rather it is the self that does the ordering. The subject takes the matter and forms it into a unity. Thus the subject's activity annihilates the matter's power of determining the subject to a specific moment, space, and sensation and, instead, orientates the subject to the universal, orderly, and formal which structures the object.

However, there is a danger of going too far in the direction of pure reasoning, i.e. of rejecting all determination or matter. "Aber, indem ich bloß einen Ausgang aus der materiellen Welt und einen Übergang in die Geisterwelt suchte, hat mich der freie Lauf meiner Einbildungskraft schon mitten in die letzere hineingeführt. Die Schönheit, die wir suchen, liegt bereits hinter uns, und wir haben sie übersprungen, indem wir von dem bloßen Leben unmittelbar zu der reinen Gestalt und zu dem reinen Objekt übergingen" (AEM, xxv, p. 653). If such a step into the pure world of form is taken, man's sensuous nature will be slighted. "Die Aufgabe ist also, die Determination des Zustandes zugleich zu vernichten und beizubehalten . . ." (AEM, xx, p. 633). In short, the human mind must participate in orderly activity without leaving the sensual world. "Die Schönheit ist allerdings das Werk der freien Betrachtung, und wir treten mit ihr in die Welt der Ideen

- aber, was wohl zu bemerken ist, ohne darum die sinnliche Welt zu verlassen, wie bei Erkenntnis der Wahrheit geschieht" (AEM, xxv, 653). How is this done?

Reflection gives distance from sensuous determination by ordering the manifold and making this order the object of rational interest. The main tools used in the ordering process are the categories or pure concepts of the understanding. It is because of these categories that the mind is able to have a priori knowledge of objects without any reference to their sensuous matter. The pure concepts of the understanding are independent of any empirical content. But these pure concepts are not the only types of order. For example, Kant himself recognized Zweckmäßigkeit as the formal order of the self as Selbsttätigkeit. The mind can be, therefore, conscious of this type of pure teleological form as Kant showed in his aesthetics. Insofar as the mind is directly conscious of any type of order as order, it is only through contemplation. Since beauty involves the working together of both of man's faculties, it must involve contemplation. But the mind does not contemplate concepts in aesthetic experience, rather it contemplates a different type of order which is a reflection of the mind's own teleological activity. Indeed, the relationship between feeling and contemplating is even closer. In aesthetic experience feeling is the condition for the contemplative activity of the subject and contemplation is the condition for the feeling activity of the subject. Feeling and contemplation merge together to form a new experience. "Die Schönheit ist also zwar Gegenstand für uns, weil die Reflexion, die Bedingung ist, unter der wir eine Empfindung von ihr haben; zugleich aber ist sie ein Zustand unsers Subjekts, weil das Gefühl die Bedingung ist, unter der wir eine Vorstellung von ihr haben" (AEM, xxv, p. 653). The special experience of beauty involves a mutual interdependence. It is order mediated through feeling and a feeling through order. Both contemplation and feeling merge into one another. "In unserm Wohlgefallen an der Schönheit hingegen . . . [zerfliesst] die Reflexion . . . hier so vollkommen mit dem Gefühle, daß wir die Form unmittelbar zu empfinden glauben" (AEM, xxv, p. 653). Reflection demands consciousness of unity, form or Gestalt, and feeling demands consciousness of a variety of content, i.e. life. The aesthetic experience is such that both reflection and feeling are mutual prerequisites. What is felt (Leben) is the unity (Gestalt) of sensuous manifold insofar as it reflects the pure forming activity (power) of the Person. Reason, so to speak, inserts itself into feeling: ". . . denn der Gedanke rührt die innere Empfindung, und die Vorstellung logischer und moralischer Einheit geht in ein Gefühl sinnlicher Übereinstimmung über" (AEM, xxv, p. 753). Insofar as aesthetic experience requires reflection it involves Gestalt =objectification of the transcendental unity of the Person) and insofar as it requires feeling it involves Leben. "[Die Schöheit] ist also zwar Form, weil wir sie betrachten, zugleich aber ist sie Leben, weil wir sie fühlen" (AEM, xxv, p. 653). When Leben and Gestalt are the necessary and hence transcendental grounds of an experience, the mind universally experiences lebende Gestalt. "So lange wir über [eines Objekts] Gestalt bloß denken, ist die leblos, bloße Abstraktion; so lange wir sein Leben bloß fühlen, ist es gestaltlos, bloße Impression. Nur, indem seine Form in unserer Empfindung lebt, und sein Leben in unseren Verstande sich formt, ist [das Objekt] lebende Gestalt, und dies wird überall der Fall sein, wo wir [es] als schön beurteilen" (AEM, xv, p. 614).

Lebende Gestalt: as a Higher Reconciliation

Above, I noted that Kant's reconciliation of empiricism and rationalism implied a peculiar recasting of the notion of life. Within a Kantian framework life can be conceived not as merely sensuous pleasure, rather as the forming power of the self which possesses the form of Zweckmäßigkeit. It is precisely this formative power and its teleological activity that constitutes the higher notion of life and represents a higher synthesis. Schiller himself went so far at one point as to identify this power as "göttlich." "[S]o muß man doch eine Tendenz göttlich nennen, die das eigentlichste Merkmal der Gottheit, absolute Verkündigung des Vermögens... und absolute Einheit des Erscheinens... zu ihrer unendlichen Aufgabe hat. Die Aufgabe zu der Gottheit trägt der Mensch unwidersprechlich in seiner Persönlichkeit in sich..." (AEM, pp. 602-603).

Gestalt is not something external to Leben, rather it is the heart of Leben, it is objectified form of life (activity). Conversely, Leben is not exterior to Gestalt, rather it constitutes the contents that are acted upon by Gestalt and hence mediate awareness of Gestalt. In aesthetic experience, the inner divinity of man - human freedom or forming power is felt as the Gestalt of empirical objects. Indeed, it is precisely such an awareness that is the aesthetic. Concerning the nature of the object of aesthetic experience Schiller writes:

> Gäbe es aber Fälle, wo [der Mensch] diese doppelte Erfahrung zugleich machte, wo er sich zugleich seiner Freiheit bewußt würde und sein Dasein empfände, wo er sich zugleich als Materie fühlte und als Geist kennen lernte, so hätte er in diesen Fällen, und schlechterdings nur in diesen, eine vollständige Anschauung seiner Menschheit und der Gegenstand, der diese Anschauung ihm verschaffte, würde ihm zu einem Symbol seiner ausgeführten Bestimmung...(AEM, xiv, p. 612).

It will be recalled that Schiller's basis for his transcendental grounding of aesthetics is the concept of man's "Menschheit." Insofar as this "Menschheit" has become the content of an "Anschauung," i.e. has become "Erscheinungen," the percipient subject is aware of the transcendental conditions of his being, i. e. of his inner life as the universal power of form.[40]

F. The Structure of the Beautiful Object

Beauty as the "Objective" Appearance of Freedom

Schiller's contention that aesthetic experience entails the feeling of man's "Gottheit" viz. "Menschheit" in an object can function as a transition to Schiller's contention that aesthetics is objective (in opposition to Kant). Neither Vergnügen nor Urtheile about pleasure constitutes the locus of the aesthetic for Schiller. Notions such as Gefühl or fühlen refer for Schiller not only to the experience of pleasure, but also to the object experienced. More specifically, fühlen as an aesthetic category intends the way that an object appears. This "way" is the situs of the aesthetic. In the case of beauty, this way evinces the structure of lebende Gestalt. In the previous section I have focused upon lebende Gestalt in its relationship to the transcendental conditions of experience in the subject. But lebende Gestalt also refers to the object aesthetically experienced. Indeed, lebende Gestalt is the very structure of the aesthetic (and hence also of Schönheit). How is this possible?

Above I cited Korff's thesis concerning the meaning of Kant's philosophy, namely: "[U]nser Geist will ja nichts wissen, sondern formen bzw. wissen, was er geformt hat." This thesis holds also for Schiller. However, the inner impulse entails two aspects: (1) the forming power and (2) the self that forms. Schiller's doctrine of beauty focuses upon the first aspect. The specific or finite self does not simply want to become aware of its own specific subjectivity. The object of its universal need is the universal forming power per se. Such power must, of course, necessarily be experienced as the power of self, or rather, of selfhood per se. It is precisely this universal power of self-determination that is the object of the aesthetic need, of the Spieltrieb.

Just as the Formtrieb is only satisfied by the formal aspects of objects and just as the Stofftrieb is only satisfied by the purely material aspects, so the Spieltrieb is only satisfied by an object whose material aspects seem to be ordered by its formal aspects. This, of course is a variant of Kant's doctrine of Zweckmäßigkeit. Schiller writes about "ein Bedürfnis nach der Vorstellung des Voninnenbestimmtseins" (KB, p. 599). Such a representation is equivalent to a "Vorstellung des Durchsichselbstbestimmtseins" (KB, p. 402). Furthermore, such a representation is simply the form of the will (or of practical reason). "Reine Selbstbestimmung überhaupt ist die Form der praktischen Vernunft" (KB, p. 599). In other words, a Voninnenbestimmtsein is the way that man's inner formative power functions and hence it is the form of this function. It is precisely this form as it appears (i.e. structures an empirical manifold) that attracts the Spieltrieb and constitutes the objectivity of the aesthetic. An object that appears in its sensuous fullness to be determined by its very form constitutes an analogy to man's subjective freedom. And this is beauty. "Analogie einer Erscheinung mit der Form des reinen Willens oder der Freiheit ist Schönheit (in weitester Bedeutung). Schönheit also ist nichts anders als Freiheit in der Erscheinung" (KB, p. 400). Expressed differently:

> Zeigt sich nun ein Objekt in der Sinnenwelt bloß durch sich selbst bestimmt, stellt es sich den Sinnen so dar, daß man an ihm keinen Einfluß des Stoffes oder eines Zwecks bemerkt, so wird es als ein Analogon der reinen Willensbestimmung... beurtheilt. Weil nun ein Wille, der sich nach bloßer Form bestimmen kann, frei heißt, so ist diejenige Form in der Sinnenwelt, die bloß durch sich selbst bestimmt erscheint, eine Darstellung der Freiheit...Die Freiheit in der Erscheinung ist also nichts anders als die Selbstbestimmung an einem Dinge, insofern sie sich in der Anschauung offenbart" (KB, p. 401).

According to Alexander Baumgarten beauty is an analogon rationis. The heart of ratio is, of course, unity, the unum. Perfectio, as the structure of the plura by the unum, is the ground of beauty. When perfectio, both in form and in content, is the object of "undeutliches Erkennen," the resultant experience is one of beauty. Schiller, following Kant, grounded the unum itself in the unifying activity (Selbsttätigkeit) of the knowing self.

Insofar as such self-activity structures man's volitional and actional life, it has the form of the Wille. It is through the Wille that the absolute demand for unity becomes operational in human life. It is precisely the form of this Wille, namely Durchsichselbstbestimmtsein, not an ontological unum, that constitutes the model, relative to which a specifically formed sensate manifold appears as an analogon. Kant's objectivity criterion, namely Verbindung in its dynamic aspect, is thereby easily seen as the aesthetic criterion, as the measure of beauty in Schiller's aesthetics. The aesthetic universe of beauty appears an analogy to the moral universe of Vernunft. "Entdeckt nun die praktische Vernunft bei Betrachtung eines Naturwesens, daβ es durch sich selbst bestimmt ist, so schreibt sie demselben... Freiheitähnlichkeit oder kurzweg Freiheit zu...[S]o ist diese Analogie eines Gegenstandes mit der Form der praktischen Vernunft [=Form des Willens], nicht Freiheit in der Tat, sondern bloβ Freiheit in der Erscheinung, Autonomie in der Erscheinung" (KB, p. 400).[41]

The Beautiful Object

I shall now briefly seek to show how an object can appear free, i. e. as a lebende Gestalt. Any object (or complex of objects) that appears as pure "Stoff" consists of sensations. Sensations, apart from the form imposed upon them by space and time, are essentially atomistic. As such they do not constitute an object, rather the stuff of an object. An object is generated when the empirical contents are subsumed under the categories of reason of reason (e.g. causality and substance). However, such categories only produce an object in general. A specific object must have empirical determinations, e. g. a rock, mountain, vase, or table. In other words, any empirical object entails certain specific features. A table, for instance, has legs and a surface. Such an empirical structure was called by Schiller the "Technik" of the object. When an object possesses all essential features of its Technik, it possesses Vollkommenheit. In other words, when the manifold of determinations agree with the Technik of an object, a unity in a variety arises and this is perfection. "Alles Vollkommene...ist unter dem Begriff der Technik enthalten, weil es in der Übereinstimmung des Manngifaltigen zu Einem besteht" (KB, p. 419).

Vollkommenheit constitutes for Schiller the form of being (albeit a phenomenal, not ontological being). Schiller correctly applied the traditional (i.e. rationalistic) definition of perfection as the Übereinstimmung des Mannigfaltigen zu Einem to the Technik of an object. However, Schiller did not consider the mere formal agreement of the parts relative to the whole to constitute beauty. Mere technical perfection is not an ingredient of aesthetic objectivity. A building, for instance, can be ugly and yet possess all its technical features, i.e. exhibit technical perfection. Beauty resides not in Vollkommenheit, rather in the form whereby the features of perfection are ordered together. "Die Vollkommenheit ist die Form eines Stoffes, die Schönheit hingegen ist die Form dieser Vollkommenheit; die sich also gegen die Schönheit wie der Stoff zu der Form verhält" (KB p. 395). This "Form einer Form" shows itself as the "free" agreement of the elements of Technik to each other. "Die Technik selbst muβ wieder durch die Natur des Dinges bestimmt erscheinen, welches man den freiwilligen Konsens des Dinges zu seiner Technik nennen könnte (KB, p. 414). When technical perfection is perfected according to the structure of freedom, the object itself appears to possess a Person (viz. freedom, forming power, Geist). "Es ist gleichsam die Person des Dings, wodurch es von allen andern Dingen, die nicht seiner Art sind, unterschieden wird" (KB, p. 411). And the essence of a Person is freedom, autonomy, or simply Selbsttätigkeit.

What Schiller means can be seen clearly in his discussion of the Schlangenlinie. Schiller, like most of his contemporaries, judged the Schlangenlinie to be a beautiful shape. However, Schiller could not accept the usual explanation as to why this is so. For example, Baumgarten, Schiller reminds his readers, will maintain that a Schlangenlinie is beautiful because is is sinnlich vollkommen. "Es ist eine Linie, die ihre Richtung immer abändert (Mannigfaltigkeit) und immer wieder zu derselben Richtung zurück (Einheit)" (KB, p. 423). This, claims Schiller, is a false explanation. Schiller draws two lines to illustrate what he means:
(1)   (2)

Schiller asserts that line one (1) is vollkommen, i.e. there is a plurality within a unity of the direction k⟶1. Furthermore, the line is perceivable by the senses. Nevertheless, line one (1) is not as beautiful as is line two (2). Schiller explains why:

> Was ist aber eine plötzlich veränderte Richtung anders als eine gewaltsam veränderte? Die Natur liebt keinen Sprung. Sehen wir die einen tun, so zeigt es, daß ihr Gewalt geschehen ist. Freiwillig hingegen erscheint nur diejenige Bewegung, an der man keinen bestimmten Punkt angeben kann, bei dem sie ihre Richtung abänderte. Und dies ist der Fall mit der Schlangenlinie, welche sich von der oben abgebildeten bloß durch ihre Freiheit unterscheidet (KB, p. 424).

What Schiller means can be graphically represented in the following manner. If line one (1) is conceived as a flow in one direction, the abrupt change will appear (show the form) as if it had been forced to do so by a force external to the line:

Force is outside
of flow

Line two (2), on the other hand, gives the appearance as if the force of change lay within the dynamics (Leben) of its flow!

Force is within
flow

Line one (1) appears, accordingly, as if it were vonaußenbestimmt and line two (2) as if it were voninnenbestimmt. Line two (2) exhibits the Gestalt of Freiheit in its Leben (= flow), and therefore, constitutes an analogue to freedom.

Schiller gives other examples of what he means. Take two vases:
(1)   and (2)

The first vase appears, "als ob die Schwere der Länge genommen hätte, was sie der Breite gegeben, kurz als ob die Schwerkraft über die Form, nicht die Form über die Schwerkraft geherrscht hätte (KB, p. 412). Conversely, if the vase narrows at the base it appears as if the form were dominating gravity. The vase is therefore experienced as beautiful. "Dagegen nehmen wir überall Schönheit wahr, wo die Masse von der Form und...von den lebendigen Kräften...völlig beherrscht wird" (KB, p. 413). For Schiller, the most impressive example of what he is talking about is a bird in flight. "Ein Vogel im Flug ist die glücklichste Darstellung des durch die Form bezwungenen Stoffes, der durch die Kraft überwundenen Schwere. Es ist nicht unwichtig zu bemerken, daß die Fähigkeit, über die Schwere zu siegen, oft zum Symbol der Freiheit gebraucht wird" (KB, pp. 413-414).

In short, when the structure determining the relationship of the technical features of an object gives the appearance that these parts are determined by a principle internal to the object, the object (or, more accurately, the presentation of the object) possesses a form that is analogous to the form of man's inner "Gottheit," namely his Selbsttätigkeit. This divinity assumes structure in man as the Gestalt of his will (Leben). When the form of an object is analogous to the form of the will, the object possesses "objective" beauty, i.e. lebende Gestalt.

Footnotes - Chapter IV

[1] Cf. Die deutsche Schulphilosophie im Zeitalter der Aufklärung (Hildesheim, 1964), pp. 265-341.

[2] Concerning the evolution of German philosophy before the critical Kant see Chapter Two, Footnote 4. For specific discussions of Kant's pre-critical philosophy see: Lewis White Beck, Early German Philosophy. Kant and His Predecessors (Cambridge, 1969), pp. 438-456; Edward Caird, The Critical Philosophy of Immanuel Kant (Glasgow, 1889), I, 104-160; Kuno Fischer, Immanuel Kant und seine Lehre. Erster Teil. Entstehung und Grundlegung der Kantischen Philosophie, 6th ed. (Heidelberg, 1928), pp. 165-329; Herman-J. Vleeschauwer, The Development of Kantian Thought. The History of a Doctrine, trans. A. R. C. Duncan (Toronto/New York, 1962), pp. 1-61; and T. D. Weldon, Kant's "Critique of Pure Reason" (Oxford, 1958), pp. 56-73.

[3] Ueber die Evidenz in metaphysichen Wissenschaften (1763) in Schriften zur Philosophie, Aesthetik und Apologetik (Hildesheim, 1968), I, 70. Hereafter referred to in the text as Ueber die Evidenz plus volume and page number.

[4] Cf. Hamburgische Dramaturgie (1766-1767) in Gesammelte Schriften, ed. Paul Rilla (Berlin, 1954), VI, 358-359.

[5] Betrachtungen über die Schrancken der menschlichen Erkenntniß (Halle, 1755). Hereafter referred to in the text as Betrachtungen über die Schrancken plus page number.

[6] Philosophia definitiva, hoc est, Definitiones philosophicae ex systemate Lib. Bar. a Wolf in unum collectae succinctis observationibus exemplisque perspicuis illustrate (Viennae, 1776), p. 13. An earlier version was first published in 1735.

[7] Entwurf der nothwendigen Vernunft-Wahrheiten, wiefern sie den zufälligen entgegen gesetzet werden (Leipzig, 1745), §8, pp. 13-14. Concerning the meaning of Crusius in the evolution of German philosophy see Heinz Heimsoeth, Metaphysik und Kritik bei Chr. A. Crusius: Ein Beitrag zur ontologischen Vorgeschichte der Kritik der reinen Vernunft im 18. Jahrhundert (Berlin, 1926).

[8] Untersuchung von den Monaden und einfachen Dingen, worinnen der Ungrund derselben gezeiget wird, als die Ausarbeitung der Aufgabe, so die Königli. Preußische Hochpreißliche Academie der Wissenschaften zu Berlin, denen auswärtigen Gelehrten auf das Jahr 1747 vorgeschreiben hat (Berlin, 1748), pp. xiii-xiv.

[9] De mundi sensibilis atque intelligibus forma et principiis (1770) in Kants Werke. Akademie-Textausgabe (Berlin, 1968). II, 392.

[10] Cf. Kants Werke, II, 76. Hereafter referred to in the text by volume and page number.

[11] Prolegomena zu einer jeden künftigen Metaphysik, die als Wissenschaft auftreten können (1783) in Kants Werke, IV, 260. Hereafter referred to in the text as Prolegomena plus volume and page number.

[12] For a detailed comparison of Hume and Kant see Henri Lauener, Hume und Kant. Systematische Gegenüberstellung einiger Hauptpunkte ihrer Lehren (Bern/München, 1969), pp. 11-136.

[13] Cf. A Treatise of Human Nature: Being an Attempt to introduce the experimental Method of Reasoning into Moral Subjects (London, 1739), Book I, Part 3, Section 6. Hereafter referred to in the text as Treatise, plus Book, Part, and Section number.

[14] For a similar critique of Hume see Harry Prosch, The Genesis of Twentieth Century Philosophy. The Evolution of Thought from Copernicus to the Present (Garden City, 1964), p. 113. For a detailed and devastating critique of Hume's concept of causality see Alfred North Whitehead, Process and Reality. An Essay on Cosmology (New York, 1957), pp. 263-274.

[15] Cf. Kants Briefe, ed. F. Ohman (Leipzig, 1911), pp.45-46.

[16] The literature on Kant's mature philosophy is enormous. I shall make no attempt to list the works. Below I will indicate some works I found particularly illuminating. See Caird, The Philosophy of Immanuel Kant, I. 227-654; Fischer, Immanuel Kant und seine Lehre, pp. 388-477; Justus Hartnack, Kant's Theory of Knowledge, trans. M. Holmes Hartshorne (New York, 1965); Martin Heidigger, Die Frage nach dem Ding. Zu Kants Lehre von den transzendentalen Grundsätzen (Tübingen, 1962), pp. 92-188; and Josiah Royce, Lectures on Modern Idealism (New Haven/London, 1964), pp. 1-62.

[17] Cf. "Vorrede zur zweiten Auflage," Kritik der reinen Vernunft, 2. Auflage (1787) in Kants Werke, III, xvi of the 1787 edition. Hereafter referred to in the text as KdrV, and, as is common, as B for the page number of the second edition. The first edition (1781) is printed Kants Werke, IV.

[18] Concerning the dynamic and static meaning of Kant's notion of unity see Gottfried Martin, Kant's Metaphysics and Theory of Science, trans. P. G. Lucas (Westport, 1974), pp. 122-128.

[19] Cf. Geist der Goethezeit. Versuch einer ideellen Entwicklung der klassisch-romantischen Literaturgeschichte, 7th ed. (Leipzig, 1964), II, 85-86. For a similar analysis of the cognitive process in Kant's thought see Samuel J. Todes, "Knowledge and the Ego: Kant's Three Stages of Self-Evidence," in Kant. A Collection of Critical Essays, ed. Robert Paul Wolff (Garden City, 1967), pp. 156-171. Also for some reflections on Kant's concept of mental activity as entailing "creativity" see Oscar W. Miller, The Kantian Thing-in-Itself and the Creative Mind (New York, 1956), pp. 71-115.

[20] System der Aesthetik. Erster Band (Leipzig, 1790). Hereafter referred to in the text as System plus page number. From Heydenreich's "Vorrede" it is clear that he had recently read Kant's Kritik der Urteilskraft, though not soon enough to make any use of it.

21 Cf. J. Koller, Entwurf zur Geschichte und Literatur der Aesthetik von Baumgarten bis auf die neueste Zeit (Regensburg, 1799), p. 102.
22 Beyträge des Geschmacks (Wien, 1797). Hereafter referred to in the text as Beyträge plus page number.

23 "Schreiben des Herrn Salomon Maimon an den Herausgeber" in Annalen der Akademie der Künste und mechanischer Wissenschaften (1791), pp. 78-85 as reprinted in Gesammelte Werke, ed. Valerie Verra (Hildesheim, 1970), III, 337. Despite using Kantian categories, Friedrich Bouterwek (like David, Heydenreich, and Maimon) utilizes a rationalistic paradigm when it comes to defining beauty. According to Bouterwek, beauty is "nichts weiter als Einheit im Mannigfaltigen." Cf. Aesthetik (Leipzig, 1806), p. 119. And on the same page Bouterwek explains himself. "Nach der Einheit im Manngifaltigen zielt alles Denken....Das Gesetz der Einheit im Mannigfaltigen ist aber eben deßwegen ein Grundgesetz des guten Geschmacks, weil es ein Grundgesetz aller Vernünftigkeit ist. Nur muß die Vernunft, wenn dieses Gesetz eine ästhetische, nicht logische Anwendung finden soll, die Anschauung nicht auflösen in eine systematische Einheit von Begriffen. Die Einheit muß, wie die Mannigfaltigkeit, empfunden werden..." Meier, Baumgarten, or any other rationalist could have written the words just cited.

24 Ibid., p. 336. Cf. also Maimon's discussion of "Schönheit" in Philosophisches Wörterbuch oder Beleuchtung der wichtigsten Gegenstände der Philosophie in alphabetischer Ordnung (1791) in Gesammelte Werke, III, 127-129.

25 The secondary literature on Kant's aesthetics is quite extensive. I shall only note a few works I found specifically helpful. See Alfred Baeumler, Das Irrationalitätsproblem in der Ästhetik und Logik des 18. Jahrhunderts (Darmstadt, 1967), pp. 264-307; H. W. Cassirer, A Commentary on Kant's "Critique of Judgment" (London, 1938); Donald W. Crawford, Kant's Aesthetic Theory (Madison, 1974); Hans-Georg Juchem, Die Entwicklung des Begriffs des Schönen bei Kant. Unter besonderer Berücksichtigung des Begriffs der verworrenen Erkenntnis (Bonn, 1970); and Theodore Edward Uehling, The Notion of Form in Kant's "Critique of Aesthetic Judgment" (The Hague/Paris, 1971).

26 Cf. Kritik der Urtheilskraft (1790) in Kants Werke, V. p. xxix of the original edition. Hereafter referred to in the text as KdU plus page number of the original 1790 edition.

27 For further discussion see Todes, "Knowledge and the Ego," Kant, pp. 161ff.

28 For further discussion of the Urtheilskraft as entailing a judgment of the subject about itself see Richard Kroner, Von Kant bis Hegel (Tübingen, 1921), I, 231ff.

29 For secondary sources on the relationship between Kant and Schiller see: Anton Appelmann, Der Unterschied in der Auffassung der Ethik bei Schiller und Kant (New York, 1917); H. A. Korff, Geist der Goethezeit, II, 428-487; P. Menzer, "Schiller und Kant," Kant-Studien, XLVII (1955-1956), 113-147, 234-272; Willi Rosalewski, Schillers Aesthetik im Verhätnis zur

Kantischen (Heidelberg, 1912); Eva Schaper, "Schiller: Adventures of a Kantian," British Journal of Aesthetics, V (1964), 348362' Alfred Smid, "Schiller als theoretischer Philosoph," Kant-Studien, X (1905), 261-286; Karl Vorländer, Kant, Schiller, Goethe: Gesammelte Aufsätze (Leipzig, 1907); and Carl Wilm, "The Relation of Schiller to Postkantian Idealism," The Journal of English and Germanic Philosophy, IX (1910), 20-24.

[30] Kallias Briefe in Sämtliche Werke, 4th ed., ed. Gerhard Fricke and Herbert Göpfert (München, 1967), V, 394. Hereafter referred to in the text as KB plus page number.

[31] For some secondary sources that discuss Schiller's aesthetics with particular emphasis upon the AEM see: Gottfried Baumecker, Schillers Schönheitslehre (Heidelberg, 1937), pp. 57-111; Karl Berger, Die Entwicklung von Schiller's Aesthetik (Weimar, 1894), pp. 254-306; Melitta Gehard, Schiller (Bern, 1950), pp. 240-267; Paul Geyer, Schillers aesthetisch-sittliche Weltanschauung aus seiner philosophischen Schriften gemeinverständlich erklärt (Berlin, 1908), pp. 14-44; Hennis Kössler, Freiheit und Ohnmacht: Die autonome Moral und Schillers Idealismus der Freiheit (Göttingen, 1962), pp. 83-135; Friedrich Ueberweg, Schiller als Historiker und Philosoph. ed Moritz Brasch (Stuttgart, 1963). pp. 478-503; and Elisabeth M. Wilkinson, "Reflections after Translating Schiller's Letters on the Aesthetic Education of Man" in Schiller, Bicentary Lectures, ed. F. Norman (London, 1960), pp. 48-62.

[32] Über die ästhetische Erziehung des Menschen in einer Reihe von Briefen in Sämtliche Werke, V, letter x, 600. Hereafter referred to in the text as AEM, plus letter and page number.

[33] For a further discussion of Schiller's notion of time and space as a priori forms in a Kantian sense see Bertha Mugdan, Die theoretischen Grundlagen der Schillerschen Philosophie (Berlin, 1910), pp. 38-43.

[34] In another work Schiller writes: "Und durch Reflexion über diese sukzessiv angestelle Synthese erkenne ich die Identität meines Ich in der ganzen Reihe derselben (reines Selbstbewußtsein): dadurch erst wird das Quantum ein Gegenstand für mich. Ich reihe A an B und B an C usf., und indem ich diesem Geschäft gleichsam zusehe, sage ich mir: Sowohl in A als in B und in C bin Ich das handelne Subjekt." See Zerstreute Betrachtungen über verschiedene ästhetische Gegenstände (1793), Sämtliche Werke, V, 556.

[35] For instance, Kant writes: "Die Neigungen selber aber als Quellen der Bedürfnisse, haben so wenig einen absoluten Wert, um sie selbst zu wünschen, daß vielmehr, gänzlich davon frei zu sein, der allgemeine Wunsch eines jeden vernünftigen Wesens sein muß." See Grundlegung zur Metaphysik der Sitten (1785) in Kants Werke, IV, 428.

[36] For two psychological interpretations of Schiller's attempted reconciliation of the Formtrieb and the Stofftrieb see C. G. Jung, Psychological Types or the Psychology of Individuation, trans. H. Goodwin Baynes (New York, 1924), pp. 123-162 and Herbert Marcuse, Eros and Civilization: A Philosophical Inquiry into Freud (New York, 1955), pp. 157-179.

[37] Concerning Schiller's attempt to reconcile two opposed drives Jung writes: "Opposites can be reconciled practically only in the form of compromise...wherein a _novum_ arises between them, which, though different from both, has the power to take up their energies in equal measure as an expression of both and of neither," Psychological Types, p. 133. For a discussion of the sociological dimension of Schiller's attempted reconciliation see Michael Böhler, Soziale Rolle und ästhetische Vermittlung. Studien zur Literatursoziologie von A. G. Baumgarten bis F. Schiller (Bern/Frankfurt/M., 1975), pp. 238-310.

[38] Unfortunately Schiller's term Spieltrieb has led some investigators to think that, in the end, Schiller's aesthetics is no more than trivia. For instance, Israel Knox writes: "There are rich kernels in Schiller's philosophy of art. But they are lost in the husk which envelops them. Upon the most generous interpretation the play-theory and the doctrine of aesthetic semblance are an evasion of the problems of life, are an escape from reality, are a mere conversion of art into an amusing toy, into a highly-valued plaything." See The Aesthetic Theories of Kant, Hegel, and Schopenhauer (New York, 1958), p. 76. Such an interpretation is a complete misrepresentation of both Schiller's intentions and achievements. Schiller is extending certain characteristics of game playing to all of life's activities. "A play or game," writes Katherine Everett Gilbert and Helmut Kuhn, "is conducted in accordance with rules. But these rules are a free creation...they suspend the never ceasing conflict between the law of nature and the law of reason, between force and freedom." See A History of Esthetics (Bloomington, 1953), p. 366. "Aesthetic play for [Schiller] is not the play of animals or children, or of adults in their sport and games" writes Leonard Ashly Willoughby, "but the free play of man's whole nature when he is in command of himself." See "Schiller on Man's Education to Freedom through Knowledge," Germanic Review, XXIX (1959), 107. It is not freedom from law, but within law. The Spieltrieb entails, in essence, the absence of any oppressive constraint. As R. D. Miller writes: "The term 'free play', although it is not used to deny the part played by law in aesthetics, serves above all to emphasize the need of freedom from constraint." See Schiller & The Ideal of Freedom: A Study of Schiller's Philosophical Works With Chapters on Kant (Harrogate, 1959), p. 107. It is for this reason that Schiller writes: "Denn, um es endlich auf einmal herauszusagen, der Mensch spielt nur, wo er in voller Bedeutung des Wrotes Mensch ist, und er ist nur da ganz Mensch, wo er spielt"(AEM, xv, p. 618).

[39] Concerning the fulfillment of the Spieltrieb, S. S. Kerry has aptly commented that "in this Schiller advances, in effect, an aesthetic imperative, complementary to the categorical imperative of Kant. The ideal is an unconscious beauty of the whole person, where duty and inclination are lost to one another." See Schiller's Writings on Aesthetics (Manchester, 1961), pp. 102-103.

[40] Schiller was not the only postkantian theorist to attempt to ground aesthetics as an expression of human nature. Karl Ludwig Pörschke attempted to derive beauty from human nature. Pörschke writes: "Alle Grundbestimmungen des Menschen sollen Erscheinungen möglich machen; daher lehrt die Metaphysik des Seyns die reine Möglichkeit der Natur, die Metaphysik des Sollens, die reine Möglichkeit der Kunst im weitesten Verstande. Hier bedeutet das Wort

Kunst überhaupt: die Methode nach Ideen Erscheinungen zu machen
....Spontaneität ist der Grund von Beyden, sie sind Produkte des menschlichen
Geistes; jene ist Produkt des reinen Verstandes, diese der reinen Vernunft.
Die Natur hat also nothwendige Gesetze, die Kunst hat nothwendige Gesetze,
die der Mensch gibt, die im seinem Wesen liegen." Cf. Gedanken über einige
Gegenstände der Philosophie des Schönen (Libau, 1794), pp. 73-75. Beauty is
an expression of man's essence, i. e. of his "Spontaneität."

[41] Similarly Pörschke writes: "[D]ie Dinge sollen die Abdrücke der
Göttlichkeit (der Freyheit) seyn. Wir nennen die Gesetze für diese
Abdrücke...Schönheit...[D]ie Schönheit [könnte man] die Totalsumme des
Ausdrückens nennen," cf. Gedanken über einige Gegenstände, pp. 69-70.
Heinrich Schreiber developed similar ideas: "[D]er Geist [des Menschen] ...
will das Sinnliche oder die Erscheinungen so gestalten, daß sie ihn
vollkommen ausdrücken, möglischst vollendete Bilder von ihm liefern, ihn
darstellen. Hier erscheint ihm als höchstes Ziel das Schöne." "[Das Schöne
besteht] in vollendeter Aeußerung des Geistes im Sinnlichen, der Darstellung
desselben in einem Gesamtblicke, der höchsten Durchdringung des
Mannigfaltigen durch die Einheit [des Geistes]." Die Wissenschaft vom
Schönen. Grundzüge zu akademischen Vorlesungen (Freiburg im Breisgau, 1823),
pp. 7 and 26. For comments upon "Schönheit" as being the fulfillment of
Schiller's transcendental grounding of aesthetic experience see Fretz Heuger,
Darstellung der Freiheit. Schillers transzendentale Frage nach der Kunst
(Wien, 1970), pp. 156-157.

BIBLIOGRAPHY

Primary Sources

Addison, Joseph. "The Pleasures of the Imagination" (1712), The Spectator in The Spectator: With a Historical and Biographical Preface by A. Chalmers. New York, 1881. Vol. VI, 121-178, No. 404-421.

Akenside, Mark. The Pleasures of the Imagination (1744) in The Poetical Works of Mark Akenside. London, 1894.

Alison, Archibald. Essays on the Nature and Principles of Taste. Edinburgh 1790.

André, Yves M. Versuch Über das Schöne, da man untersuche, worinnen eigentlich das Schöne in der Naturlehre, in der Sittenlehre, in den Werken des Witzes und in der Musik bestehe. Trans. Ernst Gottlieb Baron. Altenburg, 1757.

Baille, John. An Essay on the Sublime. London, 1747.

Baumeister, Friedrich Christian. Philosophia definitiva, hoc est, Definitiones philosophicae ex systemate Lib. Bar. a. Wolf in unum collectae succinctis obervationibus exemplisque perspicuis illustrate. Viennae, 1775.

Baumgarten, Alexander Gottlieb. Aesthetica (Erster Theil). Frankfurt/O., 1750.

_____. Acroasis Logica in Christianum L.B. de Wolff. Helae, 1761.

_____. "Kollegiumhandschrift" (ca. 1750) printed in: Bernard Poppe, Alexander Gottlieb Baumgarten. Seine Bedeutung und Stellung in der Leibniz-Wolffischen Philosophie und seine Beziehung zu Kant. Nebst Veröffentlichung einer bisher unbekannten Handschrift Baumgartens. Borna/Leipzig, 1907.

_____. Meditationes philosophicae de nonnullis ad poema pertinentibus quas amplissimi philosophorum ordinis consensu. Halae, 1735.

_____. Metaphyica. Editio VII. Halae, 1779.

_____. Metaphysik. Trans. Georg Friedrich Meier. Halle 1766.

Beattie, James. Dissertations Moral and Critical. London, 1783.

Bendavid, Lazarus. Beyträge des Geschmacks. Wien, 1797.

Bouterwek, Friedrich. Aesthetik. Leipzig, 1806.

Buhle, Johann Gottlieb. Grundzüge einer allgemeinen Encyklopädie der Wissenschaften. Lemgo, 1790.

Burke, Edmund. A Philosophical Enquiry into the Origin of our Ideas of the Sublime and Beautiful (1756). Ed. J. T. Boulton. London/New York, 1958.

Büsching, Anton Friedrich. Geschichte und Grundsätze der schönen Künste und Wissenschaften im Grundriß. Erstes Stück. Berlin, 1772.

Crusius, Christian August. Entwurf der nothwendigen Vernunft-Wahrheiten, wiefern sie den zufälligen entgegen gesetzet werden. Leipzig, 1745.

Dommerich, Johann Christoph. Entwurf einer Deutschen Dichtkunst zum Gebrauch der Schulen abgefasset. Braunschwieg, 1758.

Eberhard, Johann August. Allgemeine Theorie des Denkens und Empfindens. Berlin, 1776.

_____. Handbuch der Aesthetik für gebildete Leser aus allen Ständen. Halle, 1807.

_____. Theorie der schönen Wissenschaften. Halle, 1783.

Eschenburg, Johann Joachim. Entwurf einer Theorie und Literatur der schönen Wissenschaften. Zur Grundlage bey Vorlesungen. Berlin/Stuttgart, 1783.

Flögel, Carl Friedrich. Einleitung in die Erfindungskunst. Breßlau/Leipzig, 1760.

Gäng, Phillip. Aesthetik oder allgemeine Theorie der schönen Künste und Wissenschaften. Salzburg, 1785.

Gerard, Alexander. An Essay on Taste. London, 1759.

Gottsched, Johann Christoph. Erste Gründe der gesamten Weltweisheit, Darin alle philosophische Wissenschaften in ihrer natürlichen Verknüpfung abgehandelt werden, Zum Gebrauch Academischer Lectionen entworfen. 2 vols. Leipzig, 1733-1734.

_____. Versuch einer Critischen Dichtkunst durchgehends mit den Exempeln unserer besten Dichter erläutert. Vierte sehr vermehrte Auflage. Leipzig, 1751.

Hartley, David. Observations on Man, His Fame, His Duty, and His Expectations. In Two Parts. London, 1749.

Heydenreich, Karl Heinrich. System der Aesthetik. Erster Band. Leipzig, 1790.

Hißmann, Michael. Anleitung zur Kenntniß der auserlesenen Litteratur in allen Theilen der Philosophie. Göttingen/Lemgo, 1778.

Home, Henry (Lord Kames). Elements of Criticism, With Analyses and Translations of Ancient and Foreign Illustrations (1762). New Edition. New York, 1847.

Hume, David. An Abstract of a Book lately Published; Entitled a Treatise of Human Nature, &c. wherein the Chief Argument of that Book is farther Illustrated and Explained. London, 1740.

_____. An Enquiry Concerning Human Understanding (1748). Reprinted from 1777 edition in Enquiries Concerning Human Understanding and Concerning the Principles of Morals. Ed. L. A. Selby-Bigge. 3rd edition. Oxford, 1975.

_____. An Enquiry Concerning the Principles of Morals (1751). Reprinted from 1777 edition in Enquiries Concerning Human Understanding and Concerning the Principles of Morals. Ed. L. A. Selby-Bigge. 3rd edition. Oxford, 1975.

_____. A Treatise of Human Nature: Being An Attempt to Introduce the Experimental Method of Reasoning into Moral Subjects. London, 1739.

_____. "Of the Standard of Taste" (1757), Essays Moral, Political, and Literary. Ed. T. H. Green and T. H. Grose. London/New York/Bombay, 1898. Vol. I, pp. 266-284.

Hutcheson, Francis. An Inquiry into the Original of our Ideas of Beauty and Virtue. London, 1725.

Justi, Johann Gottlob. Untersuchung von den Monaden und einfachen Dingen, worinnen der Ungrund derselben gezeiget wird, als die Ausarbeitung der Aufgabe, so die Königli. Preußische Hochpreißliche Academie der Wissenschaften zu Berlin, denen auswärtigen Gelehrten auf das Jahr 1747 vorgeschrieben hat. Berlin, 1748.

Kant, Imannuel. Kants Werke. Akademie-Textausgabe. Berlin, 1968. 6 vols. Band II:
Der einzig mögliche Beweisgrund zu einer Demonstration des Daseins Gottes (1763), pp. 63-164.
De mundi sensibilis atque intelligibus forma et principiis (1770), pp. 385-420.
Band III:
Kritik der reinen Vernunft. Zweite Auflage (1787), pp. 1-552
Band IV:
Kritik der reinen Vernunft (Erste Auflage) (1781), pp. 1-250.
Prolegomena zu einer jeden künftigen Metaphysik, die als Wissenschaft auftreten können (1783), pp. 253-384.

Grundlegung zur Metaphysik der Sitten (1785), pp. 385-464.
Band V: Kritik der Urhtheilskraft (1790), pP. 165-486.

_____. Kants Briefe. Editor F. Ohman. Leipzig, 1911.

Ladrone, Konrad. Uiber einfache und zusammengesetzte Schönheit nach Engels und Mendelssohns Grundsätzen. Mainz, 1784.

Leibniz, Gottfried Wilhelm. Die philosophischen Schriften von Gottfried
    Wilhelm Leibniz, Ed. C. J. Gerbardt. Hildesheim, 1960-1961 (reprint of
    the 1875-1885 edition). 6 vols.
    Band II (1960):
    Briefwechsel
    Band III (1960):
    Briefwechsel
    Band IV (1961):
    Essais de Theodicee sur la bonte de Dieu, la liberte de l'homme et
    l'origine du mal (ca. 1710), pp. 21-436.
    Principes de la Nature et de la Grace, fondes en raison (1714), pp.
    598-606.
    La Monadologie (1714), pp. 607-623.

    _____.Opuscules et fragments inedits de Leibniz.
    Ed. Louis Couturat. Paris. 1903.
    Primae veritates (n.d.), pp. 518-523.
    Introductio an encyclopaediam arcanam (n.d.), pp. 511-515.

    _____. Opera philosophica quae exstant latina,
    gallica, germanica omnia. Ed. J. E. Erdmann. Aalen, 1959 (reprint of
    1840 edition).
    Da la sagesse (ca. 1693), pp. 673-675.
    "Note sur les possibles" pp. 529-530.
    "Resume de metaphysique" pp. 533-535.

Lessing, Gotthold Ephariam. Hamburgische Dramaturgie (1766-1767) in
    Gesammelte Schriften. Editor Paul Rilla. Berlin, 1954. Vol. VI.

Locke, John. An Essay Concerning Human Understanding, 4th edition (1700).
    Ed. Peter H. Nidditch. Oxford, 1975.

Koller, J. Entwurf zur Geschichte und Literatur der Aesthetik von Baumgarten
    bis auf die neueste Zeit. Regensburg, 1799.

Konig, Johann Ulrich. Eine Untersuchung von dem guten Geschmack in der
    Dicht- und Rede-Kunst. Leipzig/Berlin, 1727.

Maimon, Salomon. Gesammelte Werke. Ed. Valerio Verra. Hildesheim,
    1967-1976. 7 vols.
    Band III (1970):
    Philosophisches Wörterbuch oder Beleuchtung der wichtigsten Gegen-

    stände der Philosophie in alphabetischer Ordnung (1791). pp. 1-246.
    "Schreiben des Herrn Salomon Maimon an den Herausgeber" (1791), pp.
    332-339.

Meier, Georg Friedrich. Anfangsgründe aller Schönen Wissenschaften.   3
    vols. Halle, 1748-1750.

    _____. Auszug aus der Vernunftlehre. Halle, 1752.

165

_____ . Betrachtungen über den ersten Grundsatz
aller schönen Künste und Wissenschaften. Halle, 1757.

_____ . Betrachtungen über die Schrancken der
menschlichen Erkenntniß Halle, 1755.

_____ . Beurtheilung der Gottschedischen Dichtkunst.
Halle, 1747.

_____ . Beweis der vorherbestimmten Uebereinstimmung.
Halle, 1743.

_____ . Metaphysik. 4 vols. Halle, 1755-1759.
Erster Theil. Die Ontologie (1755).
Zweyter Theil. Die Cosmologie (1756).
Dritter Theil. Die Psychologie (1757).
Vierter Theil. Die natürliche Gottesgelahrtheit (1759)

_____ . Vertheidigung der Baumgartischen Erklärung
eines Gedichts, wider das 5 Stück des I Bandes des neuen Büchersaals der
schönen Wissenschaften und freyen Künste. Halle, 1746.

Meißner, Heinrich Adam. Philosophisches Lexicon, Darinnen die Erklärungen
und Beschreibungen aus des solu. tit. tot. Hochberühmten Welt-Weisen,
Herrn Christian Wolffens sämtlichen teutschen Schriften seiner
Philosophischen Systematis sorgfältig zusammen getragen worden.
Bayreuth/Hof, 1737.

Mendelssohn, Moses. Schriften zur Philosophie, Aesthetik und Apologetik.
Ed. Moritz Brasch. Hildesheim, 1968 (reprint of 1880 edition). 2 vols.
Band I:
Ueber die Evidenz in metaphyischen Wissenschaften (1763), pp. 45-104.
Morgenstunden, oder Vorlesungen über das Dasein Gottes (1785), pp.
299-460.
Band II:
Briefe über die Empfindungen (1755), pp. 3-96.
Ueber die Hauptgrundsätze der schönen Künste und Wissenschaften (1757),
pp. 141-168.

Mengs, Anton Raphael. Ueber Schönheit und guten Geschmack in der Mahlerei
(1762) in Sämmtliche hinterlassene Schriften. Ed. G. Schilling. Born,
1843. Vol. I, 196-250.

Porschke, Karl Ludwig. Gedanken über einige Gegenstände der Philosophie des
Schönen. Libau, 1794.

Priestly, Joseph. A Course of Lectures on Oratory and Criticism. London,
1777.

Reid, Thomas. Philosophical Works. 2 vols. Introduction by Harry M.
Bracken. Hildesheim, 1967 reprint of 1895 edition.
Vol I: Essays on the Intellectual Powers of Man (1785), pp. 215-508.

Reimarus, Hermann Samuel. Die Vernunftlehre, als eine Anweisung zum
    richtigen Gebrauche der Vernunft in dem Erkenntniß der Wahrheit, aus
    zwoen ganz natürlichen Regeln der Einstimmung und des Widerspruchs
    hergeleitet. Vierte Auflage. Hamburg, 1782.

Sayers, Frank. Disquisitions, Metaphysical and Literary. London, 1793.

Schwab, Johann Christoph. Preisschriften über die Frage: Welche Forschritte
    hat die Metaphysik seit Leibnitzens und Wolffs Zeiten in Deutschland
    gemacht? Berlin, 1796.

Schiller, Friedrich. Sämtliche Werke. 4th edition. Editors Gerhard Fricke
    and Herbert G. Göpfert. München, 1965-1967. 5 vols. Band V (1967):
    Kallias oder über die Schönheit (1793), pp. 394-432.
    Zerstreute Betrachtungen über verschiedene ästhetische Gegenstände
    (1793), pp. 543-569.
    Über die ästhetische Erziehung des Menschen in einer Reihe von Briefen
    (1795), pp. 570-669.

Schott, Andreas Heinrich. Theorie der schönen Wissenschaften. 2 vols.
    Tübingen, 1789-1790.

Schreiber, Heinrich. Die Wissenschaft vom Schönen. Grundzüge zu
    akademischen Vorlesungen. Freiburg im Breisgau, 1823.

Schütz, Christian Gottfried. Lehrbuch zur Bildung des Verstandes und des
    Geschmacks. Erster Band. Halle, 1776.

Smith, Adam. The Works of Adam Smith. 5 vols. London, 1811-1812. Vol. I
    (1811): The Theory of Moral Sentiments (1759), pp. 1-611.

Stewart, Dugald. The Works of Dugald Steward. 7 vols. Cambridge, 1829.
    Vol. IV: Philosophical Essays (1810), pp. 51-394.

Sulzer, Johann Georg. Allgemeine Theorie der schönen Künste in einzeln, nach
    alphabetischer Ordnung der Kunstwörter auf einander folgenden, Artikeln
    abgehandelt. Neue vermehrte zweyte Auflage. 4 vols. Leipzig, 1792-1794.

Tour, Seran de la. L'art de sentir et de juger en matiere de gout. 2 vols.
    Paris, 1762.

Wolff, Christian. Der Anfangs-Gründe aller Mathematischen Wissenschaften.
    Erster Theil, Welcher einen Unterricht von der Mathematischen Lehr-Art,
    die Rechen-Kunst, Geometrie, Trigonometrie und Bau-Kunst in sich
    enthält, Zu meherem Aufnehmen der Mathematik so wohl auf hohen als
    niedrigen Schulen aufgesetzt worden. Frankfurt/Leipzig, 1750.

    _____. Ausführliche Nachricht von seinen eigenen Schriften, die
    er in deutscher Sprache von den verschiedenen Theilen der WeltWeißheit
    heraus gegeben, auf Verlangen ans Licht gestellt. Frankfurt/M., 1735.

    _____. Philosophia prima sive ontologia, methodo scientifica
    pertractata qua omnis cognitionis humanae principia continentur. Editio
    nova. Francofurti et Lipsiae, 1736.

. Vernünftige Gedanken von den Kräften des menschlichen Verstandes und ihrem richtigen Gebrauche in Erkenntnis der Wahrheit (1713) in Gesammelte Werke, ed. Hans Werner Arndt. Hildesheim, 1965. I Abteilung, Band I.

Secondary Sources

Aaron, R. I. John Locke. London, 1947.

Altmann, Alexander. Moses Mendelssohns Frühschriften zur Metaphysik. Tübingen, 1969.

Appelmann, Anton. Der Unterschied in der Auffasung der Ethik bei Schiller und Kant. New York, 1917.

Baumecker, Gottfried. Schillers Schönheitslehre. Heidelberg, 1937.

Baeumler, Alfred. Das Irrationalitatsproblem in der Ästhetik und Logik des 18. Jahrhunderts bis zur Kritik der Urteilskraft. Darmstadt, 1967.

Bayer, Raymond. Historie de l'esthetique. Paris, 1961.

Beck, Lewis White. Early German Philosophy: Kant and His Predecessors. Cambridge, 1969.

Berger, Karl. Die Entwicklung von Schiller's Aesthetik. Weimar, 1894.

Bergmann, Ernst. Die Begründung der deutschen Ästhetik durch A. G. Baumgarten und G. Fr. Meier. Leipzig, 1911.

Birke, Joachim. Christian Wolffs Metaphysik und die zeitgenössiche Literatur und Musiktheorie (Gottsched, Scheibe, Mizler). Berlin, 1966.

Bissinger, Anton. Die Struktur der Gotteserkenntnis: Studien zur Philosophie Christian Wolffs. Bonn, 1969.

Blackwell, Richard. "Christian Wolff's Doctrine of the Soul," Journal of the History of Ideas, 22 (1961), 339-354.

_____. "The Structure of Wolffian Philosophy," The Modern Schoolman, 37 (1961), 203-218.

Böhler, Michael. Soziale Rolle und Ästhetische Vermittlung. Studien zur Literatursoziologie von A. G. Baumgarten bis F. Schiller. Bern/Frankfurt a. M., 1975.

Böhm, Hans. "Das Schönheitsproblem bei G. F. Meier," Archiv für die gesamte Psychologie, 56 (1926), 117-252.

Bormann, Alexander von. "Einleitung," Vom Laienurteil zum Kunstgefühl. Texte zur deutschen Geschmacksdebatte im 18. Jahrhundert. Ed. Alexander von Bormann. Tübingen, 1974. pp. 1-16.

Boulton, J. T., "Editor's Introduction," to Edmund Burke, A Philosophical Enquiry into the Origin of our Ideas of the Sublime and Beautiful. London/New York, 1958. pp. i-cxxvii.

Braune, Frieda. Edmund Burke in Deutschland. Heidelberg, 1917.

Brett, George Sidney. Brett's History of Psychology. Ed. R. S. Peters. London/New York, 1953.

Broad, C. D. Leibniz. An Introduction, Ed. C. Lewy. London, 1975.

Caird, Edward. The Critical Philosophy of Immanuel Kant. Glascow, 1889. 2 vols.

Cassirer, Ernst. Das Erkenntnisproblem in der Philosophie und Wissenschaft der neueren Zeit. 3 vols. 1922-23.

_____. Idee und Gestalt. Darmstadt, 1971.

_____. Philosophie der symbolischen Formen. 3 vols. Berlin, 1923-1929.
Band II: Das mythische Denken (1925).

Cassirer, H. W. A Commentary on Kant's "Critique of Judgment." London, 1938.

Cohen, Felix. "What is a Question?" The Monist, 39 (1929), 350-264.

Coleman, Francis X. The Aesthetic Thought of the French Enlightenment. N.P., 1971.

Copleston, Frederick. A History of Philosophy, 9 vols. Garden City, 1962-1977.
Vol. 6: Modern Philosophy, Part One: The French Enlightenment to Kant (1964).
Vol. 5: Modern Philosophy: The British Philosophers, Part One: Hobbes to Paley (1964).

Coreth, Emerich. Einführung in die Philosophie der Neuzeit; Band I: Rationalismus Empirismus, Aufklärung. Freiburg, 1972.

_____. Metaphysics. Trans. Joseph Donceel. New York, 1968.

Crawford, Donald W. Kant's Aesthetic Theory. Madison, 1974.

Croce, Benedetto. Aesthetic as Science of Expression and General Linguistic. Trans. Douglas Ainslie. New York, 1956 (first edition 1909).

Delbos, Victor. "Le 'Cogito' de Descartes et la philosophie de Locke," L'Annee philosophique, 24 (1914), 1-14.

Dessoir, Max. Geschichte der neueren deutschen Psychologie. 2nd ed. Berlin, 1902.

_____. Outlines of the History of Psychology. Trans. Donald Fischer. New York, 1912.

Fischer, Kuno. Gesichichte der Philosophie. Band II: Leibniz und seine Schule. 2nd edition. Heidelberg, 1867.

_____. Immanuel Kant und seine Lehre. Erster Theil. Entstehung und Grundlegung der Kantischen Philosophie. 6th edition. Heidelberg, 1928.

Franke, Ursula. Kunst als Erkenntnis. Die Rolle der Sinnlichkeit in der Ästhetik des Alexander Gottlieb Baumgarten. Wiesbaden, 1972.

Funke, Gerhard. "Einleitung," Die Aufklärung in ausgewählten Texten dargestellt. Ed. Gerhard Funke. Stuttgart, 1963. pp. 1-92.

Gaede, Friedrich. Poetik und Logik. Zu den Grundlagen der literarischen Entwicklung im 17. und 18. Jahrhundert. Bern/Munchen: Francke Verlag, 1978.

Gehard, Melitta. Schiller. Bern, 1950.

Geyer, Paul. Schillers aesthetische-sittliche Weltanschauung aus seiner philosophischen Schriften gemeinverständlich erklärt. Berlin, 1908.

Gibson, J. Locke's Theory of Knowledge and Its Historical Relations. Cambridge, 1917.

Gilbert, K. F. and H. A. Kuhn. A History of Esthetics. Bloomington, 1954.

Gilson, Etienne. Being and Some Philosophers. 2nd ed. Toronto, 1952.

Gilson, Etienne and Thomas Langan. Modern Philosophy: Descartes to Kant. New York, 1963.

Gomperz, H. Philosophical Studies. Boston, 1953.

Hartnack, Justus. Kant's Theory of Knowledge. Translator M. Holmes Hartshorne, New York, 1965.

Heidigger, Martin. Die Frage nach dem Ding. Zu Kants Lehre von den transzendentalen Grundsätzen. Tübingen, 1962.

Heimsoeth, Heinz. Metaphysik der Neuzeit. München, 1967.

_____. Metaphysik und Kritik bei Chr. A. Crusius: Ein Beitrag zur ontologischen Vorgeschichte der Kritik der reinen Vernunft im 18. Jahrhundert. Berlin, 1926.

Henn, T. R. Longinus and English Criticism. Cambridge, 1934.

Hermann, Hans Peter. Naturnachahmung und Einbildungskraft. Zur Entwicklung der deutschen Poetik von 1760 bis 1740. Bad Homberg Berlin/Zurich, 1970.

Heuer, Fritz. Darstellung der Freiheit. Schillers transzendentale Frage nach der Kunst. Wien, 1970.

Hipple, Jr., Walter John. The Beautiful, the Sublime, and the Picturesque in Eighteenth-Century British Aesthetic Theory. Carbondale, 1957.

Hulme, T. E. Speculations. Ed. Herbert Read. New York, n.d. (first printed 1924).

Juchem, Hans-Georg. Die Entwicklung des Begriffs des Schönen bei Kant. Unter Besonderer Berücksichtigung des Begriffs der verworrenen Erkenntnis. Bonn. 1970.

Kallich, Martin. The Association of Ideas and Critical Theory in Eighteenth-Century England. A History of a Psychological Method in English Criticism. The Hague/Paris, 1970.

_____. "The Association of Ideas and Critical Theory: Hobbes, Locke and Addison," A Journal of English History, 12 (1945), 290-315.

Kerry, S. S. Schiller's Writings on Aesthetics. Manchester, 1961.

Kivvy, Peter. The Seventh Sense. A Study of Francis Hutcheson's Aesthetics and Its Influence in Eighteenth-Century Britain. New York, 1976.

Klein, Hannelore. There is no Disputing Taste. Untersuchung zum englischen Geschmacksbegriff im 18ten Jahrhundert. Münster, 1967.

Klemmt, Alfred. John Locke: Theoretische Philosophie. Meisenheim, 1952

Knox, Israel. The Aesthetic Theories of Kant, Hegel, and Schopenhauer. New York, 1958.

Kössler, Hennig. Freiheit und Ohnmacht: Die autonome Moral und Schillers Idealismus der Freiheit. Göttingen, 1962.

Korff, H. A. Geist der Goethezeit. Versuch einer ideellen Entwicklung der klassisch-romantischen Literaturgeschichte. 7th edition. Leipzig, 1964. Band II.

Kraus, John L. John Locke: Empiricist, Atomist, Conceptualist, and Agnostic. New York, 1968.

Kronenberg, M. Geschichte des Deutschen Idealismus. 2 vols. München, 1909.

Kroner, Richard. Von Kant bis Hegel. 2 vols. Tübingen, 1961.

Kuhn, Thomas. The Structure of Scientific Revolutions. 2nd. ed. Chicago, 1970.

Kroner, Richard. Von Kant bis Hegel. 2 vols. Tübingen, 1961.

Kuhn, Thomas. The Structure of Scientific Revolutions. 2nd ed. Chicago, 1970.

Langer, Susanne. Philosophy in a New Key. A Study in the Symbolism of Reason, Rite and Art. New York, 1961.

Linn, Marie-Luise. "A. G. Baumgartens 'Aesthetica' und die antike Rhetorik" Deutsche Vierteljahrsschrift für Literaturwissenschaft und Geistesgeschichte, 41 (1967), 424-443.

Lotze, Hermann. Geschichte der Ästhetik in Deutschland. München, 1868.

Lovejoy, Arthur. The Great Chain of Being. A Study of the History of an Idea. New York, 1960.

Lüthje, Hans. "Christian Wolffs Philosophiebegriff," Kant-Studien, 30 (1925), 29-66.

McGuinness, Arthur E. Henry Home, Lord Kames. New York, 1970.

Malek, James. The Arts Compared. An Aspect of Eighteenth-Century British Aesthetics. Detroit, 1974.

Marcuse, Herbert. Eros and Civilization. A Philosophical Inquiry into Freud. New York, 1955.

Maritain, Jacques. Distinguish to Unite or The Degrees of Knowledge. Trans. Gerald Phelan. New York, 1959.

Martin, Gottfried. Kant's Metaphysics and Theory of Science. Translator. P. G. Lucas. Westport, 1974.

Maud, Constance. Hume's Theory of Knowledge. A Critical Examination. London, 1937.

Menzel, Norbert. Der anthropologische Charakter des Schönen bei Baumgarten. Wanne-Eickel, 1969.

Menzer, Paul. "Zur Enstehung von A. G. Baumgarten's "Aesthetik," Zeitschrift für Deutsche Kulturphilosophie. Logos. N.F. 4 (1938), 288-296.

_____. "Schiller und Kant," Kant-Studien, 47 (1955-1956), 111-147, 234-272.

Metz, Rudolf. David Hume. Leben und Philosophie. Stuttgart, 1929.

Meyer, Hans Georg. Leibniz und Baumgarten als Begründer der deutschen Ästhetik. Halle, 1874.

Miller, Oscar. The Kantian Thing-in-Itself and the Creative Mind, New York, 1956.

Miller, R. D. Schiller & the Ideal of Freedom: A Study of Schiller's Philosophical Works with Chapters on Kant. Harrogate, 1959.

Monk, Samuel H. The Sublime: A Study of Critical Theories in XVIIICentury England. Ann Arbor, 1960.

Moore, Addison Webster. The Functional versus the Representational Theories of Knowledge in Locke's Essay. Chicago, 1902.

Mugdan, Bertha. Die theoretischen Grundlagen der Schillerschen Philosophie. Berlin, 1910.

Murphy, Gardner. An Historical Introduction to Modern Psychology. New York, 1930.

Nagel, Ernest. The Structure of Science: Problems in the Logic of Scientific Explanation. New York, 1961.

Nivelle, Armand. Kunst-und Dichtungstheorien zwischen Aufklärung und Klassik. Berlin, 1960.

Pepper, Stephen. World Hypotheses. A Study in Evidence. Berkeley/Los Angeles, 1961.

Peters, Hans Georg. Studien über die Ästhetik des A. G. Baumgarten unter bes. Berůchsichtigung ihrer Beziehungen zum Ethischen. Berlin, 1934.

Poppe, Bernhard. "Einleitung" in A. G. Baumgarten. Seine Bedeutung und Stellung in der Leibniz-Wolffischen Philosophie und seine Beziehungen zu Kant, Nebst einer bisher unbekannten Handschrift der Ästhetik Baumgartens. Borna/Leipzig, 1907. pp. 1-57.

Popper, Karl S. The Logic of Scientific Discovery. New York/Evanston, 1968.

Prosch, Harry. The Genesis of Twentieth Century Philosophy. The Evolution of Thought from Copernicus to the Present. Garden City, 1966.

Quinton, Anthony. "Final Discussion," The Nature of Metaphysics, Ed. D. F. Pears. London, 1957. pp. 142-163.

Randall, Jr., John Herman. The Career of Philosophy. New York/London, 1970-1977. 3 vols.

    Vol. I: From the Middle Ages to the Enlightenment (1970).
    Vol.II: From the Enlightenment to the Age of Darwin (1970).

Riemann, Albert. Die Ästhetik A. G. Baumgartens unter bes. Berůcksichtigung der "Meditationes," nebst einer Übersetzung dieser Schrift. Halle, 1928.

Rosalewski, Willi. Schillers Aesthetik im Verhältnis zur Kantischen. Heidelberg, 1912.

Royce, Josiah. Lectures on Modern Idealism. New Haven/London, 1964.

_____. The World and the Individual. First Series: The Four Historical Conceptions of Being. New York, 1959 (reprint of 1899 edition).

Saame, Otto A. Der Satz vom Grund bei Leibniz. Ein konstitutives Element seiner Philosophie und ihrer Einehit. Mainz, 1961.

Saintsbury, George. A History of Criticism and Literary Taste in Europe. 3 vols. London, 1902-1906. Vol. III: Modern Criticism (1906).

Schaper, Eva. "Schiller: Adventures of a Kantian," British Journal of Aesthetics, 5 (1964), 348-362.

Schasler Max. Kritische Geschichte der Aesthetik. Grundlegung für die Aesthetik als Philosophie des Schönen und der Kunst. Berlin, 1872. 2 vols. Erste Abtheilung. Von Plate bis zum 19. Jahrhundert (1872).

Schmidt, Johannes. Leibniz und Baumgarten. Ein Beitrag zur Geschichte der deutschen Aesthetik. Halle, 1975.

Schweizer, Hans Rudolf. "Asthetik als Philosophie der sinnlichen Erkenntnis. Eine Interpretation der 'Aesthetica' A. G. Baumgarten's mit teilweiser Wiedergabe des lateinischen Textes und deutscher Übersetzung. Basel/Stuttgart, 1973.

Schwitzke, Heinz. Die Beziehungen zwischen Aesthetik und Metaphysik in der deutschen Philosophie vor Kant. Berlin, 1930.

Smid, Alfred. "Schiller as als theoretischer Philosoph," Kant-Studien 10 (1905), 261-286.

Snider, Denton J. Modern European Philosophy: The History of Modern Philosophy, Psychologically Treated. St. Louis, 1904.

Sommer, Richard. Grundzüge einer Geschichte der deutschen Psychologie und Aesthetik von Wolff-Baumgarten bis Kant-Schiller. Amsterdam, 1966 (reprint of the 1896 edition).

Stein, Karl Heinrich von. Die Entstehung der neueren Aesthetik. Hildesheim, 1964 (reprint of 1886 edition).

Sutter, Monika. Die kunsttheoretischen Begriffe des Malerphilosophen Anton Raphael Mengs. Versuch einer Begriffserläuterung im Zusammenhang mit der geistegeschichtlichen Situation Europas bis hin zu Kant. N.P. 1968.

Taylor, A. E. Elements of Metaphysics. London/New York, n.d. (first printed in 1903).

Todes, Samuel J. "Knowledge and the Ego: Kant's Three States of Selfevidence," Kant. A Collection of Critical Essays. Editor Robert Paul Wolff. Garden City, 1967. pp. 156-171.

Tuveson, Ernst Lee. The Imagination as A Means of Grace: Locke and the Aesthetics of Romanticism. Berkeley/Los Angeles, 1960.

Ueberweg, Friedrich. Schiller als Historiker und Philosoph. Ed. Moritz Brasch Stuttgart, 1963.

Uehling, Theodore Edward. The Notion of Form in Kant's "Critique of Aesthetic Judgment." The Hague/Paris, 1971.

Vleeschauwer, Herman-J. The Development of Kantian Thought. The History of a Doctrine. Translator. A. R. C. Duncan. Toronto/New York, 1962.

Vorländer, Karl. Kant, Schiller, Goethe: Gesammelte Aufsätze. Leipzig, 1907.

Warren, Howard C. A History of the Association Psychology. New York, 1921.

Wechter, Dixon. "Burke's Theory of Words, Images and Emotions," PMLA, 40 (1940), 167-181.

Weischedel, Wilhelm. Der Gott der Philosophen. Grundlegung einer philosophischen Theologie im Zeitalter des Nihilismus. 2 vols. Darmstadt, 1971.

Weldon, T. D. Kant's "Critique of Pure Reason." Oxford, 1958.

Wellek, Rene. A History of Modern Criticism: 1750-1950. 4 vols. New Haven, 1955-1965. Vol. 1: The Later Eighteenth Century (1955)

Wessell, Jr., Leonard P. "Alexander Baumgarten's Contribution to the Development of Aesthetics, The Journal of Aesthetics and Art Criticism, 30 (1972), 333-342.

Whitehead, Alfred North. Process and Reality. An Essay in Cosmology. New York, 1960.

Wildermuth, Arnin. Wahrheit und Schöpfung. Ein Grundriss der Metaphysik des Gottfried Wilhelm Leibniz. Winterhur, 1960.

Willoughby, Leonard Ashly. "Schiller on Man's Education to Freedom through Knowledge," Germanic Review, 29 (1959), 163-174.

Wilkinson, Elizabeth. "Reflections after Translating Schiller's Letters on the Aesthetic Education of Man," Schiller, Bicentary Lectures. Editor F. Norman. London, 1960. pp. 48-62.

Wilm, Carl. "The Relation of Schiller to Postkantian Idealism," The Journal of English and Germanic Philosophy, 9 (1910), 20-24.

Wundt, Max. Die Schulphilosophie im Zweitalter der Aufklärung. Hildesheim, 1964 (reprint from 1945 edition).

Zeller, Edward. Geschichte der deutschen Philosophie seit Leibniz. München, 1873.

Zimmermann, Robert. Geschichte der Aesthetik als philosophischer Wissenschaft. Wien, 1858.

GOETHE ZEIT

Elisabeth Genton
LA VIE ET LES OPINIONS DE
HEINRICH LEOPOLD WAGNER (1747–1779)

Frankfurt/M., Bern. 1980. 516 S.
Europäische Hochschulschriften: Reihe 1, Deutsche Sprache und Literatur. Band 300
ISBN 3-8204-6541-3   br. sFr. 89.—

Als Sohn eines Strassburger Bürgers hat Wagner die Entstehung jener Sturm und Drang genannten Bewegung in ihren Anfängen miterlebt. Für ihn, der seine Heimatstadt und ihr Zunftwesen nur als Symbol des mittelalterlichen Obskurantismus ansah, galten die Bemühungen der 'Goethianer' nur als Erfüllung der Aufklärung. Er glaubte fest, dass ein Dichter nichts Besseres vollbringen könnte, als durch seine Werke die moralischen Vorurteile und damit ihre verheerenden Folgen zu bekämpfen.

Der Autorin, Prof. f. Germanistik an der Universität Nancy, eilt, u.a. durch die aufsehenerregende Rekonstruktion von J.W. v. Goethes verschollener Dissertation, ein vorzüglicher wissenschaftlicher Ruf voraus. Sie wendet die Methoden der monographischen Studie an, um anhand von Wagners Leben die bedeutenden Aspekte der Epoche (1770–1780) aufzufinden und stützt sich dabei auf eine Anzahl bislang unbekannt gebliebener zeitgenössischer Dokumente.

Aus 'Germanistik', Tübingen:

«Die umfängliche Monographie, die auf einen ebenso strengen wie subtilen Positivismus verpflichtet ist, zielt auf eine gründliche Korrektur des seit der Darstellung durch Erich Schmidt (1875) zum peinlichen Klischee verkommenen W.-Bilds ab. Nicht zuletzt die Fülle der auswahlweise angefügten Dokumente, die die Verf. in diversen. z.T. entlegenen Archiven und Nachlässen entdeckt und identifiziert hat, erhärtet die These, dass dem Strassburger Freund Goethes und Lenzens als Stürmer und Dränger minderer poetischer Gaben keineswegs Genüge geleistet zu werden vermag. Vielmehr präsentiert er sich als ein 'homme de lettres', der sich keiner Schule oder Sekte zuordnen lässt und dessen 'realistische' Schreibart dementsprechend eher an ethischen als an ästhetischen Normen gemessen sein will. Die Verf. begreift *Die Kindermörderinn*, unstreitig das bedeutendste Werk W.s, als eben nur eine, gewiss mit fortschreitenden Jahren variierte, präzisierte Form, die Leitideen der Aufklärung(!) zu popularisieren und eine politisch-soziale Ordnung zu propagieren, die sich füglich an individuellen Fähigkeiten und an allgemeingültigen sittlichen Maximen orientieren sollte. — Diese reformerische Konzeption wird mit bestechender Akribie in ihrer Genese einsichtig gemacht. Mitsamt dem kaum oder gar nicht bekannten Quellenmaterial komplettieren die minuziösen Auflistungen der Entstehungs- und Wirkungsgeschichte des W.schen Werks die — unbeschadet partieller Irritationen — schwerlich überschätzbare Abhandlung.»   Wolfgang Kuttenkeuler, Köln

Peter Lang

Forschungsberichte zur Internationalen Germanistik

Umfassende und kontinuierliche Information über die vielfältigen Forschungen auf allen Gebieten der Germanistik ist das Ziel der im Rahmen der Jahrbuch-Reihe C erscheinenden Forschungsberichte, die von international renommierten Fachvertretern erarbeitet und betreut werden. Als Band 1 dieser Reihe ist erschienen:

Deutsche Literatur des 19. Jahrhunderts (1830–1895)
Erster Bericht: 1960–1975
Von Gotthart Wunberg in Zusammenarbeit mit Rainer Funke
Jahrbuch für Internationale Germanistik: Reihe C · Band 1
387 Seiten. Brosch./Lam. Fr. 138.–

Der vorliegende Bericht präsentiert in drei grossen Teilen die Forschung der Jahre 1960–1975 auf dem Gebiet der Literatur vom Jungen Deutschland bis zum Naturalismus. Der eigentliche Forschungsbericht (Teil 1) umfasst 12 Abteilungen, in denen u.a. folgende Themen behandelt werden: Theorie, Wissenschaftsgeschichte, Theorie- und Methodendiskussion – Arbeiten zur Literaturgeschichte des 19. Jahrhunderts im engeren Sinn – Die einzelnen Autoren einschiesslich Literaturkritiker – Autorenübergreifende Themen (Stoff-, Symbol-, Toposforschung etc.) – Gattungen und Textsorten – Literaturkritik und Zeitschriften – Literarisches Leben – Einflüsse und Wechselbeziehungen fremdsprachiger Literatur – Grenzgebiete von Literatur und Literaturwissenschaft. Der zweite Teil des Berichts (Abteilung 13–16) bietet eine – zumeist annotierte – Bibliographie, während die abschliessenden Literaturnachweise (Teil 3) der genauen bibliographischen Erfassung aller in den Bericht aufgenommenen Titel (ca. 1 700) dienen.

«Der von G. Wunberg in Zusammenarbeit mit R. Funke herausgegebene Forschungsbericht ist ohne Einschränkung als eine hervorragende Leistung zu werten. Die Berichterstatter haben eine gewisse Vollständigkeit angestrebt – 'dies freilich um den Preis subjektiver Akzentuierung einerseits und mangelnder Ausführlichkeit in bezug auf die einzelnen Titel andererseits'. Dieses Konzept ist angesichts der schier ausufernden Flut von Sekundärliteratur zweifellos richtig. Die streng durchgeführte systematische Gliederung [...] ermöglicht ein [angesichts des stattlichen Bandes nicht selbstverständliches] rasches Nachschlagen [...]» (F. van Ingen in Deutsche Bücher' 1980/4)

Verlag Peter Lang · Bern und Frankfurt am Main
Auslieferung: Verlag Peter Lang AG, Jupiterstr. 15, CH-3000 Bern 15
Telefon (0041/31) 32 11 22, Telex verl ch 32 420